Cervantes, Raphael and the Classics

FREDERICK A. DE ARMAS

CAMBRIDGE
UNIVERSITY PRESS

PUBLISHED BY THE PRESS SYNDICATE OF THE UNIVERSITY OF CAMBRIDGE
The Pitt Building, Trumpington Street, Cambridge, United Kingdom

CAMBRIDGE UNIVERSITY PRESS
The Edinburgh Building, Cambridge CB2 2RU, United Kingdom
40 West 20th Street, New York, NY 10011-4211, USA
10 Stamford Road, Oakleigh, Melbourne 3166, Australia

First published 1998

Printed in the United States of America

Typeset in Baskerville 10/13

*A catalog record for this book is available from
the British Library*

Library of Congress Cataloging-in-Publication Data

De Armas, Frederick Alfred.
    Cervantes, Raphael and the classics / Frederick A. de Armas.
        p.   cm. — (Cambridge studies in Latin American and Iberian
literature)
    Includes bibliographical references and index.
    ISBN 0-521-59302-6 (hardcover)
    1. Cervantes Saavadra. Miguel de. 1547–1616 – Knowledge – Civilization.
Classical.   2. Civilization. Classical, in literature.   3. Raphael. 1483–1520 –
Influence.   I. Title, II. Series.
P95358.C5704   1998   97-30187
883'.3–DC21   CIP

ISBN 0-521-59302-6

Contents

Illustrations

Preface

This book is about a journey to Rome, a journey Cervantes undertook for religion (and politics) when he was in the service of Cardinal Acquaviva. It was a sojourn that led him to consort with the philosophers and writers of antiquity as seen through the eyes of the Renaissance. When he left the city, he took with him the memories of a past he wished to resurrect. If this artistic, literary, religious and political pilgrimage led him to open the doors of perception to new ways of viewing, writing, and thinking, his future *stasis* as writer allowed him to bring together the different steps of the journey into a coherent yet kaleidoscopic artistic vision. Even memories of war would be infused with a memory of the classics. Reminiscing on the battle of Lepanto he would compare it to the glories of Salamis. On remembering Rome he would eventually perceive not only the classical and Renaissance city but also Troy and Numantia.

Ironically, it was the seat of Catholic power, the Vatican, that led him to glimpse the power of the pagan past. Through the archeological work done by Renaissance painters and displayed in order to praise the papacy, Cervantes came to visualize the possibilities inherent in the recuperation of the ancients. Vasari's *Lives of the Artists*, a sixteenth-century text that molded the way Renaissance art was perceived then and is even seen today, describes one of the artists who brought Italian art to the summit of perfection thusly: "One can claim that artists like Raphael are not simply men but, if it be allowed to say so, mortal gods" (1971, 284). Vasari's praise of this artist clearly shows the syncretism of the Renaissance, where the gods of Greece and Rome could seemingly coexist with Christianity. The pious Raphael could as easily revel in the wisdom of the ancients (which he seeks to capture in *The School of Athens*) as represent the triumphant power of the papacy (as in *The Liberation of Saint Peter*). Admired by Renaissance popes, Raphael often portrayed the greatness of the church through the authority of the ancients. Christianity he saw as completing the vision of pagan Rome. In *The Fire in the Borgo*, for example, he includes Aeneas saving his father, Anchises, from the fires of Troy. But this fresco conveys the notion that the fires of destruction can be put

ix

out. The pope making the sign of the cross in the background will bring about a miracle.

It was to Rome, "infected" with paganism (as Lutherans and even Erasmians would have it), that Cervantes journeyed some sixty years after the triumphs of Raphael. The syncretism of the Renaissance had given way to a more dogmatic and strict method of looking at things. For some Counter-Reformation thinkers, the Sistine Chapel was nothing more than "a bathroom full of nudes" (Hersey 1993, 25). But for a young poet who had undergone a humanist education and who had just come in contact with the masterpieces of Renaissance art and the archeological impetus to bring back that ancient culture, these works were precious gifts from the heavens. Raphael's frescoes taught Cervantes to envision the heavens as both pagan (*Parnassus*) and Christian. The Renaissance artist also taught him that such visions balanced wisdom with politics, beauty with power. Indeed, the four great *halls* by Raphael at the Vatican Palace have as their purpose the glorification of the power of the papacy. But Raphael made them much more than that. This contest between laudatory program and the artist's personal vision may have been translated into Cervantes's mixture of tones, from the acclamatory to the subversive. If Raphael saw Christianity as completing the classics, Cervantes would represent his religion as competing with the ancients in *La Numancia*.

It is puzzling that so little has been said about Cervantes and Renaissance art. Cervantes learned from it the way of the ancients and the politics of imitation. It is even stranger that his interest in the classics has received so little attention. Perhaps because *Don Quijote* consistently breaks with *auctoritas* and seems to turn to the romances of chivalry rather than to the classics as the object of imitation, studies on the relationship between Cervantes and the literature of Greece and Rome have been few and far between. This book, however, is not an odyssey through the treacherous seas of classical imitation in *Don Quijote*. Rather, it is a briefer (although not necessarily a safer) voyage, one that takes as a point of departure the critical belief that Cervantes's *La Numancia* is a work akin to classical tragedy. In this study, I would like to open up the discussion of Cervantes and the classics by focusing mostly (although not exclusively) on this play and by extending imitation to include not only ancient tragedy but also other classical genres – the epic, in particular. An understanding of the levels, methods, and politics of imitation should be of use to those who wish to expand this approach to *Don Quijote* and other works by Cervantes.

My first encounter with *La Numancia* and the classics goes back more than twenty years. In 1974, I published an essay on the relationship between classical tragedy and Cervantes's play. Focusing on Aeschylus's *The Persians*, I showed how the Greek tragedy had departed from the norm by representing the defeat of the Persians rather than the triumph of the Greeks. The enemy, embodied in the Persian ruler Xerxes, thus became the tragic hero. This led me to argue that it was possible to conceive of the tragic elements of *La Numancia* from the point of view of the Roman enemy rather than from the perspective of the "Spanish" city. In showing how an enemy is worthy of admiration and even sorrow, I knew I was going against the traditionally accepted imperialist and patriotic conceptions of the work. But shortly after writing this essay I came to realize that I had touched upon just one of the many levels of imitation in *La Numancia* and that I had not fully pursued how and why Cervantes utilized even this particular model.

Having turned in the 1980s to the relationship between myth and empire in Calderón's theater, I also began to conceive of new ways of thinking about Cervantes and the politics of imitation. These ideas remained just that until the appearance of two articles in 1987 and 1990: the first, by Paul Lewis-Smith, is a "sequel and riposte" to my 1974 piece, and the second, by Jane Tar, tries to chart a middle course between my conception of *La Numancia* and the one advanced by Lewis-Smith in the 1987 essay. These two publications led me to formulate my thoughts on Cervantes, empire, and the classics. A fortuitous letter from Barbara Simerka inviting me to contribute an article in which I would reconsider my thesis on *La Numancia* confirmed that it was time to embark upon a detailed study of Cervantes's canonical tragedy. A book length study would allow me to bring together the different thoughts and insights I had been gathering over the years on the politics of imitation in *La Numancia*. It would also be a way to open up the vast topic of the relationship of Cervantes's texts to Greek and Roman literature. If the phantom of *Don Quijote* haunts this book, it is here so that others will either exorcise it or bring it back to life – its numinous presence should encourage others to take a stand on classical imitation in Cervantes's novel.

In this study, I approach Cervantes's tragedy through a constellation of classical writers whom I believe he consciously and conscientiously imitated. Very much like the *Tempest*, where Shakespeare "situates his writing between two authorities, the poet Virgil and the monarch James I" (Hamilton 1990, ix), *La Numancia* situates itself between a constella-

tion of classical writers and a vision of imperial power. Classical views of
cosmology, heroism, and empire serve to evaluate a present in which
Spain wishes to carry the mantle of imperial authority. After an intro-
ductory chapter, I turn to Cervantes's Italian sojourn, when his interest
in archeology, the classics, and politics was heightened through his careful observation and appreciation of a series of frescoes in the Vatican by
Raphael (Chapters 2 and 3) and his disciple Giulio Romano (Chapter
4). Chapter 5 revisits my 1974 piece and attempts to answer questions
that have been raised in the last twenty years concerning the link
between Cervantes and Aeschylus. Even though in my early essay I did
not take up the question of direct imitation, I now believe that Cervantes
could well have had the Greek play in mind as a model. I then dedicate
one chapter to each of other classical authors whose writings are
inscribed in the play: Homer, Virgil, Lucan, and Cicero/Macrobius.
Plato's numerology and Aristotle's *Ethics* and *Poetics* will serve to further
comprehend the architecture of the play.

Sections of this book are derived from previously published material,
but all have been revised, rethought and expanded: "Classical Tragedy
and Cervantes' *La Numancia*," *Neophilologus* 58 (1974): 34–40; "Achilles
and Odysseus: An Epic Contest in Cervantes' *La Numancia*," in *Cervantes.
Estudios cervantinos en la víspera de su centenario*, ed. Kurt Reichenberger
(Kassel: Edition Reichenberger, 1994), vol. 2, pp. 357–70; "The Necromancy of Imitation: Lucan and Cervantes' *La Numancia*," in *El arte nuevo
de estudiar comedias: Literary Theory and Spanish Age Drama*, ed. Barbara
Simerka (Lewisburg: Bucknell University Press, 1996), pp. 246–58; and
"Painting and Graffiti: (Sub)Versions of History in Golden Age Theater
(Notes on Cervantes and Claramonte)," *Gestos* 11 (1996): 83–101. All
citations in the Romance languages have been left in the original. However, references to the Greek and Roman classics are given in English
translation. When citing *Don Quijote*, I always give the part and the chapter number in addition to the page for those using other editions. References to Homer, Ovid, Seneca, and Virgil include not only the page
number of the actual edition used but also, after a slash, the standard
book and line numbers.

I would like to thank *Gestos*, *Neophilologus*, Edition Reichenberger, and
Bucknell University Press for permission to include material from these
essays. I would also like to express my indebtedness to James Nicolopulos, since it was while reading the manuscript of his book *Prophecy, Empire
and Imitation in the "Araucana" in the Light of the "Lusiadas"* that I came to

realize the importance of Lucan's necromancy for the study of how Cervantes subverted imperial and heroic concerns in *La Numancia*. Many *comediantes* and other colleagues have helped me to focus and rethink my arguments through discussions and letters. I would like to thank in particular Timothy Ambrose, Mary Barnard, William R. Blue, Anne J. Cruz, Robert Fiore, Edward H. Friedman, Eric Graf, Daniel L. Heiple, Robert Lima, Leon Lyday, Charles Oriel, James Parr, Mary Beth Rose, and Anthony Zahareas for their encouragement, support, and suggestions. I owe a debt of gratitude to James Mandrell and Christopher Weimer for their careful reading of the manuscript. I would also like to thank my graduate research assistants Marie Gillette and Ron Friis for all their valuable assistance. My thanks also to Mary Malcom Gaylord, to Carmen Peraita, and to Edward Dudley for sharing with me their latest work on Cervantes in manuscript. The research for this book has been made possible by a fellowship from the National Endowment for the Humanities, the Audrey Lumsden Kouvel Fellowship in Renaissance Studies at the Newberry Library, and a sabbatical leave from Pennsylvania State University.

1

The politics of imitation

Throughout his literary career Cervantes was engaged in a conversation and a contest with the classical authors of Greece and Rome. From his early pastoral romance *La Galatea* (1585), whose very title evokes the mythology of Polyphemus's love for the nymph Galatea, to his posthumously published *Los trabajos de Persiles y Sigismunda* (1617), by which Cervantes sought to ensure his fame by rivaling Heliodorus's *Aethiopica*,[1] his works constantly call upon the textual remains of the ancients. Indeed, Cervantes's poetic career imitates the intellectual and artistic journey of the ancient poet whose compositions move from the pastoral to the higher genres, and particularly the epic. This movement through the genres was well known to the Renaissance. Petrarch, who was particularly conscious of his antique predecessors, proceeded from pastoral (*Bucolicum carmen*) to epic (*Africa*). In Renaissance England, Spenser begins as a "young bird" proving his tender wings with pastoral (*The Shepheardes Calender*) and then moves to epic (*The Faerie Queene*).[2] It is thus no coincidence that Cervantes begins his career with pastoral (*Galatea*) and ends it with *Persiles y Sigismunda*. Since this romance is an imitation of Heliodorus, it was viewed during the epoch as a work akin to epic. As Alban K. Forcione explains, the discovery of Heliodorus's romance came at a key moment in European fiction: "Educated circles, from the early sixteenth century on, universally condemned the popular romances of chivalry . . . and seized upon the newly discovered *Aethiopica* of Heliodorus as an alternative type of prose fiction" (1970, 85–6). Indeed, the Greek romance was equated with the epic. In Spain, López Pinciano's *Philosophía antigua poética* (1596) compares Heliodorus's work with the epics of Homer and Virgil, showing how it at times surpasses those of the epic masters. Aware of this situation, then, Cervantes turned to Heliodorus. As he explains in the prologue to Part 2 of *Don Quijote*, this future work would be "o el más malo o el mejor que en nuestra lengua se haya compuesto" (1978, 2.38). He thus hoped to compete and even surpass Heliodorus's epic.

And yet, there are very few studies that deal with Cervantes and the classics. As early as 1780 Vicente de los Ríos argued that Cervantes's novel was an imitation of the Homeric epic, but his view was criticized through-out the nineteenth century. Early in this century, Arturo Marasso revived Cervantes's connection with the classical epic, this time discovering par-allels with Virgil. His studies also failed to convince the critics. Even Michael D. McGaha's 1980 essay on Cervantes and Virgil has failed to stimulate critical response. Perhaps *Don Quijote*'s anticlassical bias, its fore-grounding of the chivalric romances, may have contributed to this disre-gard. The juxtaposition of Cervantes and Aristotle, for example, leads Forcione to proclaim an "anticlassical stance" in the Spanish author (1970, 343). It is certainly true that literary classicism gives way to "the historical stuff of everyday experience" in *Don Quijote* (Forcione 1970, 224). A similar claim has been made for the *Viaje del Parnaso*. In his edi-tion, Vicente Gaos compares *Don Quijote* with this poem: "si aquél es la parodia del mundo caballeresco, éste lo es del mundo mitológico del clasicismo" (Cervantes 1984b, 32). Gaos claims that Cervantes enjoys debasing the gods of mythology: "se regocija presentándonos unos dioses apeados de su majestuoso pedestal, trasmutados en seres corrientes y mo-lientes, a más de anacrónicos, pues su atuendo, costumbres y lenguaje son los de los españoles vulgares de la época" (1984b, 32). And yet, this critic also asserts that the ambience of the work is Lucianesque (1984b, 32). In depicting the gods, then, Cervantes is not turning away from the classics but is imitating a specific tradition within antique literature. Cer-vantes's playful tone is somewhat removed from the many burlesque works on mythology written during the Golden Age. His gods, although closer to sixteenth-century Spaniards, often retain a certain aura of divin-ity, which is rather striking in a poem that has been called an "epopeya burlesca" (1984b, 31). The *Viaje del Parnaso* contains careful descriptions of the ancient gods,[3] verbal reminiscences of ancient texts,[4] and numer-ous references to the writers of classical antiquity.[5] Although playful in tone, the poem's construction reveals a clear knowledge of the classics.

Other works by Cervantes evince a more obvious reverence for the classics. *La Galatea* is imbued with classical mythology and ancient pas-toral formulas. And, as Forcione masterfully shows, Cervantes's *Persiles y Sigismunda* is constantly reacting to conceptions, constructions, and images from the ancients. Thus Cervantes's anticlassical bias is a red her-ring, a deceptive veering away from the ancients. The prologue to Part 1 of *Don Quijote* shows that Cervantes has not ignored the classicist position regarding fiction. The author's friend states that the work aims to "der-ribar la máquina mal fundada destos caballerescos libros" (1978, 1.58).

Although this intention simplifies ad infinitum the polyvalence of the work, it is precisely what the imitators of Heliodorus sought to do, and what many Renaissance humanists sought to accomplish.[6] More than this, *Don Quijote* may have been conceived as an apprenticeship in the epic genre. Indeed, a recent study on the ideology of figure in the epic includes Cervantes's masterpiece along with Homer's *Iliad*, Virgil's *Aeneid*, Milton's *Paradise Lost,* and Spenser's *The Faerie Queene.* It even labels *Don Quijote* as an "'epic' in prose" (Wofford 1992, 1). Of course, Wofford recognizes a difference in narrative technique between the traditional epic and *Don Quijote.* Cervantes's narrator "uses no epic similes, avoids invocations . . . resists personifying the landscape or the settings of his poem; his principal figure, one might say, is don Quixote himself, a walking (or riding) machine of figuration" (1992, 398). Indeed, don Quijote often has the epic in mind as he pursues his adventures. When the knight decides to do penance in the Sierra Morena, for example, he wonders whether to imitate the melancholy penance portrayed in *Amadís de Gaula* or the choleric madness found in *Orlando furioso.* But, as he debates this question, the knight also recalls two ancient heroes: Homer's Odysseus and Virgil's Aeneas (1978, 1.25.303; McGaha 1980, 43). Beneath the chivalric surface, a deeper subtext can be perceived, one that derives from antiquity. *Don Quijote*'s playfulness is a way of approaching the unapproachable, of turning to epic without being engulfed in its monumentality. Revising and rethinking classical motifs, Cervantes is preparing himself for *Persiles y Sigismunda.* The irony, of course, is that in playing with the ancients, Cervantes can display his own sense of authority, his own originality, whereas in *Persiles y Sigismunda,* he is at times the victim of a tradition. But *Don Quijote* may not have been his first attempt at epic themes. One of the purposes of this study is to show the epic elements in his early tragedy, *La Numancia.* The "playful" opposition between the prudence of Odysseus and the valor of Aeneas in *Don Quijote* was a theme that had already been utilized by Cervantes in *La Numancia* – but more on this when we discuss the Homeric epic.

In the prologue to the first part of Cervantes's *Don Quijote,* the "author" bemoans the fact that his book (as well as his prologue) is lacking in learning and instruction whereas other works are "tan llenos de sentencias de Aristóteles, de Platón y de toda la caterva de filósofos, que admiran a los leyentes y tienen a sus autores por hombres leídos, eruditos y elocuentes" (1978, 1.52). This allusion, as will be explained in Chapter 2, may have been triggered by Raphael's fresco *The School of Athens,* in which Plato and

Aristotle stand at the center of a whole "caterva" of classical thinkers. When faced with the majesty of Raphael's evocation, all subsequent attempts at imitations fail. Consequently, the fictional author portrays himself in a melancholy pose with "la mano en la mejilla" (1978, 1.52), not knowing how to proceed. His friend's counsel allows him to emerge from this state of sadness and inaction. The friend advises him, among other things, to sprinkle or adorn his text with Latin *sententiae* and classical allusions so as to include in the margins (*acotaciones*) or in footnotes (*anotaciones*) the sources for these bits of erudition (1978, 1.54–5). Ruth El Saffar claims: "The friend's discussion, in fact, is nothing more than a criticism of the typical inflated, pompous and irrelevant prologue and the manner in which such a prologue can be imitated" (1975, 36). James Parr goes even further: "The 1605 prologue is a subordinate text that serves as a transition . . . , while at the same time mirroring both the structure and the ironic texture of the story of Don Quijote" (1984, 23). Although the "author's" attitude is one of anxiety over ancient texts and Renaissance evocations of these, the friend's response adds a playfulness that breaks through the barriers of authority.

There is yet one more contextual level. The friend's discussion is not just a criticism of prologues but also a criticism of the uses of imitation. Not only in *Don Quijote* but throughout his works, Cervantes criticizes those who would cloak themselves in robes of learning by using a sprinkling of classical *sententiae* and allusions. A case in point is the interlude *El retablo de las maravillas* where the villagers' honor and the pretensions of learning are satirized. The swindlers Chanfalla and Chirinos, posing as puppeteers, use adulation to confound the villagers. By sprinkling their speeches with Latin phrases, they establish their knowledge and authority. When Chirinos uses the phrase "ante omnia" (1982a, 221), Capacho, one of the villagers, proudly translates the Latin. He even corrects Benito Repollo's reference to Cicero (1982a, 219). As Michael Gerli astutely observes, *El retablo* is "an elaborate theatrical mirror which reflects not only insights into the ontology of the theater but, more specifically, Cervantes' opposition to some of the prevailing theatrical theories and practices of his day. *El retablo* especially shows Cervantes' rejection of Lope de Vega's poetics as set down in the *Arte nuevo de hacer comedias* (1609)" (1989, 478). Cervantes's interlude portrays Lope's plays as "failed, indeed bogus commercial fabrication – an art form which, if it succeeds, does so not because of its aesthetic perfection, its ability to imply a relation to reality, but because of its compromise with social delusions"

(Gerli 1989, 481). For Cervantes, honor and wisdom are displayed in these plays through certain outer trappings and disguises that have more to do with delusion than with innate or acquired worth.

The same attitude prevails in the prologue to Part 1 of *Don Quijote*. As Clemencín noted long ago, many of the erudite strategies proposed by the friend appear in Lope de Vega's works. *El Isidro* (1599), for example, contains a wealth of citations in the margins and a list of 267 authors cited, while *El peregrino en su patria* has a table of more than 150 authors (Clemencín 1933, 1.1.liv). In order to appear as properly erudite, the "author" of *Don Quijote* need only follow very specific advice: "Si tratáredes de ladrones, yo os diré la historia de Caco, que la sé de coro; si de mujeres rameras, ahí está el obispo de Mondoñedo, que os presentará a Lamia, Laida y Flora, cuya anotación os dará gran crédito; si de crueles, Ovidio os entregará a Medea; si de encantadores y hechiceras, Homero tiene a Calipso, y Virgilio a Circe; si de capitanes valerosos, el mesmo Julio César os prestará a sí mismo en sus *Comentarios*, y Plutarco os dará mil Alejandros" (1978, 1.56). Even though such advice serves to satirize Lope de Vega's practices, *Don Quijote* incorporates at least some of the (fictional) "friend's" advice. The Innkeeper is described as being thievish as Cacus (1978, 1.84). This thief from antiquity, caught by Hercules, appears, for example, in the eighth canto of the *Aeneid*. After reading the prologue, a reader may be inclined to disregard the importance of such a reference as a type of eclectic imitation that is mere adornment or show. And yet, Arturo Marasso has shown that in addition to being an imitation of books of chivalry *Don Quijote* contains "un Virgilio intencionalmente contrahecho, pero no por eso es menor el estímulo del gran poeta" (1954, 52). Among the episodes which imitate Virgil in Part 1, Marasso points to the windmills (the Cyclops in *Aeneid* 3), the pastoral episode of Grisóstomo and Marcela (Dido and Aeneas in *Aeneid* 4), the catalogue of armies (*Aeneid* 7), the fulling hammers (*Aeneid* 8), and the adventure of the corpse (*Aeneid* 11) (Marasso 1954, 54ff.). But there is much more than this. As Carolyn Nadeau has shown, the friend's advice to include references to Ovid's Medea, Virgil's Circe, and Homer's Calypso is carried out in the text of the novel. Utilizing Ovid's *Metamorphosis* and *Heroides*, Cervantes builds Dorotea's conflict between passion and loyalty and Zoraida's decision to leave her homeland from these Ovidian models. Dulcinea as a Circe-like enchantress and Maritornes as a Calypso figure show Cervantes's "respectful acknowledgement of ancient sources, and also a gesture of departure from those texts" (Nadeau 1994, 139). How can Cervantes satirize Lope's learning and yet turn to such classical stories himself in the construction of *Don Quijote?*

In criticizing Lope de Vega's stance on honor and learning, Cervantes is only pointing to the false uses of these terms. Honor, as defined in *Don Quijote*, is an attribute of the soul, not a social commodity. Learning, as Don Quijote well knows, comes with intense study and is acquired at great peril.[7] Cervantes portrays Lope as entranced by outer trappings, while *Don Quijote* exhibits an apparent simplicity and a textual integrity. While Lope commits the sin of "pretentiousness,"[8] Cervantes carefully covers up his own learned subtext, appearing to deauthorize imitation through the friend's advice. Salvador J. Fajardo explains: "The first author does not say that he undertook to follow his friend's advice but that his friend's words left an imprint on him. . . . Thus, he adopts his friend's statement as worthy of imitation because it has been voided of authoritative content" (1994, 11). Critics since Américo Castro have pointed out that the prologues to Parts 1 and 2 were written after the novel: "En realidad se trata de epílogos, redactados después de conclusa la obra . . . su sentido no se revela sino a quien posea noticia muy cabal del libro" (Castro 1960, 231).

One of the "senses" of the prologue as a commentary on Part 1, I would argue, is the sense of what constitutes true or appropriate uses of learning. Two types of knowledge are exhibited, each leading to a very different disorder: don Quijote's brings on madness, while the friend's advice on the uses of erudition denotes vanity and pretentiousness. Don Quijote knows almost too much but is unable to transform the books of chivalry into a social reality, while the "author's" friend knows so little that he boasts of his erudition. This contrastive approach lends an ethical dimension to the uses of learning. There is no obvious moralizing here. Rather, the contrastive approach becomes, in Aníbal González's words, "una invitación a reflexionar sobre los problemas Eticos de la literatura" (1994, 498).[9] It also points to the ethics of writing. Does erudite adornment serve to create a fictional representation of an author as authoritative? Are the writers of chivalric fictions guilty of poisoning don Quijote's mind?[10] Is don Quijote's madness contagious? Does it lead him to heroism or foolishness?

Although the knight's life may be deemed a failure in terms of the chivalric ideals, it succeeds when viewed in terms of its textuality. Don Quijote seeks to "vivir la vida como obra de arte" (Avalle Arce and Riley 1973, 53), and the text shows how countless imitative strategies serve to flesh out an "original" character whose search for an elusive truth is more important than his attainments.[11] In *Don Quijote*, knowledge in the guise of imitation allows the author and his audience to delve deeper into actions and ideas, thus leading the reader to reenvision herself in the light of past heroes and fools. This contrastive type of imitation that takes an ancient model and juxtaposes it to an unworthy modern frame is evinced through the novel's Virgilian subtext and the construction of women characters after Medea, Circe, and Calypso. A number of other ancient building blocks can also be found in the novel. At the very center of Part 1, for example, the interpolated tale "Curioso impertinente" develops out of the tale of Gyges in Plato and Herodotus (see de Armas 1992b; de Armas Wilson 1987). Don Quijote's own intrusion into the interpolation when he slays the giants/wineskins is but an imitation of Lucius's similar "feat" in Apuleius's *Golden Ass*. Both ancient and modern novel foreground curiosity and invisibility through interpolations – the tale of Cupid and Psyche is thus refashioned into the "Curioso impertinente" (de Armas 1992b). If the center of Part 1 deals with Gyges' vision and Psyche's curiosity, the center of Part 2, the Cave of Montesinos, is based on the epic *catabasis*, the descent to the underworld made by antique heroes in order to attain a certain knowledge. Even the prologue itself imitates the ancients. As Francisco J. Martín suggests, the friend that comes to counsel the "author" is none other than "Prologus," an ancient Latin character (1993, 80).

The rivalry between Cervantes and Lope de Vega led the former to fashion a negative portrait of his successful opponent. Although there are some factual elements in this fashioning, it does not allow for Lope's own successes in classical imitation. It also obscures the curiously similar attitude toward imitation held by both of these writers.[12] Even though Lope de Vega's *Arte nuevo de hacer comedias* begins with a rejection of Aristotelian precepts and classical models,[13] the poem is framed in such a way that the reader is constantly reminded of the classics. Indeed, Lope introduces his subject with a comparison between a Spanish academy and those of Plato and Cicero. Lope, along with many other playwrights of the period, is resisting the pressures to imitate what were then considered to be the authoritative models, the Greek and Roman "classics." Thomas M. Greene documents both "resistance and ambivalence toward imitation" throughout the Renaissance, showing them to be a "congenital feature of humanism" (1982, 43). What Greene calls "Leonardo's heresy" is not very different from Lope's stance. The Italian painter asserts: "One must never imitate the manner of another, because as an artist he will be called the grandchild and not the son of Nature" (Greene 1982, 44). Lope de Vega also invokes nature when he goes against the imitation of Aristotelian precepts, claiming that the tragic and the comic should not be separated since variety is part of nature ("Buen exemplo nos da naturaleza" [1971, 291]). What Cervantes criticizes is Lope de Vega's pretentiousness in showing off his learning. Although Lope de Vega often points to classical models, in reality he has not read many of the primary works but derives his seeming erudition from Renaissance compendia.[14] But there is much more to Lope. His plays deliberately break with classical notions while at the same time cleverly concealing a series of mythical layers. Lope de Vega's texts resist the classics in the sense that they do not follow particular classical models. They simply retell and reinvent classical mythology, using not only classical authorities but also the many Renaissance mythographers who allegorized, euhemerized, and transformed gods into natural forces.[15] This type of approach will be imitated by many of Lope's followers. If Spanish theater is different from that of the rest of Europe during this period,[16] it is not because it fails to imitate the classics, but because, through a greater resistance to imitation, it cleverly hides or pretends to reject its models – and it also accepts the gods of the ancients in their medieval and Renaissance incarnations.

La Numancia, however, differs from both Don Quijote and Lope de Vega's theater in that it hides this resistance while exhibiting a series of classical models. It also turns its back on the mythographers and prefers to deal with classical authorities, albeit through translations or refashionings of many of these. La Numancia thus becomes both an archive of the past and an archeological site that demands attention. As Willard F. King has shown, Cervantes rejects "fallacious half-fictionalized chronicles or ballads" (1979, 202) as historical sources and turns instead to Ambrosio de Morales's Corónica general de España since this author was "the first to combine the aim of writing an imperial history with the new humanist standards of historiographical rigor" (King 1979, 203). In the prologue to his Corónica, Morales is careful to differentiate his approach to history from those of his predecessors: "Corónicas tenemos en España, en que se cuenta destos tiempos de los Romanos, mas son muy defectuosas, faltándoles muchas cosas" (1791, 3.iv). Indeed, Morales claims that they are "desconformes de la verdad" (1791, 3.iv). In order to arrive at a more accurate history, Morales utilizes a number of "archeological" approaches. Ancient inscriptions on Spanish stones, for example, are scrutinized for data (1791, 3.xx). He also searches for historical information on ancient coins: "Ayudéme tambien en muchas partes de las monedas antiguas, y déstas no puse ninguna que no la tenga, o por lo ménos la haya visto" (1791, 3.xxi).

Quite unlike the *ventero* in *Don Quijote* (1978, 1.32.394–6) who confuses history with fiction, Morales is very careful to scrutinize ancient histories looking for the "true" events. For example, speaking of Scipio Africanus (the grandfather of the Scipio who laid siege to Numantia), Morales attempts to ascertain his title when he first went to Spain. In order to do this, he compares the different ancient accounts: "Solo Paulo Osorio dice, que vino Scipion con oficio y título de Procónsul, y Plinio que tuvo cargo de Prétor: pero yo creo mas á Tito Livio y á Valerio Máximo, que dan despues manifiesta razón, según verémos en su lugar de come no truxo oficio ninguno ordinario, sino solo título y cargo de Capitan General" (1791, 3.33). Thus, Cervantes would have been well informed of all the classical accounts of the battle of Numantia by Ambrosio de Morales, who repeatedly compares ancient accounts.

In modern times, a number of scholars have reviewed the classical historians that deal with the battle, and some have compared these accounts with Cervantes's play.[17] Santiago Gómez Santacruz (1914), for example, examines numerous accounts from Roman times that deal with Numantia. He asserts that Appian of Alexandria is the most reliable, since he learned of the events from Polybius, who was present at Numantia. Unfortunately, Polybius's own account is lost – although in a recent work of fiction Carlos Fuentes imagines that the Greek historian only pretended to lose his papers on Numantia.[18] Morales, like modern historians, uses Appian as his primary source on matters of Numantia, bemoaning the fact that Titus Livius's accounts also are lost (1791, 3.305). Other accounts of the events are found in the works of Valerius Maximus, Lucius Anneus Florus, Paulus Orosius, Julius Frontinus, and others. These chronicles differ significantly on the fate of the city. While Appian, for example, relates that a number of the Numantians committed suicide when the order was given to surrender,[19] later narratives describe how the inhabitants of the city decided on a collective suicide after setting fire to all their possessions. Some believe that this second account arose out of an anecdote found in Valerius Maximus in which a certain Retógenes led the citizens in his neighborhood to set fire to their buildings and possessions and to kill each other instead of surrendering (Gómez Santacruz 1914, 143).[20] It is interesting to note that Morales, when dealing with the final suicide, rejects Appian of Alexandria's account, even though up to this point Appian has been his main source for the siege of Numantia.[21] In this choice, Morales may have influenced Cervantes to accept the legendary collective suicide as historical. Anneus Florus's narrative, for example, is certainly more heroic and more amenable to being turned into a tragedy than Appian's more measured account: "not a single Numantine was left to be led in triumph as a prisoner . . . their arms they themselves burned" (1929, 157). It would seem, then, that Cervantes's archeological interest in the reconstruction of Numantia was mediated by his readings of Ambrosio Morales and by his desire to re-create an extreme example of tragic valor. In this, Cervantes may have also followed Juan Luis Vives's *Vigilia al margen del sueño de Escipión.* Although praising Scipio, Vives shows how the city, in the end, becomes a mere simulacrum, a source of neither prisoners nor booty.

Although Cervantes may have turned to a number of historical accounts from classical antiquity, Morales's own discussion of the ancients may have been all he used. After all, Morales carefully listed his ancient sources and debated their merits. Having said all this, we can now turn to more pertinent matters, since this book is not about Cervantes and classical history. I am interested in the literary texts he imitated rather than the historical ones. Or to put it another way, I would like to envision the literary adumbrations of history that can be gleaned from the play. This is not to say that I have not taken Morales into account. When historical and literary models seem to coalesce, I will point to Morales's contribution. But the main thrust of the book has to do with Renaissance art and classical literature. Cervantes's play conjoins the historical edifice with a series of literary allusions, images, and structures from the literature of classical antiquity and from the reenvisioning of antiquity by Renaissance artists. It is as if he were reconstructing Numantia using other ancient cities as models. His archeology of the Celtiberian city is based on visions of Troy and Rome by the foremost classical writers.

Cervantes, I will argue, derived this interest in the archeology of the ancients not only from his early humanistic studies but, more important, from his trip to Rome, where he saw the frescoes of Raphael and his disciples, and where he must have read Giorgio Vasari's account of many of the paintings and other works of art he viewed. Indeed, Vasari's conception of art history did not differ significantly from Morales's careful reconstruction of the "truths" of ancient history. As Patricia Lee Rubin has shown, in the second edition Vasari carefully revised his work to reflect

Vincenzo Borghini's distinction between legend and history, including a more "rigorous critical evaluation of sources" (1995, 190). This extensive revision resulted in the removal of many anecdotal accounts, epitaphs, and commemorative verses, as well as "the elimination of much, but not all, apocrypha" (Rubin 1995, 227). Although Cervantes would have been guided by Vasari's critical evaluation of art, he would deviate from *Lives of the Artists* in some cases where Vasari's description of the paintings was inaccurate. But Vasari could well have provided Cervantes with the initial impetus to search for accuracy in historical and artistic narratives. Indeed, the parallel between literature and painting may have been suggested to Cervantes by Vasari (among others), since Vasari was a painter who also succeeded as a writer and who showed how much he valued poetry in his histories and in his art.[22]

For Vasari, Raphael was the new Apelles, the exemplary painter of modern times.[23] Thus, he became Cervantes's main subject of imitation in *La Numancia*. Raphael's interest in reconstructing the Greek and Roman past through the visual arts led Cervantes to envision his tragedy as a truly "classical" work, one that re-created moments of epic and/or tragic grandeur such as the destruction of Numantia/Troy/Rome. And yet, Cervantes differs from Raphael in that he does not consistently demand authenticity and origins. While Raphael searches for remnants of classical art in order to recapture a vision of the world, Cervantes accepts the mediation of more recent writers and artists. Nevertheless, this study will disagree with Rudolph Schevill's statement that "the author of *Don Quixote* and the *Novels* betrays nowhere that he had ever given the ancients prolonged and sympathetic study" (1919, 170). Although this Hispanist was correct in assuming that Cervantes's knowledge of classical writers often came from "secondary sources" (1919, 174), this does not mean that the author of *La Numancia* did not have a keen interest in the classical past and that he did not read certain key texts in the Latin original. Cervantes's quixotic yet realized dream was to reconstruct the classical past through the means available to him. His resulting vision is a bridge that joins an ancient culture with a new empire, using both chronological ends to reach for an understanding of the complexities of culture, and in particular of the heroic and political spheres in classical and Spanish letters.

The structure of *La Numancia* derives in many ways from Raphael's own structuring of the ancients. And, although Cervantes points to Greek literature, he does not read it in the original language but constructs his perception of its meanings through translations, summaries, and adaptations. Even when dealing with some of the Latin writers, mediation is utilized: Cicero is seen through Macrobius's commentary and Juan Luis Vives's *Vigilia al margen del sueño de Escipión*. Perhaps Cervantes did read Lucan, Seneca, and Virgil in the original, but he also read translations and commentaries that impinged upon his models. The purpose of this book is not to search for the specific mediators (although a number of them will be pointed out) but to look at the classical authors to which the text points and discover their uses in the play. After all, they are the authorities, the acknowledged myth of origins of the text. A look at how these models are inscribed and imitated may give us a better understanding of the means and purposes of imitation.

A surprising number of classical allusions, concepts, and patterns are carefully hidden in the text. But concealment carries with it a persistent movement toward unveiling, toward the acknowledgment of a genealogical line. Thomas M. Greene asserts that even though we know that "the intertextual roots of each masterpiece are infinitely more entangled" than it acknowledges, and that "the unconfessed genealogical line may prove to be as nourishing as the visible," there is still a "special status" granted to the work's "self-constructed myth of origins" (1982, 19).

Consequently, this study will first look at classical tragedy as the "myth of origins" for *La Numancia*, simply because of the play's formal structure. But this study will also search for deeper textual mysteries veiled by the text. Although Chapter 5 will deal with Aeschylus as a possible origin for Cervantes's praise of the enemy, the play's construction does not depend upon the Greek tragedian. Chapters 2 through 4 focus on Cervantes's interest in archeology as derived from his Italian sojourn. It was in Rome around 1570 that Cervantes, while gazing at the frescoes painted by Raphael in the Vatican, gained new perspectives that would lead to the construction of *La Numancia* many years later. The elemental design of each of the four *halls* decorated by Raphael points to earth, water, air, and fire as keys to their placement and meaning. Cervantes will also emphasize this elemental quaternity. Chapter 4 will show that even frescoes by Raphael's disciples, particularly by Giulio Romano, led Cervantes to envision certain scenes in the play. Through the prism of time, history, and experience, Cervantes came to visualize Roman power and Roman ruin as a point of departure for the re-creation of a city whose ruins could rival those of Rome – a Celtiberian city that defied Rome's power. Visualizing Raphael through the art of memory and the prism of experience, Cervantes was able to construct an elemental play that incessantly questions the past, turning archeology from an enterprise of praise to an examination of power and empire. But the four elements and the conjoining of classical poets as found in Raphael's *halls* in the Vatican did evolve into a new program for the imitation and disinterment of the classics.

La Numancia points to a quaternity of authorities from the past: Homer, Virgil, Lucan, and Cicero/Macrobius. As shown in Raphael's *Parnassus*, Virgil looks at Homer for his construction of the *Aeneid*. The Roman writer wishes to equal and even surpass the Greek master. As Juan Luis Vives explains, Virgil strives to vanquish "con una más moderna invención, la rudeza primitiva" (1947, 1.547). This *aemulatio*, or contest, is also found throughout *La Numancia*, as Cervantes develops new ways in which to present antique materials. But *La Numancia* not only competes with the ancients but also shows them vying with each other for superiority. In a clever maneuver, the text contrasts the two canonical epic poets (Homer and Virgil) with the "Spanish" writer Lucan, whose *Pharsalia* has been labeled an anti-epic. At a time when Senecan horror was pervasive in the theater, the impact of this Roman tragedian must also be considered. Ambrosio de Morales had foregrounded both Lucan and Seneca as "Spanish" writers in his *Corónica* (1791, 4.398–436). In *La Numancia* Seneca contaminates the action of acts 3 and 4. Ambrosio Morales's comparison of Lucan and Virgil may have led Cervantes to establish a contest of epics and voices in his play. For Morales, Lucan's *Pharsalia* is much inferior to Virgil's *Aeneid* (1791, 4.433). In Cervantes, however, the competition is much keener. While Virgil provides the trappings for empire, Lucan is used to question and even subvert some of the notions ascribed to the canonical epics. Three other classical Greek authors in addition to Homer serve to construct the frame of the work, Aeschylus, Plato, and Aristotle. While Aeschylus, as stated, allows Cervantes to fashion a tragedy from the enemy's perspective, the Homeric epics prepare the reader/audience for a debate as to who is the perfect hero: the Numantians or the Roman general Scipio (Achilles or Odysseus). Plato's numerology and Aristotle's ethics and poetics contribute other building blocks.

This variety of ancient models utilized in one play may lead to criticism of Cervantes's dramatic architecture. After all, in the prologue to the *Andria*, perhaps the best-known Roman play in medieval and Renaissance times, Terence has to rebut the charge of "contaminare fabulas." His play, which was intended as an imitation of Menander's own *Andria*, is "contaminated" with Menander's *Perinthia*. He has thus been charged with "ruining his Greek originals by creating inappropriate mixtures, hybrids made up from different texts" (Conti 1988, 99). Ever since Terence had to defend himself from the charge of *contaminatio*, authors, critics, and theorists have debated the value of the "technique of crossing different literary models in a single text" (Conti 1988, 99). Thomas Greene, for example, seems to equate *contaminatio* with what he calls eclectic or exploitative imitation, where "echoes, phrases, and images from a large number of authors jostle each other indifferently" (1982, 39). This is not Cervantes's technique, nor is it Terence's imitative strategy. I will be using the term *contaminatio*, in contradistinction to Greene, to indicate the blending of a discrete number of ancient texts: either two or three key texts or one central text and a sprinkling of subsidiary ones. Only once in *La Numancia* will Cervantes go beyond *contaminatio* and enter upon the exploitative or eclectic manner. I hope to show in Chapter 9 how even here, Cervantes's uses of imitation transcend hybridization. As for the play as a whole, its structure is such that it places each model in a different *locus*. Contained within each act,[24] each of the four key models of Cervantes's tragic and epic action will battle each other without succumbing to hybridization. Contamination is thus kept to a minimum in *La Numancia*'s elemental construct based on Raphael's art.

These ancient authorities (Aeschylus, Aristotle, Cicero, Homer, Lucan, Plato, Seneca, and Virgil) provide Cervantes with the frame for his imperial edifice. His tragedy deals, among other things, with power and how to wield it. Through the doubling of history, through the representation of several dual presents such as Troy/Numantia, pre-Christian Spain/Golden Age Spain, and imperial Rome/imperial Spain, Cervantes is able to elucidate startling correspondences and thus establish a series of contrastive models through which he can engage the reader/audience in a debate over the uses and abuses of power. In looking at the siege of Numantia through the siege of Troy, in writing a foundation myth of the Spanish Empire through the Virgilian foundation myth of Rome, Cervantes is not only donning the authoritative mantle of the ancients for a bellicose and imperialistic agenda but also pointing to the foibles of his predecessors and thus to the pitfalls of contemporary imperialism. Through imitation, the text acquires a much richer texture, one where the borrowed threads of the classics run both toward praise and toward correction not only of the models but also of the political vision which those models seem to espouse. Cervantes is writing not only a text of discovery but also one of rediscovery of the ancients. As Michael Riffaterre explains: "One writes according to models, so that one's reader will simultaneously experience the pleasure of discovery and the pleasure of rediscovery" (1983, 133). Discovery of the complexities of power and imperial rule comes from a rediscovery of the ancients. And Cervantes's text goes one step further. In addition to ancient texts, he inscribes in his theater images of Renaissance art. Knowing that Raphael's political agenda in the *halls* at the Vatican was the celebration of papal power and the representation of how the heavens protected such power, Cervantes could clearly perceive how the frescoes fulfilled this role but went beyond it. A vision of the ancients which was supposed to endow the papacy with added authority was in itself so compelling that it could even subvert the political agenda. Cervantes thus came to understand the subversive nature of beauty – it can destabilize even the most carefully thought-out ideology.

La Numancia, I would argue, goes beyond any fixed ideology to set the mind questing through the labyrinths of power in search of ways to deal with humanity's bellicose desire for acquisition. Every authority, every move toward closure, is followed by a countermove in a tapestry so rich that aesthetic pleasure constantly ruptures the political vision, enabling the work to sustain even more deadly ruptures and oppositions within its frame. Cervantes's archeological feats, his necromantic ability to summon Numantia/Troy/Rome, alert us to his concept of the poet as a being that is often associated with the devil. His alluring vision of the classical past and of an epic of imperial Spain is nothing more than a virtuoso display of the trappings of earthly power. This illusory richness lays bare the mechanisms of mythmaking (how Numantia is fashioned after Rome) and the ways in which human beings seek transcendence through the very forces of death and decay. By having his characters evoke the fear of Pompey's son, the lament of the Trojan women, the valor of Achilles, the cleverness of Odysseus, and the piety of Aeneas, the work points to questions of ethics, to right action as a means to construct the immortal within the mortal. To the alluring vision of power and empire, Cervantes adds the individual's reconstruction of the self through a glimpse of the infinite potential of a life lived beyond the four elements.

2

Raphael
A Vatican of the mind

At a time when the poetry of ruins was enjoying increasing popularity due to the Renaissance's interest in remnants from the classical past and, specifically, the archeology of ancient Rome,[1] Cervantes evokes the ruins of Numantia. This chapter will place Cervantes in Rome viewing the ruins of the ancient past not only in their disintegrating physical form but also through the frescoes of Raphael at the Vatican. Very much like Castiglioni's *Superbi colli* and Du Bellay's *Antiquités de Rome*, Cervantes's play participates in a textual necromancy,[2] in bringing back through written representations the human, artistic, and architectural remnants of the ancients. Cervantes's evocation of the old Celtiberian city is not significantly different from Villamediana's vision of Rome: "Estas de admiración reliquias dinas / tumbas, anfiteatros, coliseos" (1990, 424, no. 338). Both writers revel in *admiratio*. For Villamediana, Rome's remains, its body, is as admirable as the relics of Christian martyrs. This analogy is even clearer in Castiglioni's sonnet where *reliquie* is explicitly linked to the *martir* of the fourth stanza (Foulché-Delbosc 1904, 225–6).[3] In Part 2 of *Don Quijote*, an extended discussion of Rome's ruined ancient monuments leads to questions of fame, sainthood, and relics (1978, 2.8.95–9). Cervantes again echoes the sacred elements of the poetry of ruins in the fourth book of *Persiles y Sigismunda*. When the pilgrims arrive in Rome, one of them intones a sonnet in praise of the city: "La tierra de tu suelo, que contemplo / con la sangre de mártires mezclada, / es la reliquia universal del suelo" (1969, 426).

The relationship between Rome and the Christian martyrs in Castiglioni, Cervantes, and Villamediana not only points to the contrast between Rome's second life (fame) and the martyrs' third life (heavenly bliss) but also serves to contrast pagan and Christian ways of life. The first line of Cervantes's sonnet in *Persiles y Sigismunda* describes the city as "poderosa" (1969, 426). The Renaissance and Baroque poetry of ruins often contrasts the pride of ancient Rome with the virtue of the new Christianized Rome. In Cervantes's *La Numancia* the contrast is translated into the opposition between Roman pride and Numantia's sacrifice. Cervantes includes both the life of Fame and the sacrifice or martyrdom of the city, which leads to "esa alegría final cristiana de la muerte que es vida, vida inmortal," as Casalduero (1966, 281) aptly put it many years ago, but his innovation is to be found in a fourth life, an imperial and glorious present that has become possible by the sacrifice and ruin of the past. Just as a Christian martyr gives his life for heavenly immortality, Numantia sacrifices its people to unify Spain and create a great empire under Charles V and Philip II.

It has been claimed that Villamediana's interest in the ruins of Rome dates from his voyage to Italy (1610–16). I would argue that Cervantes's concern with the ruins of Numantia derives from reminiscences of his trip to Italy forty years earlier, when, as Luis Andrés Murillo explains: "Su espíritu se abre y rebosa en la deslumbrante claridad de la cultura humanística, pinturas, arquitectura, literatura, que han venido formando varias generaciones de artistas, poetas y filósofos italianos" (Cervantes 1978, 20). Although such memories of Italy are inscribed in his play, they have been altered by time and experience. In *La Numancia*, Cervantes's Italian sojourn appears refracted through the prism of a series of reverses in life: captivity led to a questioning of the glories of war when he returned to Spain virtually forgotten. In a period when, as Foucault claims, "resemblance played a constructive role in the knowledge of Western culture," when analogy reigned supreme (1973, 17, 21),[4] reminiscences on the glories of Cervantes's imperial conquests could quickly turn into a reflection of the glories of imperial Rome. Vestiges of past personal triumphs could recall the ruins of the Eternal City. After all, personal and urban destruction come together in poems where the "Tú mortal" coalesces with "polvo" and Roman ruins (Villamediana 1990, 424, no. 338). Cervantes is a forgotten war hero in the 1580s. His own "trofeos imperiales" have turned to dust. Has the empire followed suit? Ruin and necromancy; martyrdom and resurrection; archeology and art; war, *ekpyrosis,* and imperial *renovatio*: these are the subjects of his own reflections on the relics of Rome that are artfully and cleverly metamorphosed into the ruins of Numantia. These reflections, I will argue, transport the writer from the dusty roads of Spain, where he seeks to make a living, to the palaces and ruins of Italy, where once lived the great exponents of an ancient culture. This art of the ancients experiences a rebirth through the medium of Renaissance art and archeology. Classical and Renaissance voices, ancient ruins and artful palaces, impinge upon a present that Cervantes seeks to transform.

In *La Galatea*, Cervantes tells us how he served "al cardenal de Acquaviva, siendo yo su camarero en Roma" (1968, 1.2). We know that Cervantes
was in Rome in the winter of 1569, and we also know that he needed and
was issued a testimonial of "unblemished origins" in December of that year
(McKendrick 1980, 55; Canavaggio 1987, 49).[5] He may well have started
working for Acquaviva at this time. McKendrick explains: "The cardinal,
after all, who was only a year older than Miguel, is far more likely to have
taken on as secretary cum-steward a young man straight from Spain with
his schooling and his burgeoning literary aspirations still close about him,
rather than a veteran soldier" (1980, 55). Rome's artistic treasures must
have had a strong impact on Cervantes. Indeed, *La Galatea*, where Cervantes reveals his trip to Rome, may well record several instances of the
poet's contact with Renaissance Italian art. George Camamis has argued
for the influence of Botticelli's *Primavera* upon this pastoral romance. He
also claims that this painting, together with *The Birth of Venus* and *Venus
and Mars*, are key to the composition of *La gitanilla*. And in an essay which
was in press when I completed this manuscript, Edward Dudley has argued
that inscribed within Cervantes's *La Galatea* is Raphael's *Il trionfo di Galatea*,
painted for the Palazzo Farnesina in Rome (1511–12).[6] Both the painting and the pastoral partake of the new Neoplatonic aesthetics, which dis-
cards Venus's lascivious voluptuousness in favor of Galatea's chastity. In
both works, the nymph, although surrounded by eroticism, is able to stand
apart from it. In Raphael's painting, "she cuts diagonally through the sce-
nario, avoiding all attempts to involve her in the goings on" (Dudley 1995,
36), while in Cervantes's romance she also performs an "evasive diagonal
movement" (1995, 38) as she "escapes from the multiple lovers' snares"
(1995, 39). Indeed, this program detected by Dudley in *La Galatea* may
also be found in *La Numancia,* where Scipio banishes Venus and her lustful satisfactions from the Roman camp. Galatea's chastity may be inscribed
in Lira's love for Marandro.

In the fourth and final book of *Persiles y Sigismunda*, the pilgrims arrive
in Rome and view great artworks from classical times and from the Italian Renaissance: "Parrasio, Polignoto, Apeles, Ceuxis y Timantes tenían
allí lo perfecto de sus pinceles . . . acompañados de los del devoto Rafael
de Urbino y de los del divino Micael Angelo" (1969, 445).[7] This passage
testifies not only to Cervantes's archeological interest (which is developed
elsewhere in the romance)[8] but also to his fascination with Michelangelo
and Raphael, artists who contributed extensively to the decoration of the
Vatican.[9] While in the service of Acquaviva in Rome, Cervantes must have

become well acquainted with the Vatican – not only with the political intrigue that may have led him to leave the city eventually[10] but particularly with the artworks found therein. Indeed, the pairing of Michelangelo and Raphael in *Persiles y Sigismunda* is significant since Raphael was commissioned to decorate the Stanza della Segnatura in the Vatican at the same time as Michelangelo began to work on the ceiling of the Sistine Chapel. As James Beck contends: "The two projects, which of course differ vastly in size and subject matter, must have instilled an air of competition between the two artists, despite a gap in their ages" (1993, 8). Spanish treatises on art discuss this competition. Francisco de Holanda's *Diálogos de la pintura* (1563), for example, compares Raphael's frescoes in the *stanze* with Michelangelo's commission in the Sistine Chapel. Holanda, an admirer of Michelangelo, places Raphael's art as a close second to Michelangelo's.[11] It is Raphael's commission that has a bearing on *La Numancia*.

Four great public *stanze* (halls) in the Vatican Palace preserve even today the frescoes[12] composed by Raphael and his disciples beginning in 1508. These halls were "papal offices and reception rooms" (Hersey 1993, 129), which Cervantes would have viewed while working for Acquaviva. That Cervantes remembered these paintings and transformed them through experience into poetry, the tragic vision of *La Numancia*, should not come as a surprise. The young poet must have been anxious to view works by the Italian masters, whose "pagan" subjects differed so much from Spanish paintings of the Golden Age. As Jonathan Brown reminds us: "It has often been obseved that Spanish painting of the Golden Age is largely restricted to religious subjects (mostly from the New Testament), portraiture, and still life, in that order. Absent, or nearly absent, are mythological and allegorical subjects" (1991, 4). The Spanish poet, taught in his youth by a humanist, must have wanted to understand how Italian artists were able to foreground the pagan while embracing the Christian at the very center of Catholic power, the Vatican.

Cervantes's artistic development would profit not only from this syncretism but also from the infusion of pictorialism into his poetics. As noted in the previous chapter, Cervantes was no doubt familiar with Vasari's *Lives of the Artists*, in which Vasari stresses visualization on the part of the reader. Patricia Lee Rubin explains: "Vasari's address to the judicious eye of his reader depended in part on a definition of imagination as the inner sense (the *imaginativa*) that formed mental images of sense experience and impressed them upon memory. The assumed link between perception and cognition made it possible for Vasari confidently to produce a book about images without illustration" (1995, 233). This type of visualization would reappear in Cervantes's narrative art, as Helena Percas de Ponseti has pointed out. This critic has found numerous visual features, leading her to conclude that Cervantes "develops his fiction along two levels simultaneously: a narrative level . . . and a visual, pictorial level" (1988, 29). Both *Don Quijote* and *Persiles y Sigismunda* stress the link between the two arts. Discussing Garcilaso's *Third Eclogue*, don Quijote recalls "los versos de nuestro poeta donde nos pinta las labores que hacían allá en su morada de cristal aquellas cuatro ninfas" (1978, 2.8.94). While the verses "paint" the nymphs (a type of representation that would be absent from Golden Age painting, which was characterized by "doctrinaire religiosity" [Brown 1991, 308] and a lack of mythological subjects), they also weave a tapestry. This double link between the verbal and the visual reinforces their "sisterly" connection. In Cervantes's Byzantine romance, an instance of ekphrasis[13] also underlines the link between literature and the visual arts. Here, two former captives from Algiers display a painting of the city and describe what is represented. Their tale, however, turns out to be a fiction. The people then ask Periandro and the pilgrims who accompany him: "¿ . . . traéis algún lienzo que enseñarnos? ¿Traéis otra historia que hacernos creer por verdadera, aunque la haya compuesto la misma mentira?" (1969, 350). Verisimilitude is thus seen as a notion utilized by both painting and narrative. More important, narrative often utilizes ekphrastic or visual elements in order to persuade.

While in Rome, Cervantes may have learned the epideictic genre of classical rhetoric favored by humanists and often used in panegyrics of the city. In this art of praise and blame, visualization was stressed: "To admire, love, and praise meant not to think but to gaze upon. Indeed, the use of ekphrasis – the detailed visual description, often of buildings or works of art . . . – aimed at bringing about 'seeing through hearing'" (Stinger 1985, 73–4). While poets and humanists sought to combine the verbal and the visual, artists evinced a similar concern. Raphael was famous for bringing poetry and painting together. In the *Comentarios de la pintura* (1560?), Felipe de Guevara tells how both Michelangelo and Raphael utilized in their art their knowledge of classical poetry and history. Of the latter Guevara states: "y así merece ser celebrada una loable costumbre de Rafael de Urbino en esta materia, de quien dicen que todo el tiempo que estaba en su oficina trabajando, tenía lección de historia o poesía" (Pérez Sánchez 1985, 30). Cervantes, then, is part of a culture "in which those who made words and pictures, as well as the patrons and connoisseurs of such enterprises, were themselves interconnected" (Barkan 1995, 328).

The linkage between poetry and the visual arts was not unique to the Italian Renaissance and the Spanish Golden Age[14] but was part of a long tradition. In England, Sidney's *Apology for Poetry*, published in the last decade of the sixteenth century, defines and defends this art through a pictorial image, describing its use of mimesis in terms of "a speaking picture" (Barkan 1995, 326). Frances Yates reminds us of the antiquity of the relationship between poetry and painting. Simonedes of Ceos, she tells us, believed that "the poet and the painter both think in visual images which the one expresses in poetry and the other in pictures" (1966, 28).[15] The transposition, then, was based on the supremacy of sight. Furthermore, transposition and visualization have to be conjoined with memory, since Cervantes returned to the subject more than ten years later. Simonides was also the inventor of the art of memory, conceiving of "poetry, painting and mnemonics in terms of intense visualization" (Yates 1966, 28). In order to have a good memory, the orator or poet must create loci in the mind to order the oration. These places contain images to remind the practitioner of specific arguments or notions. During the Renaissance, these images were often associated with paintings. In *L'arte del ricordare*, published in Naples in 1566, Giovanni Battista della Porta suggests: "It is useful to take pictures by good artists as memory images for these are more striking and move more than pictures by ordinary painters. For example, pictures by Michelangelo, Raphael, Titian, stay in the memory" (Yates 1966, 206).[16]

While Cervantes was in Rome gazing at the Vatican frescoes, Matteo Ricci was also in the city studying at the Jesuit College.[17] The future priest, who introduced the art of memory to the Chinese, learned it in college along with his fellow students. The textbook on rhetoric and grammar that he studied was probably Cypriano Soarez's *De arte rhetorica*. It includes the art of memory placing: "The students should practice creating dramatic images of various kinds, and designing locations for them: palatial buildings or spacious churches would be among the best" (Spence 1984, 5). Cervantes, then, could well have conceived of the Vatican as a place of memory – after all, churches and palaces were often recommended for such loci. And what greater hall for the mind than the center of Catholic power? Four halls, with their frescoes by Raphael and his disciples, could well have become the loci containing those striking images recommended by della Porta. Even if Cervantes had no desire to create an art of memory from these four halls, we have della Porta's assurance that paintings by Raphael were thought to be strikingly easy to remember. And visualization was key to both painting and poetry. The young writer would have treasured Raphael's images as mimetic keys for his own poetry. These images would also fill the absence of classical subjects in Spanish art.

The art of memory was well known is Spain during the sixteenth century.[18] There are also clear indications that Cervantes was preoccupied with memory: in many of his texts, Cervantes points to fame, recollection, and anagnorisis as keys to narrative. Aurora Egido has carefully studied a host of mnemonic devices in the *Novelas ejemplares*. Although she shows that Cervantes moves away from the traditional art of memory in order to "hacer novela, vale decir, para que la memoria discurra por los complejos canales del alma humana" (1994, 481), she does point out how the ancient art is inscribed in his texts. For example, Egido notes how Leocadia in *La fuerza de la sangre* "es la personificación misma de la memoria que guarda dentro de sí total recuerdo de los lugares y las imágenes de forma imborrable" (1994, 471). Such places and images are central to the art of memory. Like Leocadia, Cervantes as writer becomes the personification of memory. Let us then look at the Vatican as one of the places of memory for Cervantes and study *La Numancia* as a restructuring and revisualization of Raphael's frescoes at the Vatican. Through the prism of art and experience these places of memory would be transformed into other places, other rooms.

The Stanza della Segnatura and the Stanza d'Eliodoro were originally painted by Piero della Francesca, with later decorations by Lucas Signorelli and Giovanni Antonio Bazzi (Sodoma). But Pope Julius II interrupted the work of Signorelli and Sodoma[19] and had the earlier work of Piero della Francesca destroyed so as to redo these *halls* (Nesselrath 1992, 36). He agreed, on Donato Bramante's counsel, to give a young artist a chance: "So pleased was the pope with Raphael's work, that he was put in charge" (Hersey 1993, 129). The first hall to be decorated by Raphael was the Stanza della Segnatura (1508-11). Of the four halls that bridged the Belvedere and the Cortile del Pappagallo, this one is the only one "whose main scenes are thought to have been painted entirely by Raphael" (Hersey 1993, 130). It exhibits one of his most famous works, *The School of Athens* (Fig. 1). Frances Yates compares this painting to Cosmas Rossellius's *Thesaurus artificiosae memoria*,[20] showing how the figures of antiquity in Raphael's painting coincide with memory images suggested by Rossellius. She asks: "Are we looking at Raphael's *School of Athens* as useful

Figure 1. Raphael, *The School of Athens* (photo: Alinari/Art Resource, NY).

for memory and 'placing' his Plato as Theology, his Aristotle as Philosophy?" (1966, 164).[21] Whatever the answer may be, there is no question that Raphael's painting recalls the images of an art of memory and calls out for the orderly placement of the images in the room. Such an ordering may have also been related to the shelving of books in this hall, which served as a library under Julius II.[22]

Raphael's fresco does make it obvious that at least one ordering element is at work. At the very center of all the great thinkers of ancient Greece stands Plato, pointing to the heavens and holding in his hand the *Timaeus*. S. K. Heninger has shown that this Platonic dialogue was, for the Renaissance, "the most important single vehicle of Pythagorean doctrine" (1974, 47). This text foregrounds numerology, studying the notion of harmony through mathematical ratios and structuring the four elements (earth, water, air, and fire) into a unified system called the tetrad or quaternion.[23] In order to further underline the importance of the number 4, Raphael's fresco includes the figure of Pythagoras himself in the left fore-

Figure 2. Vault: *Stanza della Segnatura* (photo: Alinari/Art Resource, NY).

ground, holding a tablet that shows his tetractys: I + II + III + IV = X. This arithmetical formula was the "sacred symbol by which Pythagoreans sealed their oaths" (Heninger 1974, 152) since it was thought that all things were governed by the number 4, and that the sum of the numbers 1 through 4 symbolized perfection. That Empedocles is seen perched behind Pythagoras in Raphael's fresco should come as no surprise, since he was the one who codified the system of the four elements, or roots, which combine and separate through Love and Strife. His theories were associated with those of Pythagoras, who had previously used the number 4 as the focus for his mathematical philosophy and cosmology. Although many structuring principles may be found in *The School of Athens*, the number 4, as seen through the works of Empedocles, Plato, and Pythagoras, is the most obvious.[24]

Indeed, the prominence of quaternity is not restricted to this one fresco. The number 4 is highlighted in the hall not only by the presence of four large paintings but also by the four main figures in the ceiling: Poetry, Philosophy, Theology, and Justice (Fig. 2). Although a number of art critics claim that the fourfold division of the ceiling was made before

Raphael and has little to do with his program for the hall,[25] I would argue that Raphael preserved this structure to underline the importance of quaternity, which is further emphasized by four sets of paired scenes next to these larger figures.[26] The upper pictures deal with Roman history, and the lower ones have mythological subjects. As Edgar Wind has noted, each pair represents one of the four elements (1938, 75–9) and each is also linked to the four larger allegorical figures that refer to the pursuits of the mind. Although Wind does not mention them, there are also four rectangular scenes that are clearly linked to the allegories. The four allegories, the four rectangular figures that comment on these representations, the four histories, and the four mythologies that foreground the elements create four sets of four pictures each (see the table).

Table of quaternities in the Stanza della Segnatura

FIRE
  History: *Mucius Scaevola Placing His Hand in the Flame of the Altar*
  Mythology: *The Forge of Vulcan*
  Allegory: *Theology*
  Rectangle: *The Temptation and Fall of Adam and Eve*
  Fresco: *The Dispute over the Sacrament*
AIR
  History: *Pax Augusta*
  Mythology: *Amphitrite fleeing Neptune*
  Allegory: *Poetry*
  Rectangle: *Apollo and Marsyas*
  Fresco: *Parnassus*
WATER
  History: *The Leader of the Sabines Leads His Horse into Lacus Curtius*
  Mythology: *Satyr Pouring Water over Lovers*
  Allegory: *Philosophy*
  Rectangle: *Astrology*
  Fresco: *The School of Athens*
EARTH
  History: *Creation of the Campus Martius from the Tarquinian Fields*
  Mythology: *Fettered Giants*
  Allegory: *Justice*
  Rectangle: *Judgment of Solomon*
  Fresco: *The Cardinal Virtues Fortitude, Prudence, and Temperance*

This double quaternity invites the spectator not only to view and interpret this particular hall in terms of the four elements but also to consider each of the four rooms as representing a particular element, a guess that would seem to be supported by the fact that the third hall is the Stanza dell'Incendio (fire).[27] Observing this suite of rooms from the Cortile del Pappagallo, the Incendio would be at the extreme left, and the Sala di Constantino would be at the far right. They represent the two extreme elements: fire as the highest for the Incendio and earth as the lowest, represented by Constantine's donation of land to the church. In between these two stand the Stanza della Segnatura and the Stanza d'Eliodoro, with a reversed elemental order since the first foregrounds water (as seen in the fountain of Parnassus) and the latter indicates the prominence of air through the movement and flight of the figures in the frescoes.[28]

The elements were a key ordering aspect of the art of memory and attained singular prominence in Guido Camillo's (1480–1540) theater of memory (Yates 1966, 139–40). Following Camillo's *Art*, a number of treatises of the period relate memory to a theater. Robert Fludd's *Ars memoriae* even includes an engraving of the mnemonic theater.[29] If memory can be a theater and contain within it a fourfold elemental division, then a play can be structured in this manner.[30] A careful look at *La Numancia* reveals that each of its four *acts* foregrounds a particular element. They are represented in the traditional mode, separating the lower elements (earth and water) from the higher (air and fire).[31] While air and fire tend to rise, water and earth fall. Ovid's description of earth in his account of creation emphasizes the heaviness of this element: "The earth was heavier than these, and, drawing with it the grosser elements, sank to the bottom by its own weight" (1921, 1.5/1.29–30). Earth is thus the grossest of the elements, settling at the very bottom of the cosmos, followed by water. Yet, water does not uniformly cover earth. In Christian accounts, this is explained by the fact that God parted the waters from portions of the earth so that humanity would be able to breathe, thus partaking of a heavy and a light element. Even though human beings aspire to rise, as reflected in their upright stance and their breathing, they inhabit the heaviest of elements and build from its materials. The results of such creation at the lowest level are necessarily temporary, since earth, being the grossest element, is most subject to the negative force, strife, which brings about decay, as described by Empedocles.

Cervantes's meditation on the ruins of Numantia is then an affirmation of the strife and decay that are inherent in the element earth. And yet, he does not begin his play with this element. Instead, Act 1 culminates in the prophecy of the river Duero (water). Through the higher of the low elements, the text emphasizes a desire to rise above destruction. Act 2 centers on necromancy or disinterment (earth). It is here that strife and decay come together in a hopeless vision of the future, leading the Numantian priest Marquino to commit suicide. The third and fourth acts reverse the order of the higher elements just like the first two had inverted the sequence of the lower ones. The fires of war and self-destruction consume the city, its treasures, and its inhabitants in the third and the first part of the fourth act. Rather than fanning the fires, air appears at the end in order to blow away the Roman hopes of victory ("en humo y en viento son tornadas / las ciertas esperanzas de vitoria" (vv. 2261-2). Air is the element utilized by Fame in order to transmit to future generations the sacrificial glory of Numantia. The upward thrust of wind and fire also points to humanity's desire for eternity and transcendence. The four acts thus form a Pythagorean tetractys, their sum creating eternity through fame at the end of the play.

As noted above, the macro-elemental structure of the Stanza della Segnatura is replicated in a series of microstructures which again portray the four elements. Cervantes's play also exhibits these microstructures. For example, Act 2, which represents earth, also depicts all four elements in its prophesying thrust: the fire of the sacrifice, the air represented by the birds whose flight reveals the outcome of the siege, the water sprayed on the corpse, and earthen necromancy. In the Stanza della Segnatura there are elemental structures within microstructures. One of the figures in the ceiling, Philosophy (Fig. 3), is dressed, according to James Beck, in a robe that shows "four colors representative of the four elements: blue (air), red (fire), green (water) and yellow (earth)" (1993, 42).[32] *La Numancia* exhibits a similar elemental structure within a microstructure. Both allegorical figures, Spain and the river Duero, evoke the elements. The three tributary streams that accompany Duero serve to emphasize the number 4. While the Duero denotes water, Spain stands for earth. The latter speaks of the city's destruction in terms of the flames in which the phoenix is consumed, thus evoking the element fire (v. 392). Spain's lament ("que prestes a mis ásperos lamentos / atento oído" [vv. 433-4]) is carried through the medium of air and is heard by the Duero, whose prophesying waters put an end to the watery tears of España, envisioning a future where Spain's torn dress can be mended through the reunification of the peninsula ("ha de zurcirse / de nuevo, y a su estado antiguo

Figure 3. Vault: *Stanza della Segnatura: Philosophy* (photo: Alinari/ Art Resource, NY).

unirse" [vv. 520–1]). Thus, Philosophy's elemental garb is reapportioned in the play to cover the two allegorical figures who together prophesy a new and harmonious imperial tetractys which will mend previous tears in imperial unity.

Although partaking of the four elements, Philosophy is related to water in the program of the Stanza della Segnatura. Both her micro-elemental images and her link to water relate her to the river Duero in Cervantes's play. Philosophy carries a sign that reads "causarum cognitio," or a "knowledge of the causes of things" (Hersey 1993, 142), the natural aspect of philosophy. Through the prophecy of the river Duero Cervantes's text shows the causes for both the destruction of the city and the future rise of Spain. Therefore, a careful study of this speech should reveal the bases for imperial power in the sixteenth century. By including the rectangular painting of astrology within the realm of philosophy, the program of the hall further emphasizes the astral–prophetic aspects of natural philosophy. This astral component is also found in the river Duero. When the figure of Spain asks the river how the " alto, sereno y espacioso cielo" is exerting its "influencias" (vv. 353–4), the river answers in terms of "el saber que a Proteo ha dado el cielo" (v. 470). Astrology, then, plays a key role in the causes of things. The importance of this celestial art is also seen in *The School of Athens*. In the right foreground, opposite the "elemental" figures of Pythagoras and Empedocles, stands a crowned figure with his back to the spectator. Holding an earthly globe, he has been identified as the astrologer Ptolemy. Across from him, holding in his hand a globe which represents the stars, is Zoroaster. The two globes may reveal that the positioning of stars is significant in determining the fate of earthly situations. Euclid, drawing geometrical figures, may be attempting to discover the positioning and relationship of earthly to heavenly realms. Thus, in *La Numancia*, España is intent on discovering the celestial influences that are at work in the siege of the city and in her future history.

Both the twin historical and mythological representations of water on the ceiling of the Stanza della Segnatura have a thematic bearing on *La Numancia*, prophesying events in the play. The satyr pouring water over the lovers shows that the bonds of love and passion can be dissolved by the accidents of history. In *La Numancia*, Cipión argues against holding on to passion (Venus) while engaged in the pursuits of Mars; whereas in the Numantian camp, Marandro's sacrifice for Lira shows how love can shine but briefly in the moment of death and destruction. The historical episode is even more telling. Here, Mettius Curtius, leader of the Sabines, leads his horse into the waters of a swamp rather than submit to the Romans. Very much like the Numantians, this Sabine leader fails to give in to superior power and chooses death over domination. Not only does his death foreshadow Numantia's destruction, but the fact that the swamp was renamed Lacus Curtius in his honor corresponds to Numantia's new life through fame. Indeed, Numantia has also become a lake in its resistance to the Romans: "De mirar de sangre / un rojo lago" (vv. 2217–18).

Each of the four historical episodes depicted on the ceiling is taken from Titus Livius's history of Rome. The tale of Lacus Curtius, for example, is told in Book 1, Chapters 12–13 (Wind 1938, 76). Even though these historical paintings may find echoes in Cervantes's play, of equal importance is the fact that Livy's history also narrates Scipio's conquests. In Cervantes's *comedia*, the places of memory are the four acts described in terms of the elementals from the Stanza della Segnatura. But instead of being random events from Livy's history, the acts focus on one particular historical sequence, the siege of Numantia.

If water is associated with natural causes, astrology, the quenching of the passions, the forging of fame, and the utterance of prophecy, fire has very different connotations. The fire of the Stanza della Segnatura is the holy fire of theology, represented by *The Dispute over the Sacrament*.[33] The Eucharist will reappear as a central theme in *The Mass at Bolsena*, one of the four frescoes of the Stanza d'Eliodoro. Its importance will be discussed in the next chapter. Something should be said here, however, of the historical depiction that exemplifies fire. Taken from an episode in Titus Livius (Book 2, chapters 11–13), this fresco portrays Mucius Scaevola placing his hand into the fire of an altar. Although the scene may reflect the link between theology and fire, Scaevola's act had little to do with the gods. By leaving his hand on the fire until it was consumed, this Roman hero is evincing Roman valor and endurance. His deed serves to convince the Etruscan king Lars Porsena to give up his siege of Rome. The besieged Numantia also uses fire against the enemy. Both Scaevola and the inhabitants of the Celtiberian city destroy their bodies so that the community may survive. But the Numantians carry Scaevola's heroic valor to an extreme, burning not only their hands but their whole bodies and all their possessions. In other texts, Cervantes repeatedly reminds the reader that the purpose of Scaevola's deed was to gain fame. Listing a series of acts that were meant to "ganar fama," don Quijote asks: "¿Quién abrazó el brazo y la mano a Mucio?" (1978, 2.8.96). And in the *Viaje del Parnaso*, this Roman figure is portrayed as an example of the power of Vainglory. The false goddess helps to cool Scaevola's hand as he places it upon the fire.[34]

Numantia will also feel the cooling winds of glory as it consumes itself in the fires of destruction. But the reader/audience must ask if these fires are located on the false altar of immortality or on the ground of love of country and liberty. Some of the other companion pieces to *The Dispute over the Sacrament* in this hall point specifically to the fire of the destructive passions. *The Temptation and Fall of Adam and Eve* is the clearest Christian representation of the dangers of fiery passion. *The Forge of Vulcan* depicts the fire of the forge as a symbol for the dangerous flames of passion. This mythology is juxtaposed to another: *Satyr Pouring Water over Lovers*. While the satyr picture can be compared to the dissolution of sexual passion in war as exemplified by Cipión's harangue to his troops, *The Forge of Vulcan* recalls the adultery of Vulcan's wife, Venus, with the god Mars. Indeed, Mars and Venus are also central to Cipión's harangue. The general warns his troops that war cannot coexist with the pleasures of Venus, that the goddess of love must be exiled from their camp.

Much more important for the architecture of *La Numancia* is the representation of air in the Stanza della Segnatura. It is linked to poetry. Edgar Wind describes the section of the ceiling associated with this element: "The sail of Amphitrite and the winged goddess of the *Pax Augusta* are seen next to the figure of Poetry (Fig. 4), who, herself winged, bears the inscription *Numine afflatur*. To be moved by the spirit (= wind, air) is the meaning of *afflari*. Therefore, the pair of scenes representing the element of Air are meant to be associated with the genius of Poetry" (1938, 78). A rectangular painting is also part of air/poetry, representing Apollo and Marsyas. The flute, a wind instrument which Marsyas claims to play better than Apollo, recapitulates air. Apollo, the god of poetry, who was presented as a mere statue on the upper left side of *The School of Athens*, appropriately becomes the reigning deity in the fresco ruled by air, *Parnassus* (Fig. 5). Cervantes was well aware of the element and god that represented poetry, publishing his own *Viaje del Parnaso* in 1614. *La Numancia* not only reflects but also comments upon the images of air depicted in the Stanza della Segnatura. The winged figure of Peace comes to crown Augustus and his Pax Romana in the historical painting related to air. Through the prism of time, *La Numancia* transforms the peace of the Roman Empire into an apocalyptic siege where war, famine, and plague are the weapons used to attain the ancient glories and the so-called peace.[35] Through the spirit or wind of poetry, then, *La Numancia* could well be warning that winged peace is not the ally of warlike imperialism.

Figure 4. Vault: *Stanza della Segnatura: Poetry* (photo: Alinari/Art Resource, NY).

Although it has been noted that Raphael's archeological interest is at work in *Parnassus*, designing at least Apollo and the Muses after actual ancient models (Pope-Hennessy 1970, 140–4), the fresco can also be interpreted as pertaining to the spirit of poetic inspiration. Although it

Figure 5. Raphael, *Parnassus* (photo: Alinari/Art Resource, NY).

partakes of air or spirit, the painting also includes water. From beneath the god issue the waters of the Castalian Spring, the waters of inspiration. Although the river Duero's speech is associated with the waters of natural philosophy and prophecy, it can also be linked with the poet as *vates*. Raphael's fresco calls attention to a particular group of poets. Next to Apollo sits the Muse of epic poetry, Calliope. Holding a thyrsus, she looks to her right. There stands the blind poet, Homer, with Virgil dressed in green to his right. Homer is presented as an almost equal to Apollo since both the god and the poet gaze toward the heavens. The fact that Calliope is turning toward Homer shows him to be the exemplar of epic (Hersey 1993, 139).

The three figures in the right foreground of the *Parnassus* have been identified by some art critics as the three Greek tragic poets Aeschylus, Sophocles, and Euripides.[36] Chapter 5 will show how Aeschylus's *The Persians* is central to the construction of *La Numancia*. Euripides' *Trojan Women* may have also contributed some building blocks to the play, as will be seen in Chapter 9. The presence of both the epic and the tragic poets within the fresco may have provided Cervantes with the notion of mixing the genres in *La Numancia*. Although the structure of the play follows the Greek tragic model, other elements derive from Homer and Virgil. *La Numancia* develops a Homeric question: who is the greatest hero, the valorous Achilles or the wily Odysseus? This question is depicted in the fourth fresco in the hall. In the lunette representing the element earth are found the Virtues of fortitude, prudence, and temperance. The allegorical painting above these Virtues completes the quaternity with the representation of Justice. In *La Numancia*, the *valor*/fortitude of the city's inhabitants is pitted against the *prudencia* of Cipión, who is careful not to waste his troops in battle. The Roman general also exhibits temperance when he banishes Venus and Bacchus from the camp. Justice, as in the hall, lies outside. As for the play, a reader/audience might well ask if the siege of Numantia was a just war.

But there may be a deeper connection between Raphael's Virtues and the play. *The Cardinal Virtues* (Fig. 6) and the painting above relate to the numerology of the hall because they depict four Virtues. Thus they can be linked to Plato's *Timaeus*. Next to Plato in *The School of Athens* stands Aristotle, also holding a book in his hand: the *Nicomachean Ethics*. In this work, Aristotle defines virtue very differently from Plato: "Plato (in the *Republic*) takes the four cardinal virtues recognized in his day – wisdom, courage, self-control, justice – and interprets them so widely that each is in danger of overlapping the others. . . . In Aristotle the spheres of the several virtues are strictly narrowed down. . . . The order is haphazard" (Ross 1964, 202). Indeed, only two cardinal virtues are treated in the second book, and a whole series of other virtues is included. But what is of interest to us is Aristotle's general definition: "Virtue, then, is a state of character concerned with choice, lying in a mean, i.e. the mean relative to us, this being determined by a rational principle, and by the principle by which the man of practical wisdom would determine it" (1941, 959/2.6.1107a). Virtue, then, is found in the mean between extremes. For example, the mean between rashness and cowardice is courage. However, this mean is not to be found halfway between the two extremes. It is a *personal* mean determined by the practical wisdom of the individual. Indeed, another term for "practical wisdom" is "prudence."[37] Given the fact that Cipión is repeatedly labeled as prudent, it may be possible to connect Aristotle's definition of virtue with his behavior. It is also interesting to note that courage is the first virtue described by Aristotle (1941,

Figure 6. Raphael, *The Cardinal Virtues* (photo: Alinari/Art Resource, NY).

959–60/2.6.1007b). The *valor* of the inhabitants of Numantia could then be discussed in terms of a mean between cowardice and rashness. Do their deaths represent courage or rashness?

The fresco *The Cardinal Virtues* thus leads the play into a discussion of both the Homeric epic virtues and the Aristotelian virtues derived from his doctrine of the mean. Through allusion to both doctrines, *La Numancia* may be engaging in a meditation on the practical application of these different definitions of virtue. The reader would ponder on the qualities of the Romans and of the Numantians. A political reading is but an extension of such an ethical reading since an audience could well ask what are the strengths and weaknesses of the new Spanish Empire. Is it heir to Rome or to Numantia?

We have seen how Aristotle's *Ethics* is displayed at the center of *The School of Athens*, next to Plato's *Timaeus*. If the latter provides the structure of quaternity, the former defines the virtues. But both texts also have a deeper, transcendental meaning. They discuss how stillness is the greatest good and the basis of all activity. In a compelling and important book on Cervantes, Steven Hutchinson (1992) argues for the journey as a key to *Don Quijote*. Indeed, we can see how the Italian sojourn is inscribed in *La Numancia*, thus leading the reader or audience of the play to imaginatively visit the ancient sites of Numantia, Troy, and ancient and Renaissance Rome. But Cervantes's voyage is infused with meaning through a pensive recollection. It is only after the voyage, in moments of stasis, that the past journey acquires new meaning and is transformed into a work of art. Offering a corrective to Hutchinson's notion that journey is preferable to stasis, James Parr notes that in Aristotle's *Ethics*, stasis is the preferred state: "This is why God always enjoys a single and simple pleasure; for there is not only an activity of movement but an activity of immobility, and pleasure is found more in rest than in movement" (1941, 1058/14.7.27ff).[38] Parr expounds on this citation: "While activity and motion are endemic to our animal natures . . . it would follow from the preceding quotation (from a Peripatetic, no less) that if we wish to emulate God – or with greater *hubris* become Godlike – we will seek rest rather than motion" (1994, 429). Kenneth Chandler explains that in the *Timaeus* Plato "identifies the eternal with what is One and at rest."[39] Thus, both Plato and Aristotle identify stasis with divinity.

At the center of *The School of Athens* stand two figures whose books exhibit the principle of motionlessness. Artistic joy, the beauty of the fresco, they seem to be saying, comes from that vision of perfection experienced in moments of godlike stasis. The legends and accounts of Cervantes at work in the prisons of Spain seem to point to this principle also. While at rest, the writer can reenvision the world and partake of the creative principle of the divine.[40] Only through the wisdom acquired in the state of divine silence can the fractured pieces of travel and imperial politics come together in moments of infinite correlation. Plato explains that when the soul reaches "knowledge absolute of existence absolute" (*Phaedrus*, 1892, 247c),[41] it is at home even within the body and thus partakes of divine intelligence. In the *Phaedo*, the soul is perceived as concentrating "itself by itself, and to have its dwelling, so far as it can, both now and in the future, alone by itself" (1963, 67c–d). In this state the soul "passes into the realm of the pure and everlasting and immortal and changeless, and being of a kindred nature . . . consorts with it always and strays no longer, but remains, in the realm of the absolute, constant and invariable," thus attaining eternal wisdom (1963, 79d). Jowett's translation is even more explicit, showing that in this state of wisdom the soul "finds rest from her wandering" (1892, 79d). James Parr has shown how such a metaphysical return home can be located within Cervantes's texts: "These moments of metaphysical awareness are inscribed in Cervantes's works. In Cervantes's longer narratives . . . the main characters do indeed travel about, but it is always in search of something, and when that desire is satisfied or when metaphysical awareness dawns, they come to rest, whether in Rome (*Persiles*) or at home (*Quixote*)" (1994, 429).[42] The motionlessness symbolized by Rome in the *Persiles* comes to be represented by the phoenix-like Celtiberian city in *La Numancia*. The final joy in the play can be expressed in terms of both the artistic joy that comes from a godlike creation (Cervantes's composition) and the final silence of Numantia, now turned to ashes. In this silence, the city becomes all-powerful. Partaking of divinity, it creates a new future for the Iberian Peninsula.[43]

While Plato and Aristotle are at the center of *The School of Athens*, Homer and Virgil are portrayed at the center of *Parnassus*. All four figures are thus key not only to Raphael's Stanza della Segnatura but also to Cervantes's *La Numancia*. Homer's presence in the hall is further reinforced by a scene found under *Parnassus*. Here, Alexander is seen preserving the *Iliad* in a chest. Curiously, Cervantes retells this tale in *Don Quijote*, Part 1: "se haga para ello otra caja como la que halló Alejandro en los despojos de Darío para guardar en ella las obras del poeta Homero" (1978, 1.6.115).[44] Set next to this scene is the figure of Augustus, who is preventing the burning of Virgil's poetry, an anecdote that is also found in *Don Quijote*, Part 1 (1978, 1.13.179).[45]

These two scenes,[46] then, portray Homer and Virgil side by side, just as in the main fresco. In the *Parnassus*, Virgil looks back at Dante since the latter used him as a guide in the *Divine Comedy* (Hersey 1993, 140; Beck 1993, 66). If painting can represent Homer and Virgil side by side, so can poetry. *Parnassus* and the two scenes under it may have led Cervantes to bring together Homer and Virgil as authors to be imitated in *La Numancia*. The fourfold elemental division of the play can be extended to represent a wider program of *imitatio*, which could be derived from Raphael's archeological program to recast a series of ancient figures in one work. Each of the four acts of the play is presided over not only by an element but also by a poetic authority from the classical past: Virgil, Lucan, Homer, and Cicero. Plato simply stands as the originator of the quaternity while Aristotle provides the theoretical underpinnings for both the representation of virtue (*Nicomachean Ethics*) and the construction of a tragedy (*Poetics*). This second task is shared with Aeschylus. To the two great epic poets from the past (Homer and Virgil), Cervantes adds Lucan for his reputed "Spanish" origins. His inclusion is also "authorized" by Raphael's fresco. Let us recall that in *Parnassus*, Virgil looks back at Dante, thus calling up Dante's canonical comedy. Opening this book, the reader discovers that, in the *Inferno*, Virgil first leads Dante into a new limbo, where a noble castle houses the virtuous pagans.[47] Four great writers from classical antiquity come to greet them, forming a "bella scola" ("splendid school" [1982, 4.94]).[48] Not surprisingly, the leader of the ancient poets is Homer, carrying the sword "il simbolo della poesia epica" (Iannuci 1993, 23). The other three are Horace, Ovid, and Lucan (1982, 4.88–90). Raphael's emphasis on quaternity (which leads to Cervantes's fourfold division) could well derive from this meeting. And Cervantes could have added Lucan to his own quaternity of ancients using Dante's authority, which is also affirmed by Raphael through his depiction of the author of *The Divine Comedy*.

Cicero, the fourth author in *La Numancia*'s program of imitation, comes to Cervantes through Macrobius's *Commentary on the "Dream of Scipio."* His commentary looks back to Plato and has been ranked second "as a source of Platonism in the West in the Middle Ages" (1952, 46). Cicero is mentioned along with Seneca in Dante (1982, 4.141). Seneca's "Spanish" origins and his popularity as a tragedian may have led Cervantes to "contaminate" his own tragedy with certain aspects of the Cordoban's vision. After all, Ambrosio de Morales in his *Corónica* (Cervantes's main historical source) foregrounds both Lucan and Seneca as "Spanish" authors. Although Dante speaks of a "moral Seneca" who was thought to be a different person from the dramatist, by the time Cervantes composed *La Numancia* such a separation was rejected by many.[49] In addition to Seneca and Cicero, verse 141 of *The Divine Comedy* mentions "Lino." However, this may be a mistake for "Livy." If Cervantes read "Livy," it would have very much fit into his program for *La Numancia* since this Roman historian narrated the siege of Numantia.

Four classical authors, a quaternity derived from Raphael and Dante, provide *La Numancia* with the four elements out of which the play is composed. Cervantes's interest in quaternity is not unique to this play. It can be seen, for example, in his transformation of the Virgilian triad into a quaternity in *Don Quijote*.[50] The novel also foregrounds the four elements, as in Cardenio's reaction to Luscinda's wedding.[51] The authorial elemental quaternity appears years later in Cervantes's *Viaje del Parnaso*. In the second chapter, four poets are singled out for their magnificence:

"Cuatro vienen aquí en poca distancia / con mayúsculas letras de oro escritos" (1984b, 75). Quaternity is here related to memory: "De tales cuatro, siglos infinitos / durará la memoria" (1984b, 75). Furthermore, a Virgilian storm breaks out soon afterward, describing the mixture of the four elements.[52] Thus, in one of his last works Cervantes returns to quaternity as an ordering principle that is related both to the elements and to memory.

In *La Numancia*, the Virgilian storm at sea is transformed into a land battle. The waters of prophecy with their imperial currents are represented by the river Duero in imitation of the Tiber in Virgil's *Aeneid*. The earthen feats of necromancy with its "foul" republicanism are conjured up in the second act in response to Lucan's *Pharsalia*. The fires of passion burn but lightly in this play and represent a mere interlude governed by the conjunction of Venus and Mars. The play evokes a much more dangerous fire. The Homeric fire that destroys the besieged city of Troy enters Cervantes's text contaminated by Seneca's tragedies. *Ekpyrosis*, a vision of the universe consumed by flames, while averted in Virgil's vision, is a major component of Seneca's philosophy and of his tragedies. Although *La Numancia* ends with Senecan horror and fury, there is an intimation of immortality, which derives from Cicero's *Dream of Scipio*. Once again, Cervantes does not follow a pure imitative strategy but turns to Macrobius and his Neoplatonic doctrine in order to understand *The Dream of Scipio*. It is fitting that Cicero close the play since he is the ancient authority on the art of memory. The winged figure of Fame, which concerns Scipio in Cicero's dialogue, carries through the medium of air reports of the battle of Numantia.[53] Air, as fame and poetry, is the element that fulfills the tetractys. The four elementals add up to 10, the number for eternity. But Numantia's eternity goes beyond fame. As in the *Bhagavad Gita*, the collective self of the city stands unvanquished because it realizes its existence beyond the elements: "Weapons cannot cleave him, nor fire burn him; water cannot wet him, nor wind dry him away" (Maharishi 1967, 101).

From the Vatican of his mind, Cervantes forges an elemental mnemonics based on archeology and imitation, where Numantia is reenvisioned as a new Troy and a new Rome, constructed from the elements provided by epic and "moral" poets.[54] Utilizing images from the Stanza della Segnatura, Cervantes visualizes an action that goes beyond linear time, conjoining ancient epics, Renaissance visions, and the aspirations and pitfalls of a new Spanish Empire to set the mind questing through the theater of memory in search of the causes of things.

3

Raphael
The archeology of power

Moving from the Stanza della Segnatura to the Stanza d'Eliodoro (1512–14), the traveler or the practitioner of the art of memory notices a decisive change in style. The new locus contains images very different from the previous ones. The emphasis on portrait and allegory gives way to the telling of a story. Finding "la obra más tempestuosa . . . masas en movimiento" (1988, 90), Frederick Antal detects here a movement from classicism to mannerism, with its concern with chiaroscuro and "luminism" (Chastel 1983, 52). In spite of change, there is also continuity. The motif of the four elements, so prominent in the first hall, reappears here in the fourfold division of the ceiling, where each of the biblical scenes refers to one of the elements.[1] Each of the four frescoes can also be related to one of the elements. But the elemental imagery loses its power through the clarity with which the ideological program of the hall is reflected. All four frescoes serve "as an illustration of the unique protection enjoyed by the Church of Rome" (Chastel 1983, 50). More specifically, Bram Kempers claims: "In the four scenes Raphael highlighted the liturgical, fiscal, military and diplomatic aspects of the papacy" (1987, 259). The *hall* derives its name from the most famous of the four frescoes here: *The Expulsion of Heliodorus from the Temple* (Fig. 7). In the background of the painting, the priest Onias prays. The right foreground depicts the result of such an appeal to God. The thief Heliodorus is pursued by an angelic horseman and two helpers. Heliodorus is actually a tax collector sent by King Seleucus to "seize the treasures kept in the Jerusalem temple" (Hersey 1993, 145). The treasures of the church, then, are protected by the heavens and cannot be taken by earthly rulers.[2] The far left of the painting anachronistically represents Pope Julius II, who commissioned Raphael to paint the fresco. Indeed, Raphael and his disciple Giulio Romano are the two men portrayed in front of the pope (Hersey 1993, 146). As André Chastel explains: "here is the exalted defense of the papal politics then in force" (1983, 50).[3]

While the fresco may have pointed to specific secular threats to the papacy, Cervantes, in viewing it more than fifty years after its composi-

Figure 7. Raphael, *The Expulsion of Heliodorus from the Temple* (photo: Alinari/ Art Resource, NY).

tion, could not help but understand some of the new threats to the papacy as coming from Spain. Even though the Santa Liga, an alliance that included Rome, Venice, and Spain against the Turks, would lead to Cervantes's heroic exploits at Lepanto, the relations between Philip II and the papacy were far from harmonious. J. H. Elliott explains: "There existed between the two a kind of undeclared war, in which Philip did everything possible to extend his control over the Spanish Church and to exploit its financial and political resources. The Inquisition was duly reduced to little more than a department of state; the enormous revenues of the see of Toledo were appropriated by the crown" (1970, 230). The Duero's speech in *La Numancia* seems to reverse Raphael's vision of a divinely powerful papacy. The prophesying river envisions a pope (Clement VII) fleeing from the brave Spaniards ("tus bravos hijos" [v. 486]), and a second pope (Paul IV) being besieged: "blandiendo el español cuchillo / sobre el cuello romano" (vv. 490–1).[4] While two popes appear powerless when faced by Spaniards, the river speech portrays

Philip II as upholding Catholicism and ruling a vast empire. The "bien universal" (v. 515) related in these lines may well be "a universal Christianity with Spain at its center" (Tanner 1993, 141), something that all Spanish rulers since Queen Isabel had desired and that Philip fervently tried to accomplish. Cervantes's play, then, seems to reverse the center of power, claiming for the Spanish kings the authority which Raphael had granted to the papacy.

In *The Expulsion of Heliodorus from the Temple*, an ancient scene points to and reinforces present politics – the power of the papacy. Wittkower comments: "In expressing one event through the other, and *meaning both*, the painting becomes the symbol of an exalted mystery, the miraculous power of the Church, which remains the same throughout the ages" (1977, 180). It is precisely this doubling of history that has engaged the attention of critics when dealing with *La Numancia*. As Edward Friedman asserts, "In *La Numancia* Cervantes creates a temporal pattern in which he manipulates history to emphasize the historicity of a dual present, that of the siege of Numancia (pre-Christian Spain) and that of the time of composition (Habsburg Spain)" (1977, 87). Indeed, there are times in the play when multiple historical moments coalesce, the most significant being the speech by the river Duero which foretells not only the defeat of Numantia by the Romans in 133 B.C. but also Numantia's revenge to be carried out by Spaniards and Huns many centuries later (vv. 482–8). According to the prophecy, vengeance will be carried out for the first time when Attila threatens Rome and for the second time when the city is sacked by Spaniards and other soldiers. The destruction of Numantia will make possible the rise of a new Spanish Empire, which will threaten Rome. In this second onslaught, the Vatican itself will be invaded and the pope made to flee. The river Duero thus brings together a series of historical moments – 133 B.C., A.D. 450, and 1527 – culminating with the present, a vision of the glories of Philip II in the 1580s, "el segundo Felipo sin segundo" (v. 512).

I have already mentioned how these prophecies seem to reverse Raphael's support for the papacy's power in *The Expulsion of Heliodorus from the Temple* and proclaim instead the power of Spain. But why include Attila the Hun as the first of the avengers in this prophecy? He did not sack Rome. The city's fall came later. I believe that the presence of Attila in such close textual proximity to the sack of Rome of 1527 serves to inscribe another moment of Cervantine creation. Standing in the Vatican Palace sometime after 1569 and having witnessed the battle between

Figure 8. Raphael, *Leo I Stops Attila's Invasion* (photo: Alinari/Art Resource, NY).

the papacy and the secular powers in *The Expulsion of Heliodorus from the Temple*, a conflict that was later inscribed in the prophecy of the river Duero, Cervantes then moved to the next fresco. Here, Cervantes would have seen Raphael's painting of the confrontation between Attila and the pope. *Leo I Stops Attila's Invasion* of 1513 (Fig. 8) depicts the miraculous moment when the fifth-century pope, riding on a white horse, was able to persuade the "barbarian" Attila not to invade Rome. Ringed by his cardinals, the pope came to bless Attila and turn him away. Although the legendary event was supposed to have taken place by the river Mincio near Mantua, Raphael depicts Rome in the background to give his fresco more immediacy and dramatic force (Dussler 1971, 81). In the sky above, Saint Peter and Saint Paul with their swords threaten the "barbarian," who contemplates the miraculous vision while riding on his black stallion. Jacob Burckhardt praises the fresco as "a vigorous scene full almost entirely of horsemen." At the same time he asks: "must it not be merely impossible with so much animal life, so much expression of phys-

ical strength, to give sufficient prominence to the higher spiritual purpose?" (1879, 154). In reality, the scene contrasts two forms of power:
the physical power that surrounds Attila and his troops versus the spiritual force of the pope and the apostles. Whereas Attila rides a dark stallion representing unrestrained force, the pope, astride his white horse of
spirituality, is defended by celestial powers. Barbaric (dark) force is seen
as incapable of overcoming the (white) power of spirit. Contrastive oppositions leave little room for ambiguity in this fresco. What it does contain
is a doubling of history. The image of the pope in the painting is that of
Leo X,[5] thus recalling yet another historical moment, "the rout of the
French troops after the battle of Ravenna in which the Pope Leo X took
part" (Chastel 1983, 52). Although in this battle it might be more difficult to separate secular and spiritual power, that is what Raphael's program wishes to accomplish. Two events separated by hundreds of years
coalesce to underline once again the doctrine that threats to papal power
(Rome and its temples) will be met with supernatural resistance.

Standing in the Stanza d'Eliodoro, Cervantes would have viewed
Raphael's painting that demonstrated how even a barbarian (Attila)
must accept the power of the pope and spare Rome from destruction.
Ironically, the troops of the Catholic emperor Charles V had participated
in the undoing of the myth of Roman invulnerability. They had
unleashed such a savage sack of the city in 1527 that many believed that
the Apocalypse was at hand. Lutheran soldiers, who accompanied the
Spanish troops, left traces of their violent visit to the Vatican. Angered
that the pope had fled to Castel Sant'Angelo, these soldiers had "killed
and stabbed the pictures in the frescoes instead."[6] Bemoaning the many
desecrations and defacements brought about by the imperial army, Ben-
venuto Cellini wrote: "The name of Martin Luther was carved with a pike
on one of Raphael's frescoes in the Stanze" (Hibbert 1975, 245). Indeed,
a graffito has been found on the walls of the Stanza d'Eliodoro. It reads
"V. K. Imp." and "Got hab dy sela Borbons" (Chastel 1983, 93). In other
words, the victory belongs to Emperor Charles V, while Charles de Bourbon, the army's commander, now dead, is entrusted to the Christian
deity: "God keep Bourbon's soul" (Chastel 1983, 93). There may have
been other graffiti here, erased by successive restorations.[7] But in the
Stanza della Segnatura, under another "V. K. Imp.," can be read "Martinus Lutherus" (Chastel 1983, 92).[8] The graffiti, then, have been grafted
onto the paintings in order to deauthorize their program. To the argument that Rome is invulnerable since even the barbarian Attila had to

refrain from attacking the city is grafted the opposite argument, that Rome must fall since it lacks divine authority and must be cleansed of its sins. As Jonathan Culler explains, this type of structure "sets up reverberations, as does a tympanum: a membrane which at once divides and acts as a sounding board to transmit sound vibrations – connecting, by its transmissions, the inside and the outside it separates" (1982, 136).

It is out of this reverberation that the Duero's speech in *La Numancia* is constructed. The oppositions Roman/barbarian, pope/emperor, and Catholic/Lutheran are reinscribed in *La Numancia* through the juxtaposition of Attila and the sack of Rome. If the fresco represents the acceptance of the pope's authority, the graft recalls the sack when Spaniards and Lutherans united under Charles V in an attempt to destroy the temporal powers of the Vatican. By inscribing this pictorial graft within his text,[9] Cervantes not only sets up a series of reverberations that deconstruct both imperial and church histories but also places himself as the iterative artist who inscribes painting and graffiti within the prophetic and epic modes in order to transform visual arts into an aural text that compounds the tympanum's reverberations. In the double vision of Cervantes's pictorial language, neither pope nor emperor attain to exemplarity. Both partake of grievous error.

The third fresco of the Stanza d'Eliodoro perpetuates the motif of papal and church invincibility. *The Liberation of Saint Peter* portrays the supernatural protection given to the apostle described as the founder of the papacy. The fresco depicts three moments in Saint Peter's liberation, showing how an angel can deliver the head of the church from imprisonment. This vision of deliverance serves as a contrast to Cipión's designs on Numantia. The Roman general revels in incarceration. He refers to the siege as a way of keeping the fierce enemy in a cage: "La fiera que en la jaula está encerrada" (v. 1185). Only through this siege can their wild nature be tamed: "por su selvatoquez y fuerza dura, si puede allí con maña ser domada" (vv. 1186–7). Indeed, Cipión rejects a Numantian embassy, claiming that they are beasts that must remain incarcerated until they are tamed: "Bestias sois, y por tales encerradas / os tengo, donde habéis de ser domadas" (vv. 1191–2). There is no angel to come to their rescue. In what may be a deliberate attempt at contrasting the Numantian situation with that in the fresco, a devil appears in the second act, serving as an evil omen of their future. Only the prophecy of the river Duero speaks of freedom, a liberation to come about centuries after the destruction of the city. And yet, we have seen that this freedom is a problematic one, since

Figure 9. Raphael, *The Mass at Bolsena* (photo: Alinari/Art Resource, NY).

the heirs of Numantia besiege Rome in a much more cruel and savage manner than that in which Scipio had threatened the ancient Celtiberian city. Furthermore, the Spaniards seem to be threatening their very own religion in the figure of the pope. This doubling of history ruptures the connection between Scipio and the devil and places in question Spain's rise as an angelic rescuer.

The fourth fresco seems to be the one that is farthest removed from a program that strives to prove "the unique protection enjoyed by the Church of Rome" (Chastel 1983, 50). *The Mass at Bolsena* (Fig. 9) depicts German priests, whose doubts over transubstantiation trigger a miracle – blood flows from the Host. Like the previous paintings, it presents a dual moment in history because the miracle of 1263 is viewed by a pope with the features of Julius II. Consequently, the painting refers not only to the thirteenth century but also to the 1506 visit by Pope Julius to the relic at Orvieto (Pope-Hennessy 1970, 112). Although the painting does assert papal authority and continuity, it fails to make its point as strongly as the other three frescoes. But the painting does foreshadow an important motif in Cervantes's play. The thirteenth-century miracle led to the feast of Corpus Christi and to the performance of *autos sacramentales* to commemorate the event during the Spanish Golden Age. Very much like these plays, which focus on the mystery of the Eucharist, *La Numancia* deals with the fruits of sacrifice. Indeed, William H. Whitby considers sacrifice to be the central theme of the play. Variations of the motif can be found in the sacrifice of a heifer to Jupiter, Marandro's sacrifice for Lira, and the final sacrifice of the city.[10] Just as Christ sacrificed himself for humanity, the inhabitants of Numantia meet their death in order to unify the Spanish peninsula. When Marandro returns from the enemy's camp, he brings Lira bread covered with his own blood. By offering her "mi sangre vertida, / y con este pan mezclada" (vv. 1844–5), Marandro's sacrifice is seen through the lens of Christian imagery. The dying hero nourishes Lira spiritually: "la comida mejor / y de que el alma más gusta" (vv. 1858–9). The Numantians appear both as pagan worshipers of Jupiter and as Christian exemplars by means of their sacrifice. This conflation of Christian and pagan images should come as no surprise. Cervantes's play was composed during the reign of Philip II and serves as a commentary to his imperial aspirations. In his desire to restore a universal monarchy, Philip "employed an increasingly sophisticated syncretism of classical and Judeo-Christian traditions to achieve his goal" (Tanner 1993, 143). The syncretism of the Escorial, for example, presents Philip as both Solomon and Jupiter (Tanner 1993, 163). Sacrifices to Jupiter coalesce with eucharistic sacrifice in *La Numancia* since both are images of Philip's imperial powers. Marie Tanner has documented the link between the Habsburgs, and particularly Philip II, with the Eucharist. Titian's *Allegory of Lepanto* (Fig. 10) makes use of this association. In this canvas, which would have been of particular interest to Cervantes since he participated in this battle, Philip raises his child to heaven[11] in a gesture reminiscent of the priest's consecration of the Host during mass (Tanner 1993, 217).[12] Including this painting in her study of allegorical portraiture during the Renaissance and Golden Age, Emilie Bergmann describes it within the type that "places the sitter among mythological heroes and deities" (1979, 196). Philip II stands in the foreground "as if [he][13] were among the supernatural powers controlling the outcome" (1979, 196). Thus the king is more than a priestly Solomon or Abraham.[14] He can wear the laurel carried by the figure of Victory (the "angel") since he is a new Apollo and a living Jupiter.[15] Titian's painting, then, allows us to visualize the syncretism of Cervantes's play. Numantia's sacrifice is presided

Figure 10. Titian, *Allegory of Lepanto* (photo: Alinari/Art Resource, NY).

over by Philip II, a new Jupiter whose rule will bring about the pagan Golden Age, and a priestly king whose piety and bellicose prowess will attain the Christian universal peace which precedes the Millennium.[16]

During the reign of Philip IV, the link between king and Eucharist would still be lively. The preacher Hortensio Paravicino would then speak of the Habsburg's use of the Eucharist as an antidote for heresy (Tanner 1993, 221). And yet, the very notion that the Eucharist belongs to the secular powers rather than to the church and the papacy could be seen as heretical. In *La Numancia*, the city's sacrifice is both death and life, poison and antidote. It serves to create a new empire, one that will rival Rome in its thrust toward eternity. But this new empire seeks to take authority away from the papacy. It seeks to make Madrid (remade from the remnants of Numantia) and not Rome the Eternal City. After all, Philip II had been denied the title of Holy Roman Emperor and he strove to become emperor of the world without the title.

From the Vatican of remembrance, Cervantes envisions how Raphael once portrayed the power of the papacy. But he is also aware that time has changed the frescoes' tenor from propagandistic to ironic. The invading soldiers have grafted new meanings upon the Stanza d'Eliodoro. Through the juxtaposition of graphic representations and historical events from different eras Cervantes's play foregrounds the power of the *graphium* to shift the meanings of history. But the term "graft" not only derives from writing instrument but also refers to grave digging. *La Numancia* is thus a necromantic exercise that points to the city's grave as a place for imperial inscription. The play seeks to give voice to competing aspirations through an archeology of power that emulates and betrays all its models. The text juxtaposes past and present, sacred and profane, the canonical and the popular, in an epic fresco that insistently questions authority through grafting and reversal. It conjoins the ruins of the past and the vissicitudes of the present in order to set the mind questing through the theaters of history.

As viewers move from the Stanza della Segnatura and the Stanza d'Eliodoro to the third hall at the Vatican, they observe a gradual shift from paintings done exclusively by Raphael to works that more and more are conceived and executed by his assistants, and particularly by Giulio Romano. The Stanza della Segnatura (1508–11) is "the only room whose main scenes are thought to be painted entirely by Raphael" (Hersey 1993, 130). We know that Raphael's most noted assistant was already at work in the Stanza d'Eliodoro (1512–14) since he appears next to the great artist in *The Expulsion of Heliodorus from the Temple*. It is said that after Raphael completed the cartoon and part (if not all) of one of the frescoes of the Stanza dell'Incendio, "the focus of Raphael's interest shifted abruptly from the *Stanze* to the Sistine Chapel" (Pope-Hennessy 1970,

29). Consequently, only *The Fire in the Borgo* is attributed solely to Raphael, and the other three frescoes in the third hall are said to have been prepared by the artist and his assistants. Ironically, this hall had been decorated earlier by Perugino, Raphael's teacher, but Julius II and his successor, Leo X, "halted or partially destroyed Perugino's painting in the Stanza dell'Incendio" so that Raphael could continue it (Nesselrath 1992, 36).[17] The vault of the Stanza dell'Incendio preserves Perugino's frescoes on the ceiling.[18] Raphael may have wanted to honor his teacher (and his teacher's workshop) in this manner.

The Stanza dell'Incendio was used as a reception room for dignitaries during the early sixteenth century. Under Leo X it became a private dining room (Hersey 1993, 152). Instead of choosing as its topic a variety of historical and legendary moments, as was the case with the Stanza d'Eliodoro, this hall concentrates on events from the first half of the ninth century and depicts great occurrences in the lives of two popes, Leo III and Leo IV. The names of these two popes serve as laudatory references to the pope who had commissioned this room, Leo X. As in the Stanza d'Eliodoro, a dual present is invoked. As in previous halls, the program of the Incendio also foregrounds the power of the papacy, concentrating on the relationships between popes and emperors (Hersey 1993, 152). *The Oath of Leo III* depicts a debate that took place in the year 800 but which was very much alive in the Renaissance: "the pope's right to rule politically in central Italy and to appoint bishops in foreign countries" (Hersey 1993, 152). This papal right, which had been challenged by the French, was threatened by both Charles V and Philip II during the sixteenth century. This dispute between Spain and the papacy is inscribed in *La Numancia* through the description of the sack of Rome by the troops of Charles V (vv. 485–8) and through the narration of a second threat to the pope by the armies of Philip II (vv. 489–96). While Raphael and Romano's fresco defends papal political authority, the Spanish play narrates two Spanish threats to the papacy. The second fresco, *The Coronation of Charlemagne*, is a companion piece to the *Oath*: "As, in the previous scene, the emperor had sanctioned the pope's civil power, so in this the pope sanctions the emperor's" (Hersey 1993, 153). The fresco once again represents a dual present, since the alliance of Leo and Charlemagne recalls the alliance between Francis I and Leo X signed in 1515.[19] A third historical context would have come to mind to a Spaniard viewing the fresco during the sixteenth century. The coronation of Charlemagne was imitated by the emperor Charles V, one of the three kingly figures praised as the establishers of the Spanish Empire in the Duero speech in *La Numancia*. Charles V, who some ten years earlier had been elected Holy Roman Emperor and had been crowned at Aachen, where Charlemagne was buried, received two more crowns at Bologna. His third crown was the crown of the Holy Roman Empire, bestowed by Pope Clement VII on 24 February 1530.[20] This fulfilled his wish to be crowned by a pope just as Charlemagne had been. *The Coronation of Charlemagne* is reflected in *La Numancia* through images of the coronation of Charles V. But the Duero speech portrays an empire that is at war with the papacy, rather than one that is sanctioned by the pope. Indeed, when Clement VII appears in the Duero speech, it is not as a figure that will grant imperial authority but as a fearful man who is fleeing the power of Charles V: "para huir vuelva la planta / el gran piloto de la nave santa" (vv. 487–8). Spain's imperial destiny as prophesied in the play is built on the sack of Rome, on a break with the Vatican. Neither Charles nor Philip in the fluvial prophecy follows the visions of Raphael and Giulio Romano.

The relationship between kings and popes is also underlined in the caryatids and reliefs found under the four main frescoes. They depict seven kings who were loyal to the papacy, beginning with Charlemagne and ending with Ferdinand of Spain. The inscription under this last caryatid reads: "Ferdinand the Catholic, king, propagator of the Christian empire" (Hersey 1993, 157). Such an inscription is echoed in the Duero's speech in *La Numancia*:

aquel que ha de quedar instituido
por visorrey de Dios en todo el suelo,
a tus reyes dará tal apellido,
cuál viere que más cuadra con su celo:
católicos serán llamados todos.
(vv. 498–502)

The line of authority is clear. The Spanish kings receive the title of "Catholic" from the pope in acknowledgment of what they have done for the faith. The pope thus empowers earthly monarchs. But the Duero speech contrasts Ferdinand's acknowledgment and support of papal power with Charles V's threat to the papacy. In the context of the Stanza dell'Incendio, the Duero speech shows the erosion of papal authority as the Spanish monarchy rises to become a world power, a universal empire. In order to foreground this veering away from the Vatican, the fluvial speech censors the crowning of Charles V by the pope. The speech implies that neither Charles nor Philip would ever be placed next to Charlemagne and Ferdinand as defenders of the papacy.

In the third fresco in this hall, *The Victory of Leo IV at Ostia*, the Turks are in the process of being defeated by papal forces. In the left foreground the pope prays for deliverance. As in previous paintings, the double present is felt through the depiction of Leo IV as Leo X. The threat of Islam was as current in the ninth century as it was in the sixteenth, and this painting, done mainly by Giulio Romano, calls for vigilance.[21] More than that, it proclaims that the armies of Islam will be defeated by prayer and force. Such threats are a partial justification for the pope's political and military power. This fresco had a particular relevance at the time Cervantes was viewing it. Some of the differences between Philip II and the pope had been set aside so that the Santa Liga, the alliance between Venice, the Papal States, and Spain, could be formed to combat the Turkish threat. Participation in the naval battle at Lepanto, when the Turks were defeated, may have led Cervantes to reenvision the fresco he had seen only two years before at the Vatican. By the time he composed *La Numancia*, more than a decade after the battle, the author had gone through five years of captivity and had experienced how easily a country forgets its military heroes. The victory of Lepanto had been followed by other triumphs and defeats in a continuing war that was beginning to drain the will and the resources of Spain and their allies. In the Captive's tale interpolated within *Don Quijote*, we read that the defeat of the Turks did not come about even at Navarino the following year.[22] The "sins" of Christianity could well include the division between pope and secular rulers. In *La Numancia*, the Duero speech prophesies the glorious future of Spain. But Lepanto, Spain's most glorious victory in the sixteenth century, and one won with the help of Cervantes, is not even mentioned in the fluvial prophecy. What is foregrounded is the battle between pope and king. By omitting *The Victory of Leo IV at Ostia* through the absence of Lepanto, the historical prophecy emphasizes the problems of empire rather than its great victories. Although the Duero speech seems to be praising the "golden age" of Philip II, it is actually looking back at the days of Fernando and Isabel as that perfect time when spiritual and secular rules lived in harmony.

One more fresco from the Stanza dell'Incendio remains to be discussed. *The Fire in the Borgo* (Fig. 11) is set in 847, two years before the battle at Ostia, and is based on a legend from the *Liber Pontificalis*.[23] Many disparage the work, arguing that there is no real link "between the fore-

Figure 11. Raphael, *The Fire in the Borgo* (photo: Alinari/Art Resource, NY).

ground and the background" and that it consists of an "unconnected sequence of isolated episodes," leading some art critics to the conclusion that Raphael either did not prepare a cartoon for the painting or produced several smaller cartoons that were assembled on the wall.[24] There are some who would even attribute the execution of the fresco to Raphael's disciples Giulio Romano and Gian Francesco Penni, claiming that "an idea from the mind of Raphael was systematized and developed in all its details by another and radically different personality" (Hartt 1944, 69). The recent restoration of the fresco has shown that "a single cartoon existed for the entire painting" (Nesselrath 1992, 45). Furthermore, most art critics now agree that it must be Raphael's work: "The *Fire in the Borgo* appears to us to be entirely his design and in all important parts painted by him" (Jones and Penny 1983, 151).

The individual groupings within the painting "once aroused great admiration; it was in them that the greatness of Raphael's spirit was thought to be most apparent. For a long time they were accepted as out-

standing examples of the grand style and were frequently copied; some
of these copies have been preserved; Vasari and Bellori saw them in that
way" (Badt 1959, 44). Thus, when Cervantes viewed this fresco, it was in
the context of Raphael's greatness. The memory of this work (altered by
time and experience) may have been key to the elaboration of *La Numancia* in its epic, tragic, and archeological concerns. It may also have led
him to conceive of the flames of *ekpyrosis*.

An early appraisal of *The Fire in the Borgo* by Jacob Burckhardt makes
clear the problems faced by the artist and his critics: "Lastly, the famous
picture, *l'Incendio del Borgo*, is in its subject the most unfortunate of any.
Leo X, by the sign of the cross, extinguishes a fire near St. Peter's. There
was nothing to be done with the incident itself, because the causal connection of the gesture of the Pope with the cessation of the fire could not
be outwardly represented. Raphael, therefore, in place of it, created the
most powerful genre picture that ever existed" (1879, 155–6). For
Burckhardt, the worth of the painting has to do with the representation
of common people fleeing a fire. Both the fire and the people are so perfectly depicted that the work becomes a masterpiece "free from historical or symbolical considerations, in the dress of a heroic world" (1879,
156). Burckhardt then points to an epic model: "Properly it is not the
Borgo that is in flames, but Troy; in place of the legend, the second book
of the *Aeneid* is the original" (1879, 156). What unifies the fresco, then,
is an epic vision folded into a church legend, thus creating a double present that represents the burning of Troy and the burning of Rome. If we
add to this epic concept the frame of antique tragedy, then we can come
to a clearer understanding of this fresco and of how Cervantes imitated
it to create an epic tragedy in *La Numancia*.

Kurt Badt has carefully elucidated the tragic elements of *The Fire in the
Borgo*. We will follow his lead, although modifying some of his conclusions. Studying Italian stage designs for the period, Badt shows how they
were divided into three generic groups with few variations: tragic, comic,
and satiric. He concludes: "The space arrangement and architectural elements of the *Incendio del Borgo* indicate therefore that the picture was designated as a tragic scene; and this can only have been the case if the
events represented were interpreted as a tragic action. Hence the painting is doubly dependent on antique sources – Vitruvius' *De Architectura*
for its constructions and Aristotle's *Poetics* for its figures" (1959, 42). Vitruvius explains: "Tragic scenes are represented by means of pillars,
gables (*fastigia* in the sense of temples), and other royal buildings" (Badt

1959, 43),[25] while Serlio's *Perspettiva* (Paris, 1545), following Vitruvius, describes a tragic stage decor with "classical palaces, triumphal arches, obelisks, pyramids and rectangular, straight streets" (Badt 1959, 43). The foregrounding of a monumental architecture with arches, temples, and columns indicates that *The Fire in the Borgo* is a reworking of a tragic setting. The mixture of different architectural styles, including the commingling of different types of columns, serves to "emphasize the tragic character of the subject" (1959, 43). It should come as no surprise that Raphael used this type of setting since in Vitruvius's discussion of frescoes, he notes that in ancient times some of these pictures "depicted the façades of scenes in the tragic . . . style" (1960, 211).

Although we know little of the setting for Cervantes's *Numancia*, we do know that at this time the spectator's imagination was more important than the actual decor. However, the play does evoke a number of architectural elements from the fresco and from tragic settings: walls, temples, towers, arches, and streets. The walls in the fresco recall the *muralla* that surrounds the city and that is often mentioned in the stage directions (vv. 82, 121, 123). Act 2 contains numerous ceremonies and sacrifices performed by Numantian priests, which evoke pagan temples. As for towers,[26] attempting to flee the carnage, the child Bariato goes to his father's *torre* (v. 2126). Stage directions state: "Aquí se arroja de la torre" (p. 126). His fall deprives Scipio of his triumph through the streets of Rome and the erection of triumphal arches in his honor. Fire rages through both the play and the painting, bringing down many of the structures. Whereas a city street leads to Saint Peter's in the painting, roadways are dead ends in the play, serving as places of carnage during the mass suicide of Numantia.

The fresco is divided into three main scenes, according to Badt, thus providing the necessary passage of time and allowing for the action required in a classical tragedy. The "play" begins at the left-hand side of the picture. This is Act 1, which is in turn divided into three scenes, each depicting different moments of escape from the fire: "In the first phase the small child is just being handed over the wall; the youth climbing the wall in the middle shows the process in the stage of accomplishment – he will drop to the ground at the next moment; and, in front, we see the final phase – the family are already out in the street which is to lead them to safety" (1959, 46). Act 2 is found on the right-hand side of the fresco. Here, water is used to attempt to put out the fire. Once again, there are three scenes: In the foreground a "majestic" woman carries a jug of water on her head with ease and without haste; behind her, in the second scene, water is passed from hand to hand with more effort. The third scene is located "under the pillared portico, at the extreme right of the picture," where "an old man is in the process of pouring water on the flames. That is all . . . he shows the vanity of human effort" (1959, 46). The third act is located at the center of the painting. Here mothers with their children show their fear and plead with heaven (or the pope) for deliverance.

From these scenes, Cervantes's play envisions a tragedy where the flames of destruction almost become a character upon the stage. *La Numancia* also shows the terror experienced by those about to perish. The majesty of woman is portrayed in her refusal to live enslaved, while woman's terror is dramatized through the mother and child attempting to escape the fire and through a mother's attempt to save a child: "Sale una mujer con una criatura en los brazos, y otra de la mano, y ropa para echar en el fuego" (p. 100). In *La Numancia* the fear and terror are even greater than in the fresco since the mothers know that all must die in the end, be it by sword or by fire. In the fresco, a child is about to be saved as his mother hands him over to someone on the other side of the wall. A young man can also save himself by jumping from the wall. But in *La Numancia*, all those within the walls of the city will be sacrificed. The child Bariato, the last human being left alive in the city, duplicates the movement of the painting but with opposite intent. Instead of jumping from the wall to save himself, he throws himself from a tower to meet his death and prevent a Roman victory.

In contradistinction to Badt, who proposes a tripartite structure for the fresco, I would claim a fourth act for Raphael's *Fire in the Borgo*. It consists of the central background, where the pope is performing the benediction that will quench the fires. In Raphael's painting, a classical tragedy is transformed into a Christian *comedia* by miraculous intervention. *La Numancia*, like Raphael's fresco, is divided into four acts. The tragic impetus of both works are derailed by a final joyous scene. And both the fresco and the play use the four elements as a structural device which emphasizes quaternity. We have seen how Cervantes's tragedy begins with the waters of prophecy, goes on to portray earthen necromancy in Act 2 and the fires of war in Act 3, concluding with the airy figure of Fama. *The Fire in the Borgo* follows a somewhat different elemental sequence. The first scene depicts the burning fire, while the second foregrounds the water that is used to attempt to stop the destruction. Earth emerges as key to the third scene, where the women fall to their knees pleading to escape an earthen burial. As in *La Numancia*, Raphael's fresco ends with air. A sign of the cross performed upon this element does not fan the flames but quenches them. It is here that both Raphael's fresco and Cervantes's play depart from the classical ideal of tragedy. Rather than ending the work with a catastrophe triggered by fire, both texts turn to air to bring about a joyous conclusion. The pope's benediction becomes Fama's prophecy in *La Numancia*. Her voice ("Vaya mi clara voz de gente en gente" [v. 2417]) prophesies the future rise of Spain, the valorous heir of Numantia:

Indicio ha dado esta no vista hazaña
del valor que en los siglos venideros
tendrán los hijos de la fuerte España,
hijos de tales padres herederos.
(vv. 2432–5)

The children blessed by the pope in the fresco become the future sons of Spain in the play. Fame thus claims that the action has ended happily: "demos feliz remate a nuestra historia" (v. 2448). Of course, the joy is to be discovered in the future, at a time when Spain becomes a mighty empire. In Raphael's fresco, joy is also beyond the temporal setting of the work of art. We do not see the result of the pope's benediction but know contextually that it will quench the flames. Thus, although both the fresco and the play have a tragic conclusion, they point to the future and negate such a fate through the air of benediction and prophecy.

The play and the painting not only follow a tragic structure (which is negated in the end) but also imitate the epic. Renaissance artists were quite aware of Raphael's innovation in turning to a classical text for one of his models.[27] Giorgio Vasari in his *Lives of the Artists* (1568), a text Cervantes could very well have known, explains a key scene in *The Fire in the Borgo*: "On the other side is depicted an infirm old man, distraught by his weakness and the flames of the fire, being carried (as Virgil describes Anchises being carried by Aeneas) by a young man whose face expresses his strength and courage and whose body shows the strain of carrying the figure slumped on his back. He is followed by a dishevelled, bare-footed old woman fleeing from the fire, and going before them is a naked child" (1971, 308–9). In what has been called "one of the most famous incidents Raphael ever painted" (Hersey 1993, 155), the artist follows in great detail the second book of the *Aeneid*. The young man in the painting rep-

resents the epic hero who saves his aged father, Anchises, from the burning of Troy: "Come then, dear father, up on my back. I shall take you
on my shoulders. Your weight will be nothing to me" (52/2.708–9).[28]
Raphael also follows Aeneas's commands as to the departure: "Young
Iulius can walk by my side and my wife can follow in my footsteps at a distance" (52/2.710–11). We see in the fresco how the child (Aeneas's son)
walks at his side, while Creusa, his wife, walks behind him.

This classical scene was well known during the Spanish Golden Age
and appears, for example, in *El burlador de Sevilla*, where don Juan and
Catalinón are compared to Aeneas and Anchises as they emerge from the
ocean (rather than from the flames).[29] Cervantes chooses not to represent this scene but looks for other ways of imitating Virgil's epic poem.
As will be detailed in a later chapter, the Duero's speech in *La Numancia*
imitates the Tiber's prophecy in the *Aeneid*. Indeed, ancient statues of
river gods were located in the gardens just outside Raphael's *stanze*,
where Cervantes may have seen them; while inside, Virgil is provided a
prominent place in *Parnassus*. In this fresco, Dante stands behind Virgil,
indicating the Christianization of the epic. Both Cervantes and Raphael
Christianize Virgil, the first through the evocation of a Catholic empire
and the second through the blessings of the pope. However, both Cervantes's *La Numancia* and Raphael's *Fire in the Borgo* preserve the epic
nature of the destructive flames.

In Raphael's fresco, Aeneas is fleeing the destruction of Troy, guided
by fate (and by his mother, Venus). He is to found a new city, which will
eventually become the center of a new empire. Rome, then, is a second
Troy. Raphael is not confusing his cities when he depicts Aeneas fleeing
Troy while actually escaping the burning of the Borgo in Rome but is
fusing both cities as Renaissance poets often did. More than a dual present, the fresco depicts a triad of present moments: the burning of Troy
(through the figures of Aeneas and Anchises), the burning of the Borgo
in the ninth century, and the rule of Renaissance warrior popes, who are
always defending and expanding papal lands. Leo IV in the fresco brings
to mind the contemporary pope, Leo X. It is this juxtaposition of cities,
rulers, and destructive impulses that serves as model for Cervantes's *La
Numancia*. In the play, the siege of the Celtiberian city is compared to the
sack of Rome in 1527, thus evoking a series of successive destructions
beginning with Troy and including the fall of Rome to the "barbarians."
Spain seems to be the culmination of a series of cities and empires. Just
as Troy must be destroyed so that Rome will be founded, so Numantia

must meet its end so that Spain can rise. *La Numancia*'s archeology then, very much like that of Raphael's *Fire in the Borgo*, depends on the *Aeneid.*

In the epic poem, Venus, Aeneas's mother, complains to Jupiter of her son's future. The father of the gods answers Venus with a prophetic speech. He asserts that Aeneas's progeny will eventually build an empire when "Ilia the royal priestess, heavy with the seed of Mars, shall give birth to twin sons" (12/2.273–4). Romulus will found the city of Rome. As for his descendants (and consequently the descendants of Aeneas), Jupiter prophesies: "On them I impose no limits of time and place. I have given them an empire that will know no end" (12/1.278–9).[30] Mircea Eliade explains: "it was not until after the publication of the *Aeneid* that Rome was called *urbs aeterna.* . . . Then arose the hope that Rome could regenerate itself periodically *ad infinitum.* Thus it was that, liberated from the myths of the twelve eagles and of the *ekpyrosis*, Rome could increase until, as Virgil foretells, it embraced even the regions 'beyond the paths of the sun and the year'" (1954, 135). But the true fulfillment of this prophecy, according to Christian apologists, would come with the advent of Christianity. Only then would a peaceful and harmonious future be possible. In Raphael's fresco, the pope's benediction falls within this vision of *renovatio*. Rome is the eternal city that is constantly renovated by the grace of the Christian God. In contrast to the pagan Troy that must be totally destroyed so that Rome may be born, this new Virgilian and Christian Rome will endure until the end of time.

Cervantes takes up this notion of *renovatio* from Raphael's fresco but questions its implications. Like Raphael, he shows regeneration through fire. Numantia/Troy must burn in order for the Spanish Empire to be born. But he incorporates doubts as to the eternity of Rome by foregrounding the sack of the city in 1527 by Spanish imperial troops. Cervantine ambiguity arises when the spectator is led to wonder if this apocalyptic event signals the end of the myth of the eternal city. Is Virgilian authority to be discovered in a Rome that will renew itself one more time, or has this authority been transferred to the Spanish Empire? Such a *translatio* would make of Madrid a new Rome, with both its desire for eternity and its fear of *ekpyrosis*. For George L. Hersey, *The Fire in the Borgo* "suggests the phoenix-like way in which the Eternal City is born after disaster" (1993, 156). Cervantes also sees Numantia as undergoing a phoenix-like *renovatio*: "cual fénix renovándose en la llama" (v. 392). Spain is thus a new Numantia and a new Rome. The significance of the god Mars in the Spanish tragedy emphasizes the legacy of the ancient empire. As noted, Romulus, its founder, was the son of Mars. Thus, it should come as no surprise that the Roman general Scipio invokes this deity (vv. 89, 154). One of the most courageous of the Numantians, Marandro, conjoins the bellicose qualities of Mars with the amorous nature of Venus. This goddess, we will recall, is the mother of Aeneas (vv. 713ff.). The Numantians, then, appear to be the heirs of both Romulus and Aeneas.

It has been shown that, following his archeological interests, Raphael includes Corinthian columns from the temple of Mars in the Forum Augustum on the left-hand side of the fresco (Badt 1959, 43). The fact that Mars in full armor has Venus and Cupid to his right in the temple (Richardson 1992, 162) points to La Numancia's utilization of both Mars and Venus. On the left side of Raphael's fresco he has included Ionic columns from Saturn's shrine on the slope of the Capitoline.[31] I would argue that the juxtaposition of these two architectural orders serves to underline some of the key aspirations of Virgilian Rome. While Mars provides the impetus for conquest (and is thus associated with the fires on the left-hand side of the painting), Saturn evokes the vision of a golden age of peace and tranquillity. In the fresco his temple is next to the refreshing waters of life. Raphael's painting shows how the Roman popes represent the fulfillment of these two pagan deities in their drive to preserve an eternal Rome and in their vision of a Christian paradise. Renaissance syncretism sought to reconcile not only the pagan and the Christian but also war and paradise. Cervantes's own archeological exercise also seeks to juxtapose Mars and Saturn, the pagan and the Christian, the imperial bellicose spirit and the hope of a lasting peace:

Debajo de este imperio tan dichoso
serán a una corona reducidos,
por bien universal y a tu reposo,
tus reinos hasta entonces divididos.
(vv. 513–16)

The war between the Numantians and the Romans will eventually bring about a new empire and a new peace. But Cervantes's Augustan peace is punctuated by questions of war and *ekpyrosis*. The play's vision differs from that of Raphael's fresco. After all, in *La Numancia*, Rome is depicted as burning in the 1527 sack, in spite of the pope's benediction. If Aeneas, as David Quint notes, is "a hero deliberately created for political reflection" (1993, 8), then Cervantes takes up his political agenda, seeming to perpetuate the imperialist ideal. But his text, through tragic nuances, epic *ekpyrosis,* and the representation of a dual present, questions how politics can encompass eternity and asks whether either a pope's power or a warrior's fire can bring about a lasting golden age.

Only a child can envision and be envisioned as eternal harmony. Virgil claimed in his *Fourth Eclogue* that a child had been born that would change the trends of time. He would signal the dawning of the Augustan Pax Romana. Indeed, we see a child carefully saved from the flames of destruction in *The Fire in the Borgo.* Is this the Virgilian child? Will it become Cervantes's Bariato? But the pagan epiphany and the Renaissance survival are replaced by Cervantes's sacrifice of the child. It is true that Bariato's death brings a certain immortality to Numantia. And textual prophecies foretell a glorious imperial future. But this life-in-death, this sacrificial moment akin to Christian crucifixion, is very different from Cervantes's models. Bariato's only life depends upon texts that necromantically resurrect him in order that he may serve patriotic and imperialist ideals. Through a living child, both Virgil and Raphael open the world of possibilities. Cervantes's ending is less joyful, even though the term *feliz* (v. 2448) is actually used. His vision fails to glimpse eternity either in a pope's benediction or in an Augustan imperialist stance. While Virgil and Raphael point to the child as the inheritor of the golden world of all possibilities, Cervantes shows how eternity is forever compromised in the play of power. Although we are subjected to an endless repetition of the structures and destructions of imperial dominance, be they Troy/Numantia, Rome/Vatican, or Rome/Spain, the pen can eternalize certain moments through the figure of Fame. Cervantes's epic tragedy seeks to establish the foundation myth of Spain in accord with Virgil's *Aeneid.* But the endless repetition of imperial dominance lends his text a certain bittersweet quality – all empires come to an end. While Cervantes's subject is epic in nature and even transcends classical tragedy through a phoenix-like *renovatio,* it fails to capture the luminosity of Raphael's fresco and insists on the darker flames of destruction.

4

Giulio Romano
Remembering Rome

The largest of the halls and the last to be decorated was the Sala di Constantino (1519–25). Until recently it had been thought that the decorations of the fourth hall were both conceived and executed by Giulio Romano, aided by Gian Francesco Penni and Raffaellino del Colle. But new evidence suggests that even here Raphael's hand can be seen since sketches of the first two stories (*The Apparition of the Cross* and *The Battle of the Milvian Bridge*) in the painter's own hand have been preserved (Pagden 1989, 85–6). Although the title of this chapter bears Giulio Romano's name, the reader should be aware of Raphael's hand even here.

The program in this fourth hall is even more specific than in the Stanza dell'Incendio. Four moments from the life of Emperor Constantine are represented in the four frescoes. The first is *The Apparition of the Cross to Constantine,* where he is seen giving an *allocutio,* or exhortation, to his troops before a crucial battle. At this time Constantine is said to have witnessed the miraculous appearance of the cross. The second fresco portrays the battle itself. Constantine had vowed to convert to Christianity if he won the contest at the Milvian Bridge. The third fresco depicts his baptism. The fourth and last represents the legendary donation of Constantine, who gave Rome and the surrounding lands to the popes. The program is clear, and consonant with those of the other halls: to exalt the power of the papacy. Here, a pagan emperor recognizes the truth of Christianity and, more important, recognizes the right of the popes to rule politically. As Chastel states: "The victor of Ponte Milvio appears twice in a reverential pose, once before the pontiff, who baptizes him, and again before the bishop of Rome, who accepts his donation" (1983, 60). Other than the general topics of the relationship between pope and emperor, and the political rights of the papacy, which have been represented over and over again in these halls, there seems to be little in the life of Constantine that could have a bearing on *La Numancia.*

In addition, we are dealing with an artist who was never mentioned by Cervantes and who is seldom studied in terms of Spanish culture. And yet, just because Romano has been forgotten over the centuries does not mean that he was not well known in Cervantes's time. Cristina Gutiérrez Cortines Corral, in a pioneering essay, has shown that in spite of the "olvido . . . tan notorio entre los historiadores del arte" (1989, 184), the study of Romano's impact on Spanish architecture needs to be taken seriously. In the process of describing his influence in Spain, she clarifies Romano's role in developing the imperial image of Charles V: "Giulio Romano fue el artista que mejor dio forma a la imagen imperial. . . . Recordemos que el artista romano fue quien se encargó de diseñar todo el programa escenográfico de las entradas y recibimientos realizados en Mantua en 1530 con motivo de la visita regia" (1989, 170). Cervantes could well have studied him as an artist who helped develop Spain's imperial image. In a play dealing with the birth of Spanish imperialism, the Spanish playwright could very well have sought to include him.

Indeed, one of the frescoes in the Sala di Constantino may have contributed to the composition of the first major scene in *La Numancia*. Furthermore, the changes made by Giulio Romano to Raphael's sketch of the fresco may have played a significant role in Cervantes's imaginings. While *The Battle of the Milvian Bridge* closely follows Raphael's sketches, Giulio Romano intervenes radically in *The Apparition of the Cross* and is fully in charge of the *Baptism* and *The Donation of Constantine* (Pagden 1989, 85–8).[1] Romano's presence is first made clear in *The Apparition of the Cross*, and this is the fresco that may have been of special interest to Cervantes.[2] The appearance of the cross to Constantine (Fig. 12) takes place outside of Rome, the day before Constantine's battle with Maxentius for possession of the city. In the fresco the emperor stands on a raised platform to give his *allocutio* to the soldiers before battle. Such a pose may well reflect the archeological interest of Raphael and his disciples. The scene seems to have been modeled after a similar one found on the Arch of Constantine (Hersey 1993, 164–5).[3] Cervantes's own archeological interest may have led him to model Cipión's harangue after Raphael and Giulio Romano's *Apparition*. Both Constantine and Cipión are Roman leaders who wish to instill the necessary valor in their troops to win a battle. Both stand above the soldiers to deliver their *allocutio*. Constantine speaks from a pedestal, and Cipión "se sube sobre una peña que estará allí" (p. 41). Cervantes's explicit stage directions evince his desire to replicate visually upon the stage this feature found in Romano's painting. At the time Cervantes was writing for the theater, stage scenery and props were almost nonexistent. Thus, most of the features taken from Raphael's and Romano's paintings went into the structuring of the work,

Figure 12. Giulio Romano and assistants, *The Apparition of the Cross to Constantine* (photo: Alinari/Art Resource, NY).

the action and the images encountered in the *comedia*. Just as the *stanze* frescoes were conceived as part of an art of memory, the visuality of the play was to be found as much in the language as in the staging. At times, however, the action of the play put in motion the implied movement of the fresco. The Roman soldiers in Romano's painting, although frozen in the stillness of the fresco, can be seen as rushing forward to hear their leader. In the play, the *allocutio* is delivered immediately after an order is given to the soldiers to come forward: "Manda nuestro general / que se recojan, armados, luego todos los soldados" (vv. 49–51). The painting also shows that the soldiers are armed.

The Vatican fresco represents in the background the river Tiber, which flanks the city of Rome. In Cervantes's play, the river Duero appears onstage and recounts how it borders the city of Numantia. Lacking the ability to stage a river, Cervantes uses personification, borrowing the technique from epic authors such as Virgil, who characterized the Tiber as a river god. But in the mind's eye, the spectator could well have pictured the river. Like Constantine in Romano's fresco, Cipión would have as background a city and a river. The foreground would be occupied by the soldiers. Both the fresco and the play are careful to portray them "a lo antiguo" (p. 41). An archeological concern is also evinced in the representation of Rome in the fresco. As André Chastel explains: "Ancient motifs, taken from reliefs on triumphal arches and Trajan's column, appear in the views of Rome: in the *Apparition*, the bridge over the Tiber with the statues silhouetted, the reconstructed mausoleum, the pyramid of Romulus' tomb" (1983, 57–8).[4] In the second part of *Don Quijote*, the knight seems to recall two of these monuments: "las cenizas del cuerpo de Julio César se pusieron sobre una pirámide a quien hoy llaman en Roma la *aguja de San Pedro* . . . la reina Artemisa sepultó a su marido Mausoleo en su sepulcro que se tuvo por una de las siete maravillas del mundo" (1978, 2.8.97). In *La Numancia*, Cervantes's archeological concern had led him not only to specify that the soldiers should dress in antique garb but also to give an accurate location for Numantia. Cervantes would have discovered the true location while reading Ambrosio de Morales's *Corónica*: "poco mas de una legua mas arriba de donde agora está la ciudad de Soria, a la puente que llaman Garray, junto al rio Duero, y pocas leguas abaxo de su nacimiento" (1791, 3.313–14).[5] Dispelling "the mythical identification" with Zamora (King 1979, 206), the play specifies: "Soria, que en aquel tiempo fue Numancia" (p. 55). Stage directions in this instance have little to do with the visual, stressing again archeological knowledge.

In imitation of Giulio Romano's *Apparition* Cervantes's epic tragedy places Cipión on a raised platform, addressing his soldiers with river and city in the background. In his speech, the Roman general chastises the troops for having abandoned themselves to the pleasures of Venus and Bacchus. These gods, he claims, are antithetical to the pursuits of the god of war, Mars. Banning "concubinas" (v. 135), gambling, and wine Cipión declares: "En blandas camas, entre juego y vino / hállase mal el trabajoso Marte" (vv. 153–4). Although such a speech is not recorded in Ambrosio Morales's *Corónica*, nor in his sources Appian of Alexandria and Anneus Florus, this historian does record that Scipio found a cowardly and ineffective army and attributed their decline to vices such as lust: "De ser todo muy cobarde le venia estar en ocio, y de ahí como es cosa ordinaria haberse corrompido con muchas maneras de vicio" (1791, 4.28). In Appian, Scipio, "having heard that it was full of idleness, discord, and luxury, and well knowing that he could never overcome the enemy unless he should first bring his own men under strict discipline" (1962, 1.271), sought to train them properly. Florus describes how, on Scipio's arrival, "the women and camp-followers and all the baggage except what was absolutely necessary were dispensed with" (1929, 153).

However, I would argue that Scipio's speech derives from Renaissance art, and not from historical accounts. Romano's painting, as *poesía muda*, cannot give us the words of Constantine's allocution, and yet, I believe that Cipión's injunctions derive from the Vatican fresco. Daniel L. Heiple reminds us that Renaissance painters and theorists reversed the Horatian notion of *ut pictura poesis* in order to show that painting was like poetry. One way in which a painting could "speak" was through the use of "allegorical figures or mythological figures that could be juxtaposed in a variety of meaningful combinations and postures. These figures already contained deeper meanings, and their new context provided further reflections on possible meanings for the painting" (Heiple 1994, 368). Renaissance painting, then, as Edgar Wind has shown (1968, 22–5), depicts iconological mysteries, pagan truths hidden behind a thin veil of allegorized fable. Through a highly developed sense of syncretism, the "truths" of these pagan mysteries were often Christian truths, which led to hybridization. For example, "Renaissance art produced many images of Venus which resemble a Madonna or a Magdalene" (Wind 1968, 24). It should come as no surprise, then, to find a Christian miracle surrounded by pagan motifs in the *Apparition*.

A viewer who is aware of painting's role as mystery can begin to find the answer to what Constantine is saying to his troops in the emperor's gesture. Beyond the fact that it is the typical gesture of an *allocutio*, it serves to point in a particular direction. Some may argue that Constantine's gaze is more important than his gesture and would describe him as looking at the sky, where the sign "EN TOYT Ω I NIKA" ("by this sign, victory") appears below and to the right of a luminous cross surrounded by clouds. In a darkened sky, the fresco does not show the sun. Daylight seems to have as its source the cross and its rounded sphere of brightness, which resembles the celestial luminary. This may well show the conflation of two heavenly powers. Constantine was devoted to Apollo, the sun god, and had a vision of this deity attended by Victory years before the battle of the Milvian Bridge (Grant 1993, 131). Michael Grant, Constantine's most recent biographer, explains: "This connection with the Sun made Constantine's eventual transition to Christianity easier, because he may well have believed that Christ and the Unconquered Sun-god were both aspects of the highest divinity. . . . Old Testament prophecy was interpreted as identifying the 'Sun of Righteousness' with Jesus Christ, who was often called *Sol Justitiae*" (1993, 135).[6] Renaissance Neoplatonists certainly saw the sun as a mysterious representation of God. The Vatican fresco, then, juxtaposes light (the pagan sun god) and the Christian cross. If Apollo once promised Constantine victory, now it was solar Christianity that vowed to protect him. *La Numancia* has long been regarded as a text that conflates the paganism of the Numantians with a Christian vision. Casalduero, for example, speaks of "esa alegría final cristiana de la muerte que es vida, vida inmortal" (1966, 281). It is no coincidence that this final victory in death is represented in the play through solar imagery. Spain speaks of death and resurrection using the image of the phoenix, which is linked to solar forces, to pagan fame, and to Christian resurrection ("cual fénix renovándose en la llama" [v. 392]). Indeed, the river Duero also imagines the resurrection of Numantia in terms of solar imagery:

un consuelo le queda en este estado:
que no podrán las sombras del olvido
escurecer el sol de sus hazañas,
en toda edad tenida por estrañas.
(vv. 461–4)

Constantine's solar vision, according to Eusebius, was followed by a dream in which God told him to use the sign of the cross "as protection during his encounters with the enemy" (cited in Grant 1993, 140). Constantine's dream of the cross with the sign denoting victory was utilized by Philip II and his allies as an icon representing the triumph over paganism at the battle of Lepanto in 1571. The motto, translated from the Greek to the Latin (In Hoc Signo Vinces) and already adopted by the Jesuits, appeared on the banner of the Holy League. Indeed, the painting Philip II commissioned from El Greco to commemorate the victory includes this motto abbreviated as IHS (Tanner 1993, 203). Giulio Romano's fresco, then, although a part of Cervantes's repertory of images, would have been subtly transformed through his participation in the battle of Lepanto. Constantine's victory would be conflated with Cervantes's own naval triumph. Just as Christ's sacrifice would serve to construct a triumphal banner for the Holy League, Numantia's sacrifice would allow Spain to disseminate its triumphal banners. The prophetic Duero proclaims that "tenderás triunfando tus banderas!" (v. 524) in the new dawn of Spanish imperialism.

In the Vatican fresco, both the cross and Sol/Apollo can be seen in the standards held by the troops. However, legend has it that Constantine created a different device for his troops, the *labarum*, which he had displayed on as many shields as possible. What Grant calls a "miraculous amulet" (1993, 141) is made up of a long spear "joined by a transverse bar which gave it the shape of the cross" (1993, 142). The letters chi and rho were included in the wreath at the top of the standard. They carried a double meaning: "For the Christians it was the first two letters of Christos; for the pagans it stood for the Greek *chreston*, good" (Grant 1993, 142). Not only was the *labarum* a conjoining of two religions but it was also "an amalgamation of religious banner and military *vexillum* (emblem of power)" (1993, 142). It is envisioned in the Vatican fresco by the military standard that is cut horizontally by the miraculous sign in the sky, thus forming the shape of a cross. Curiously, this particular standard also carries one of the common totems for the Roman troops, the dragon.[7] This mythical beast acquired a very different meaning in Constantine's reign, being associated with the devil. The emperor was thought to have defeated the dragon and his army of demons (Grant 1993, 150). By horizontally crossing the standard of the dragon with the sign for victory, the painting reveals the mystery of Constantine's triumph. Christianity would give him the power to defeat the devils of paganism. In *La Numancia*, the Celtiberian city is able to defeat the Romans since their sacrifice prefigures the Christian sacrifice and helps pave the way for the defeat of paganism (Rome). The *demonio* which appears in the second act (p. 71) serves as a symbol of this paganism, which, on the verge of triumphing, is defeated by a Christ-like death which leads to "resurrection" both in fame and in the new Christian empire of the Spanish Habsburg, Philip II. The relationship between the fresco and the play is thus contrastive and ironic. The allocution in the Spanish play is pronounced by the "enemy," by the dragon figure, by a Constantine that never converts. Cipión is given two chances to change his mind, to show that he can embrace the Other. But he rejects two peace offerings from the Numantians, paving the way for the final sacrifice that will attest to the city's proto-Christian ideals. Once again, there is contradiction. In committing suicide, albeit a heroic one, the city confronts the Christian injunction against such a deed and comes closer to pagan ideals. This fluctuation between Christian and pagan in *La Numancia* sets the work in the context of the Renaissance, where pagan mysteries were thought to reveal Christian truths. In this context, the city's suicide is a pagan mystery that foreshadows Christ's sacrifice. By bringing together such incompatible opposites into a cohesive whole, the play seeks to transcend a particular ideology and attempts to present a Platonic vision of *discordia concors*.

But let us return to the gesture and the gaze. It is not at all clear that Constantine is looking up at the sky, and his gesture does not point upward. According to Sylvia Ferino Pagden, Giulio Romano has eliminated from Raphael's original sketch a soldier who stands in the left foreground and points to the miracle, replacing him with two youths holding the leaders' helmets and arms. There is then less of a movement upward in Romano's fresco and more of a horizontal movement than in Raphael's sketch. Indeed, Pagden claims that Giulio's composition is less religious (1989, 86). It deemphasizes the miracle through a number of insertions in the foreground. Constantine may not be looking upward at the miracle. Instead, he may be looking and pointing to the right. Following his gesture, the viewer's gaze would eventually collide with the edge of the "tapestry." The scene of the allocution appears to be randomly cut off by a column with two statues. Legs and capes are mutilated by these adornments, which in turn serve as the left side of a frame for a portrait of Pope Clement I. In reality, the *Apparition* is a false tapestry. The column and statues are also false. They are all wall paintings, done to give the impression of tapestries and sculptures. At any rate, this frame which ends the false tapestry's field of vision houses the Virtue of moderation. Hersey accurately describes her: "One breast is revealed and her thick blond hair, set with pearls, is artfully arranged. The wine jug at her feet is borrowed from the iconography of a sister virtue, Temperance, who stands for moderation in drinking" (1993, 165). This figure, then, may well hint at the subject of Constantine's allocution and serve as the subject of Cipión's speech. The pearls worn by Moderation are the emblem of Venus – they are associated with the goddess because of her birth from the sea. Edgar Wind acknowledges that the "idea of Venus as a goddess of moderation may seem mythologically odd" (1968, 130). Discussing Botticelli's *Birth of Venus*, where she rises from the ocean in a shell (which makes her the embodiment of the pearl), this critic shows how Venus "holds the powers of love in abeyance, while they are released by the wantonness of Amor" (1968, 120). Moderation, then, is an earthly Venus[8] whose dictates are in accord with Cipión's wishes to banish the "concubinas," and thus banish a Venus *vulgare*, from his camp.[9] The conflation of Temperance and Moderation in Giulio's allegory, then, is trans-

lated in Cipión's speech into an injunction against the excesses of passion and drink. The discarded wine jug and the emphasis on the pearls
of abeyance are echoed in Cipión's harangue when he argues that victory
cannot come as long as his soldiers are "con Venus y con Baco entretenidos" (v. 123).

Both the fresco and the play, through their allocutions, espouse moderation and condemn the excesses of Venus and Bacchus. Those who want
to follow the martial path cannot be given to these other gods. In order
to foreground the influence of Mars, the fresco depicts a pyramid under
the cross. If the Christian symbol will bring about victory, it is a triumph
that is also presided over by the pagan god of war. The pyramid was
thought to be Romulus's tomb (Chastel 1983, 58; Hersey 1993, 165). The
founder of Rome was the son of Mars and the city was dedicated to this
god. Indeed, Mars "figures as Constantine's special patron on his early
coins; and his troops were at first sometimes called 'people of Mars'"
(Grant 1993, 131). Cipión, as a pagan Constantine, can more clearly
invoke the power of Mars. His allocution mentions the god of war twice.
This deity's power is also represented through an animal associated with
him, the wolf: "siendo del fiero lobo acometidas" (v. 2033).[10] Cervantes's
play includes yet one more irony. Although it is Cipión, the pagan Constantine, who invokes Mars, it is his rivals, the Numantians, who take valor
to the extreme and thus come closer to the spirit of the pagan god. Cipión, like the Christian Constantine, follows the goddess Moderation in
his rejection of the weakening forces of drunkenness and lust.

One way in which ancient and Renaissance artists and writers represented moderation was through the union of Venus and Mars. Although
Cipión follows the goddess Moderation, in his allocution he forbids her
representation as a union between Venus and Mars: "La blanda Venus
con el duro Marte / jamás hacen durable ayuntamiento" (vv. 89–90). On
the other hand, the changes made by Giulio Romano to Raphael's sketch
of the *Apparition* serve to foreground moderation through the iconology
of the union of Venus and Mars. According to Pagden, Giulio made two
main changes to Raphael's sketch. The first is the introduction of the
dwarf, who is trying on a helmet. For Chastel, the dwarf's function is to
establish "a relationship with the viewer" (1983, 58).[11] Pagden argues
that he is included in order to amuse or astound the observer (1989, 86).
Such a figure would certainly have aroused Cervantes's interest. The
Spanish writer would later use the dwarf in *Don Quijote* as part of the mar-
velous and the grotesque. Eduardo Urbina (1987), who has studied this

figure in *Don Quijote*, shows how Cervantes's novel utilizes the opposing characteristics of dwarfs as found in the romances of Chrétien de Troyes and in the chivalric romances. While the former presents malicious dwarfs who oppose the hero, the latter tends to portray a more positive type who serves as messenger and mediator. Sancho Panza, Urbina argues, partakes of both traditions but emphasizes the dwarf's comic function. The *nano* in the Vatican fresco also seems to conjoin traditions. His smile is an invitation to amusement in an otherwise martial and heroic scene. Holding a helmet in his hands, he, like Sancho, creates a dichotomy between the martial ideal and the quotidian comic. After all, don Quijote, like Constantine, is a figure who claims Mars as his guide. But the dwarf's smile and facial expression seem also somewhat malevolent. He is both menacing and mirthful. The dwarf conjoins then the powers of Mars (helmet, menacing smile) with those of Bacchus. His knees are bent and he seems to be in motion, reminding the viewer: "Dwarfs love feasting and dancing" (Voegelin 1972, 331). He is thus also engaged in the pursuits of Venus/Bacchus.

Giulio Romano's interest in Rome's antiquities and customs may have also made him aware of one of the main functions of the dwarf in antiquity. They were made to take part in gladiatorial games, where they fought women. This curious spectacle was well known in Spain in the seventeenth century, as Sebastián de Covarrubias notes: "aver en Roma avido juegos gladiatorios de mugeres y de enanos" (1987, 511). He then cites a poem by Statius on Domitian's games, where these two parties are described in terms of the cruelty of Venus and the laughter of Mars ("Ridet Mars pater et cruenta Venus" [1987, 511]). The description hints at the union of these two deities since each is adopting the quality of its opposite. If this reference is indeed inscribed in the fresco, it would set up a series of fascinating parallels and connections, which would take us back to the Stanza della Segnatura. In *Parnassus*, behind the three great epic poets Homer, Virgil, and Dante, stands Statius, who according to Dante converted to Christianity. By inscribing the games between dwarfs and women immortalized by Statius, Romano may be relating a pagan poet who converted to Christianity to a pagan emperor who also embraced the new faith.

If Giulio Romano's inclusion of the dwarf on the right is the first indication of the Mars/Venus conjunction, then his emendation of Raphael on the left foreground should confirm this interpretation. Here, he substituted two youths holding helmets and a sword for Raphael's soldier who was pointing at the heavens. Once again, instruments of war are wielded by those who do not seem intent on using them. In the most famous Renaissance representation of Venus vanquishing Mars, that of Botticelli, baby satyrs play with Mars's helmet and sword while he sleeps and is watched over by Venus. Although she wears a ruby, the fiery red gem that corresponds to the god of war, it is encircled by pearls, her own gemstone. As Daniel L. Heiple asserts: "her stones completely surround and check his power" (1994, 385). In the Vatican fresco, the youths (who may very well parallel the satyrs under Venus's command in Botticelli's painting) are listening to the allocution. Their beauty may link them to the women who are forced to fight the dwarfs in the pagan arena. But a new order is being evoked. As they gaze at Constantine and the miracle above, these youths seem ready to surrender the weapons of war to their martial owners. Both the mirthful dancing dwarf and the youths of Venus stand on the same plane as the goddess Moderation, who, it should be remembered, wears the pearls of Venus. Giulio Romano has then created a foreground which defines moderation as the conjunction of opposites, be they Venus and Mars or laughter and war. Christian harmony, then, will arise out of the Platonic conjoining of contraries.

In *La Numancia* Cipión attempts to establish moderation in his soldiers through his allocution. But his effort is misdirected since he knows only how to banish the vulgar Venus: "La cipria diosa estése agora aparte" (v. 93). The Numantians, on the other hand, realize that the mystery resides in the conjoining of opposites. They would agree that subjects of Venus such as "concubinas" (v. 135), wine (v. 133), and perfumes (v. 137) should be banished. But they would claim that this does not mean that the goddess cannot be part of the martial enterprise. Leoncio, echoing Cipión's logic, berates his friend Marandro for pursuing Venus at a time for war:

Al tiempo que del dios Marte
has de pedir favor,
¿te entretienes con amor,
quien mil blanduras reparte?
        (vv. 713–16)

Through his deeds, Marandro shows that true love (as opposed to lustful passion) is actually a trigger for heroic action. Mars can gain in power when united with a "celestial" Venus.[12] The contrast between the two camps points to the fact that Cipión was ignorant of this second, more spiritual Venus. She can join with Mars to bring about a victory that will result in lasting harmony. The Vatican fresco, like the Spanish play, rejoices in the harmony established between these two gods and relates this pagan mystery to a Christian vision: the triumph of Constantine and the eventual rise of Christian Spain.

Two minor elements in the fresco and their relationship to the play remain to be discussed. Above Moderation and indeed on both upper corners of the Vatican painting are nude figures who carry banderoles with the inscription *suave*. This refers to Leo X's motto, "Jugum enim emum suave est, et onum meus leve" (My yoke is easy and my burden is light)(Hersey 1993, 166).[13] In the allocution, Constantine, like Jesus, may be asking his soldiers to follow him, claiming that his yoke and the burden he will be imposing will be light. In *La Numancia* Cipión is given a charge that is far from light. The first lines of the play attest to it:

Esta difícil y pesada carga,
que el senado romano me ha encargado,
tanto me aprieta, me fatiga y carga.
(vv. 1–3)

In order to discharge this heavy burden, Cipión's yoke will be impossible to bear. After specifying the burden, *La Numancia* shows how the heavy yoke will be imposed. This image was also present in one of the Spanish play's models, Aeschylus's *Persians*. The Greek tragedy shows Xerxes as demonstrating excessive pride through the yoking of the Hellespont, and Cipión shows a similar *hubris* by attempting to yoke the Numantians: "pusieron tan grande yugo a nuestros cuellos" (v. 247). Constantine's light yoke is based on moderation, the celestial or Christianized Venus, while Cipión's and Xerxes' yokes are based on the unchecked force of Mars.

The final element is found in the bottom left-hand corner of *Apparition*'s frame. Above the word *Aeternitas* can be seen a woman holding a rooster.[14] This bird became an important Christian symbol during the Middle Ages and continued so during the Renaissance, appearing on weather vanes and cathedral towers. It meant vigilance "tending towards eternity and taking care to grant first place to the things of the spirit, to be wakeful and to greet the Sun – Christ – even before it rises in the East" (Cirlot 1971, 51–2).[15] The rooster then reinforces the many solar images in the fresco, which are hybrid representations including both Christ and Apollo. Having his back to eternity, Constantine speaks to his troops. He will win the battle at the Milvian Bridge because he heeds a vision. He is backed by his own spiritual pursuits. There is yet one more syncretic meaning in the rooster. Although associated with Sol/Apollo, its pugilistic character links this bird with the god Mars. Covarrubias states: "es symbolo del buen guerrero, y assí le atribuyen en cuanto a esta calidad a Marte y la pintan con él" (1987, 623). The rooster thus reflects Constantine's devotion to another pagan god, Mars. But this pagan mystery has a Christian meaning. Constantine's martial pursuits, since they are based on spiritual ideals, lead him to victory. In *La Numancia* Cipión, although related to Sol/Apollo and Mars, never achieves his victory because he neglects the visionary spirit. "Eternity" is more likely to belong to the city: "Numancia . . . / merece ser eterna en la memoria" (v. 2266).

Although Cervantes seems to have modeled Cipión's exhortation to his soldiers after Giulio Romano's *Apparition* (which was based on a sketch by Raphael), a number of the positive iconological traits of the fresco are transferred to the Numantians. *Discordia concors* (the harmony that mysteriously arises in conjoining opposite traits), the foregrounding of the spiritual, and solar/Christian imagery are some of Constantine's traits that are passed on to the Numantians in Cervantes's play. Although Cipión's martial spirit and his quest for moderation serve to reform his troops, he is unable to win the final victory since, unlike his enemy, he fails to understand the mystery of the union of Mars with the "celestial" Venus and he cannot envision the quest for eternity. And yet the play does portray him as a brave and imposing figure, one who like Constantine is able to speak persuasively, galvanize his troops into an army of Mars, and transform their bad habits into courage and determination. In transforming Constantine's allocution into Cipión's, Cervantes may have been aware that the Vatican's false tapestries on Constantine have a number of features in common with a tapestry series for which Giulio Romano prepared the program and the sketches between 1532 and 1535 (Salet, Jestaz, and Bacou 1978, 5, 11). This series, "The History of Scipio," was commissioned by Francis I to exalt his own victories. Cervantes need not have seen Giulio Romano's sketches in Rome or have gone to France to view the tapestries. Seven tapestries, the oldest surviving duplicates, were bequeathed to Philip II by Mary of Austria, queen of Hungary and regent of the Netherlands (Domínguez Ortiz, Herrero Carretero, and Godoy 1991, 69).

As noted in the previous chapter, the rivalry between Francis I and Charles V has been inscribed in *La Numancia* through the transformation of Raphael's *The Coronation of Charlemagne* (where the emperor is represented with the features of Francis I) into the coronation of Charles V at Bologna. Cervantes's concern with this rivalry points to his possible utilization of Francis I's tapestries in order to praise Spanish imperialism or at least reexamine rulership and empire through such a leader. Francis's tapestries focus on the triumphs of the Scipio Africanus who defeated Hannibal: "Twelve tapestries represented major events in the Second Punic War, from the battle of Ticinum to the decisive battle of Zama. The remaining ten featured scenes of Scipio's triumph on his return to Rome" (Domínguez Ortiz, Herrero Carretero, and Godoy 1991, 69). Cervantes prefers to look at the deeds of his grandson, the second Scipio Africanus, and describe Numantian/Spanish resistance to one of the greatest generals of antiquity.

Like the portrayal of Constantine at the Vatican, the tapestries of Scipio Africanus reveal the subject's continence. Indeed, one of the twenty-two tapestries prepared for Francis I is labeled *Scipio's Continence*. It is also one of the seven tapestries in Philip II's set (Domínguez Ortiz, Herrero Carretero, and Godoy 1991, 69). It is based on the story of a beautiful woman prisoner who reveals to Scipio that she is engaged to the Celtiberian prince Allucius. Instead of taking her for himself, Scipio returns her to her lover. And instead of accepting the treasures brought as ransom by her parents, the Roman general gives these riches to Allucius (Salet, Jestaz, and Bacou 1978, 46).[16] In the tapestry, the woman prisoner stands to Scipio's left and the treasures are displayed in the right foreground. Contrasting with Scipio's continence, the *putti* of the frame engage in playful embraces and in sexual exploration. Both the fresco and the tapestry banish the lust of Venus so that the valor of Mars can shine through. It is curious to note that a sketch for this tapestry includes in the right foreground two youths holding helmets and weapons who are strikingly similar to the ones found in the left foreground in the *Apparition* (Salet, Jestaz, and Bacou 1978, 48). Their banishment to the edge of the sketch mirrors the placement of the putti in the frame of the actual tapestry. Both sketch and tapestry relegate the pleasures of the vulgar Venus to the margins. As noted, Cipión in *La Numancia* also banishes the vulgar Venus.

It could be argued that Cipión's continence in the play does not exhibit the mercy shown by the general who frees the woman prisoner in the tapestry. But Cipión's clemency in *La Numancia* does parallel that of Scipio Africanus in the artistic series. A tapestry entitled *The Clemency of Scipio* shows how once Carthage is taken, the Roman general releases his prisoners and gives them back their possessions (Salet, Jestaz, and Bacou 1978, 39).[17] In *La Numancia*, this is not possible, since the inhabitants of the city have destroyed their possessions and killed themselves. Nevertheless, echoing the tapestry and the clemency of his grandfather, Cipión exclaims:

¡Mal, por cierto, tenían conocido
el valor, en Numancia, de mi pecho,
para vencer y perdonar nacido!
                    (vv. 2312–14)

While Giulio Romano uses Scipio Africanus to praise Francis I, Cervantes revives his grandson Cipión in order to delve into the qualities of rulership, ancient and modern. At a time when power is authorized through its link to the ancients, Romano remembers the glory of ancient Rome and shows how the martial spirit of the past is at its best when it is accompanied by moderation, continence, temperance, and clemency. His Renaissance syncretism allows him to present pagan mysteries and Christian truths, one emerging from the other. *La Numancia* also turns to pagan mysteries to envision the newer religion and the rising of imperial Spain. While Giulio Romano remembers Rome, Cervantes adds the remembrance of another ancient city. In this textual and syncretic archeology of power, Numantia becomes a new Rome, a city whose eternity is ensured through "Christian" sacrifice. While a miracle led to Constantine's conversion, Cipión's own anagnorisis comes about from the sacrifice of the city. The iconology of the *Apparition*, then, is fulfilled in *La Numancia* when Cipión portrays his own would-be clemency. The new Spanish Empire should then emulate the Roman general while fashioning its own myth of power from the ruins of Numantia/Rome.[18]

5

Aeschylus
Praising the enemy

Although a number of the themes and structures of *La Numancia* arise from the frescoes by Raphael and Giulio Romano at the Vatican, Cervantes's own medium of representation is the theater, a genre which combines the visual and the verbal. In the early days of the *comedia*, when Cervantes was composing his *Numancia*, the verbal far exceeded the visual. His incorporation of visual elements from Renaissance art was a highly innovative technique. But it is now time to turn from the visual to the verbal, from the relationship between painting and drama to the nature of tragedy. Throughout the Western tradition, tragedy has consistently been regarded as one of the highest forms of literature, one that "refers to a mode of elevated subject matter."[1] Tragedies' heights have to do not only with genre, social status, and critical perceptions but also with agon and characterization. Since it combines both the rare and the intolerable, tragedy leads the audience to a catharsis of pity and fear. As R. J. Dorius asserts: "Courage and inevitable defeat: when we confront the great literature of tragedy from our everyday world, it is perhaps these two qualities that strike us most forcibly, for the first in any society is rare and the second is a prospect most men find intolerable" (1965, 860). During the Renaissance, these qualities of tragedy combined with the prestige of the ancients and imbued the genre with even greater value. Aristotle's *Poetics*, subjected to countless commentaries by Italian and French thinkers, became the blueprint for tragedy. But the lack of availability of many of the Greek dramatic texts seems to have led many Renaissance playwrights to imitate the tragedies of Seneca, which presented "a very different vision from that of Greek tragedy, and unquestionably more limited" (Braden 1985, 30).[2]

And yet, Spanish theater of the Golden Age, even more than English Elizabethan drama, showed a marked resistance toward imitation. Lope de Vega's pronouncements on imitation of the classics in his *Arte nuevo de hacer comedias* are proverbial: "y cuando he de escribir una comedia, / encierro los preceptos con seis llaves; / saco a Terencio y Plauto de mi estudio" (1971, vv. 40–2). Lope rejects Roman comedies as models, since he believes that the tragic and the comic ought to be mixed in all plays. He also moves away from the Aristotelian unities in tragedy since "aunque es consejo de Aristóteles / porque ya le perdimos el respeto" (1971, vv. 189–90).

This resistance toward imitation was one reason for the marginalization of Golden Age theater. A French traveler to Spain, François Bertaut, for example, claimed in his *Journal de voyage d'Espagne* (1659) that Calderón was unaware of Aristotelian unities.[3] However false, this conception became prevalent, because Spanish culture was suspect. The great Western tradition ended at the Pyrenees. Beyond this mountainous barrier was a liminal land, poised between European greatness, which emulated the authorities of the past, and African Otherness, which produced "wild" texts that must be tamed.[4] The *comedia*, then, became doubly marginal: it was Spanish and it rejected the classical tradition. Critical perception has tended to reinforce this view. For example, in his two influential articles on the uniqueness of the *comedia* (1959 and 1970), Arnold Reichenberger foregrounded Spain's differences by contrasting Greek tragedy with the *comedia*, noting that the ever-present movement in Spanish theater from order disrupted to order restored is the result in an overwhelming belief in faith and honor.

Other critics, however, have searched for Spanish tragedies in the Golden Age since it was thought that by using this authoritative label, the plays of the period could acquire a more dignified status. In *The Tragic Fall* (1978), Raymond MacCurdy argues that Spanish tragedy is to be found in the fall of the king's favorite; Duncan Moir sees in the peasant plays of Lope and Calderón "Spanish drama's greatest contribution to the European tragic tradition" (1965, 225); while Alexander Parker, in spite of underlining the importance of poetic justice in the *comedia*, seeks to make Calderón into a tragedian by discovering a collective hamartia in his plays: "each single error trickles down and combines with all the others to form the river that floods the tragic stage" (1962, 233). The most influential critics on Golden Age tragedy, however, are those that conceive of the honor dramas as tragic.[5] It is here that Seneca's most important link to Spanish theater can be discovered.[6] And yet, Alfonso de Toro (1985), reviewing Lope's honor plays, clearly shows that they are, not tragedies, but tragicomedies. In the *Arte nuevo de hacer comedias* Lope had stressed the importance of mixing the tragic and the comic. Arguing that nature always mixes tragedy and comedy, he develops the notion of *imitatio naturae*, which replaces Aristotelian mimesis.[7] Although comedies abound in the Spanish Golden Age, as represented by the *comedia de capa y espada* genre, most other works of the period can be labeled tragicomedies. And even some cloak-and-dagger plays include tragic elements that should grant them the label *tragicomedias*.[8] This is why Cervantes's *La Numancia* acquires such importance. It comes before the crystallization of the *comedia* into a mixed genre, but it also follows or is the contemporary of a number of experiments with the tragedy, such as Juan de la Cueva's *Tragedia de la muerte de Ayax Telamon sobre las armas de Aquiles* (1579), Cristobal de Virués's *Elisa Dido* (1580–6), and Lupercio Leonardo de Argensola's *Isabela* (1580–1).[9] It thus emerges as the single great Aristotelian tragedy of the Spanish Golden Age. As will be argued in Chapter 9, it also imitates elements from Seneca's theater.

Criticism of Miguel de Cervantes's *La Numancia* rarely fails to emphasize its tragic aspects. Raymond MacCurdy, for example, calls this drama "a rare specimen of Spanish tragedy" (1960, 100) and, in a chapter entitled "Spanish Tragedy before Rojas," considers this play the noblest and best up to that time: "Despite certain technical deficiencies, it surpasses all previous Spanish tragedies in its warm interest and nobility of sentiment" (1958, 12). Alfredo Hermenegildo speaks eloquently of this play as tragedy: "A mi modo de ver, *La Numancia* es la mejor tragedia aparecida en España, no ya en los tiempos anteriores a Lope de Vega, sino en toda la historia de nuestra literatura" (1973, 370). Most critics also agree on the identity of the protagonist. Simonde de Sismondi states: "He has taken as the subject of his tragedy the destruction of a city which valiantly opposed the Romans, and whose inhabitants, rather than surrender themselves to the enemy, preferred perishing beneath the ruins of their homes" (1853, 2.12). Angel Valbuena Prat makes an even clearer statement to this effect: "*La Numancia* es la gran tragedia nacional de la colectividad teniendo como protagonista la ciudad entera" (1968, 2.21). In a more recent article, Antonio Rey Hazas once again affirms that "el personaje individual cede su protagonismo al personaje colectivo" (1992, 71–2).

There are those, however, who reject the collective protagonist in favor of viewing the enemy general, Cipión (Scipio), as tragic hero.[10] Paul Lewis-Smith admits that at first glance Cipión can be seen as a typical protagonist of a "Tragedy of Error," where "some highly fortunate person suffers a fall when a flaw in his character causes him to make a mistake, or error of judgment" (1987, 16). However, he goes on to show that there is no true tragedy if the play is viewed from this perspective since Cipión's fall is thoroughly justified. Lewis-Smith claims that the incipient tragedy turns into a tragicomedy when Spanish valor overcomes the Fates through a collective suicide that deprives the Romans of a victory. Since drama's first purpose is to please, a tragedy becomes tragicomedy in order to celebrate the spirit of ideal Spanish patriotism. His view of *La Numancia*, then, would place it as just one more text from the Golden Age that mixes genres. Jane Tar, on the other hand, will not privilege the city over Cipión or vice versa, nor will she accept the play as tragicomedy. She speaks of a double hamartia that confers "a kind of equality on the agents, one not necessarily undermined by the glorification of the collective tragic hero at the play's conclusion" (1990, 28). This chapter will take up the question of genre; will reaffirm the notion of Cipión as tragic protagonist; will explore the question of the tragic flaw; and will propose a Greek model that reflects Cervantes's praise of the enemy.

If the city is considered to be the tragic hero of *La Numancia*, then it should possess elements which might enable us to classify it as such. Dorius's comments on courage and the inevitable defeat seems to bolster the view of the city as tragic hero. From the omens in Act 2 the inhabitants discover the inevitability of defeat and yet they behave with utmost courage. The term *valor* is constantly invoked to praise the inhabitants of the city. Furthermore, the city seems to have a hamartia, or tragic flaw: hubris. As Joaquín Casalduero notes, one of the key examples of rhetorical rhyme in the play is *arrogancia–Numancia* (1966, 283). The repetition of this rhyme foregrounds the city's central flaw. Since these major components of tragedy (courage, tragic flaw, and inevitability) lead to the final catastrophe, many assert that the audience would then experience the catharsis of pity and fear.

Menéndez Pelayo insists that such a catharsis is not precluded by collectivity.[11] And yet, many of the tragic elements do not hold up if the play is carefully scrutinized. The question of omens and the courage of the Numantians, for example, will be analyzed in Chapter 8 in order to show how necromancy and suicide subvert some of the lofty ideals represented by the city. For now, let us concentrate on catharsis and catastrophe. Both may be questioned if the ideas of Joaquín Casalduero regarding this play are accepted. One of the three themes of the play, indicates this critic, is "la caída de Numancia y el levantamiento de España" (1966, 259).[12] In this sense, the end of the play does not show catastrophe, because Numantia, which represents Spain, falls but does not fail. In the third act of the play, the Numantian leader Teágenes comes up with a plan that will deny the Romans their victory.[13] By burning and destroying all their riches and by killing all the citizens of the city, the Numantians will deprive the Romans of the glory of conquest. Furthermore, since the Romans will have no captives or booty to display, they will not be able to enter Rome in a triumphal march. Indeed, the Romans will become the witnesses of Numantia's glory. They will see how a small city has been able to deprive the mighty Roman Empire of their expected conquest. On witnessing Numantia's fate, the Roman Mario is one of the first to admit that the empire has been defeated: "pues en humo y en viento son tornadas / las ciertas esperanzas de vitoria" (vv. 2261–2). He also acknowledges that Numantia's feat is deserving of eternal fame.[14]

The figure of Fame appears at the end of the play to provide an optimistic conclusion which precludes the Aristotelian emotions of pity and fear. Gustavo Correa, aware of the role of *Fama* in the play, asserts: "La comedia nos muestra, por consiguiente, la superación del sino trágico y el triunfo sobre la muerte, en virtud de la presencia de la Fama" (1959, 289). Omens and prophecies throughout the play point to such a conclusion. The image used by Mario to describe the Roman failure (victory turned to smoke) had already been utilized in a priestly prophecy in Act 2 (vv. 822–4). The living flames of Numantia are the fires fanned by fame, which will give the city "eternal" renown. As early as Act 1, the figures of Spain and the river Duero (which have been equated by some critics with the chorus of Greek tragedy) point to the failure of the Romans and the future fame of the Iberian city:

llegada ya la hora postrimera,
do acabará su vida y no su fama,
cual fénix, renovándose en la llama.
                    (vv. 390-2)

Just like the Egyptian bird that is reborn from its own ashes, Numantia will rise again in the annals of fame.

Studying the uniqueness of the Spanish *comedia* of the Golden Age, Arnold Reichenberger finds that it departs radically from classical tragedy. This critic explains that Aristotelian catharsis occurs when the protagonist finds himself "in a situation out of which he cannot safely extricate himself and which evokes pity and fear in the spectator. The play ends with the hero's moral or physical destruction" (1970, 168). The Spanish *comedia*, however, "follows the pattern from order disturbed to order restored" (1959, 307). This movement, which has its source in Christian optimism, certainly differs from the inescapable fate of classical drama and does not convey the emotions of pity and fear. Reichenberger's conclusions are somewhat dated; most critics today recognize that the *comedia* not only celebrates but also questions the values and attitudes of the society. Although the outward movement of many of these plays can be seen in terms of a concluding optimism, a deeper look reveals fissures in the monolithic structure.

The term *comedia*, of course, refers not only to the typical cloak-and-dagger plays of the period but also to works that can be labeled tragicomedies. Thus, when Paul Lewis-Smith refers to *Numancia* as tragicomedy, he is still within the parameters of the *comedia*. For Lewis-Smith, Cervantes's play follows a particular type of tragicomedy which Giraldi Cinthio calls a *tragedia mista*: "The plot of this kind of tragicomedy followed a formula that was common to most forms of tragicomedy developed in the sixteenth and seventeenth centuries: good came into conflict with wickedness and at the end of the day the two got their just deserts: goodness prospered; wickedness was punished" (Lewis-Smith 1987, 21).[15] By invoking poetic justice, however, Lewis-Smith must turn away from catharsis, since it cannot exist when all receive what they deserve. Although I agree that Cervantes's play can be called a tragicomedy (or simply a *comedia*) when viewed from the Numantians' perspective, I will argue that within the structure of the *comedia* there is an embedded tragic structure which focuses on the Roman general's defeat at the hands of a small but valiant city. Although there is poetic justice when it comes to dealing with Numantia/Spain (and thus there is no tragedy), I do not believe that Cipión's punishment is appropriate. Rather, his is the fate of a tragic hero.

If we view *La Numancia* from the perspective of the traditional definition of the *comedia*, it can be perceived that the "order disrupted" is created by the Roman invasion which leads to the fall of the city. Yet, Numantia does not perish but lives on through *Fama*. Although the "order restored" is not attained within the time of the play, it is underscored by the joyful conclusion and implied throughout by the *caída–levantamiento* theme visualized in the prophecy of the Duero. The river prophesies the birth of a new empire out of the ashes of Numantia:

Debajo de este imperio tan dichoso
serán a una corona reducidos,

por bien universal y a tu reposo,
tus reinos hasta entonces divididos.

(vv. 513–15)

But the play, some will argue, does not achieve its triumphal conclusion solely through political *renovatio*. Although the figure of Fame serves to inspire Spaniards to attain future unity and glory, it also points to the three lives that a Christian can live: earthly life, the life of fame, and "esta otra vida tercera" of which Jorge Manrique speaks, the eternal life as reward for the virtuous Christian. After all, it can be argued that the play is imbued with Christian images. Marandro's willingness to sacrifice his own life to bring bread to his beloved can be related to the sacrifice of Christ to bring new life to humankind. But Marandro's eucharistic sacrifice is but a microcosm of the central sacrifice. By dying, the city ensures the birth of a nation. Religious theater in Spain was often linked to the feast of Corpus Christi. Very much like an *auto sacramental, La Numancia* speaks of bread, sacrifice, and a death that becomes eternal life. Joaquín Casalduero goes so far as to assert that we are confronted at the conclusion of the play with "esa alegría final cristiana de la muerte que es vida, vida inmortal" (1966, 281). Numantia can then be seen as yet another martyr to the pagan Roman Empire. Although the text is open to this type of interpretation, more subversive and suggestive elements will be discussed in later chapters. What is important for our purposes here is to show how the movement toward "order restored" permeates the surface of the text both in its political and in its religious guise.

Thus, if the city is taken as the protagonist of the work, *La Numancia* stands more as a *comedia* than as a model of classical tragedy. Yet, over and over again critics insist on discussing classical elements in the Spanish play. Although, as stated, this may point to the urge to link Spain to the European and classical traditions and thus mitigate the perception of the literature of the peninsula as a nonconforming and "wild" Other, there is a kernel of truth in all of these assertions. Beginning with Simonde de Sismondi, *La Numancia* has been compared to Aeschylus's *The Persians*. The idea of collectivity is stressed in this comparison, thus returning us to the contention that the city is the protagonist of *La Numancia*, which in turn removes the play from its classical models. It is surprising that collectivity has been shown to be the major link between both plays since modern classical criticism, as will be shown, does not accept the collective hero in *The Persians*. A study of Aeschylus's tragedy and its comparison with Cervantes's play may help us to arrive at an understanding of what constitutes tragedy in *La Numancia.*

Aeschylus's *The Persians* was presented in Athens in 472 B.C.,[16] only eight years after the Greek naval victory of Salamis, which is the subject of the play. Even though the play commemorates this triumph, "the comparative absence of patriotic bias is in keeping with the high moral tone of the play" (Broadhead 1960, xvi). The tragedy takes place in Susa, capital of the Persian Empire, at a time when Atossa, mother of Xerxes, and the chorus of elders chosen by the king to manage affairs of state during his absence anxiously await news from the king and his forces, who are battling the Greeks. From its very inception, images and feelings of doom serve as counterpoint to the catalogue of Persian heroes and a narration of the glorious exploits of the army. Contrasting the epic and martial vision – "Resistless, Persia's armed flood / and the war-joy that crests in her sons" (1981, 42)[17] – the private feelings of the chorus surface to create foreboding: "My heart's ragged beat prophesies doom" (1981, 39). This feeling is compounded when the queen comes to consult the chorus of elders about a dream/vision: Two women stood before her, one dressed in Persian, the other in Doric, garb. Her son, Xerxes, yoked them to his chariot, and while the Persian woman "kept her mouth well-governed by the reins" (1981, 48), the other tore the yoke, turning over the cart. "And he falls, / my son falls" (1981, 48), cries out Atossa. In waking she sees an eagle chased by a falcon, "and the eagle did / nothing, / only cringed and offered up its flesh" (1981, 49). The dream and the omen obviously predict the fall of the imperial power, Persia.

A messenger arrives and recounts the destruction of the Persian fleet at Salamis: "One stroke, one single stroke has smashed / great prosperity, / and Persia's flower is gone, cut down" (1981, 52). Aeschylus then focuses the action of the tragedy around the shattering news of defeat, but he glorifies the Greeks without ridiculing the Persians. In fact, the catalogue of fallen Persian soldiers is epic in nature (1981, 54–5). Understanding the strength and valor of the enemy, the Athenian audience can be proud of their victory.

The ghost of Darius, Xerxes' father, appears in order to foretell present and future catastrophe. The play ends with the arrival of Xerxes in rags lamenting his fortune. It is fitting that he should thus appear, since he (and not the Persians as a whole) is the subject of the tragedy. Throughout the play, interest is focused on Xerxes by the references to him made by Atossa, the chorus, the messenger, and even the ghost of Darius. Xerxes' portentous fall and his expressions of sorrow and loss ("My heart howls / howls / from its bony cage" [1981, 88]) move an audience to experience the catharsis of pity and fear. Thus, a play that is meant to commemorate a Greek triumph has a Persian king as the tragic hero. H. D. Broadhead acknowledges that Aeschylus is viewing the tragedy from the side of the enemy: "We expect to find that the poet has done his best to view the scene through Persian eyes, and that whatever his feelings toward the barbarian invader, he has, as a dramatist and delineator of character, entered with imaginative insight into the heart of the Persian tragedy" (1960, xxiv).

According to Philip Whaley Harsh, "A fundamental concept is that too great prosperity (*koros*, "satiety") brings on boastfulness or wanton insolence (*hybris*), which in the end results in ruin (*ate*). This conception, the most frequent basic theme of Greek tragedy, occurs repeatedly in the *Persians*" (1944, 46). Throughout the play there is emphasis on "Persia's power / her prosperity" (1981, 75). This *koros* leads the tragic hero, Xerxes, to experience a particular type of hamartia called hubris. H. D. F. Kitto states emphatically: "Xerxes' *hubris* led him to break a divine law. He sinned as Paris sinned, as Agamemnon; and like those sinners he was punished by Zeus" (1968, 39). His excessive pride and boastfulness are evinced in his reckless invasion of Greece and in his attempt to dam the Hellespont so as to cross from Asia into Europe: "Mere man that he is, / he thought, but not on good advice, / he'd overrule all gods, / Poseidon most of all" (1981, 77). Xerxes' sins against Poseidon and Zeus lead to his downfall at the hands of the Greeks.

The Persians and *La Numancia* both deal with a crucial battle. At first glance the approach is somewhat different. In Aeschylus, the Greeks win the battle, and the tragedy is that of the Persians. In Cervantes, the Romans win the battle, and the tragedy is that of Numantia. While a Greek writer envisions an enemy's tragedy, a Spanish author seems to focus on his own country's downfall (Numantia). Yet, let us reconsider. Casalduero discusses the theme *caída–evantamiento*. The Spaniards have not been defeated; the end is not tragic. Fame appears. Warning of "la fuerza no vencida" (v. 2445) of Numantia, she states: "Demos feliz remate a nuestra historia" (v. 2448). This is certainly not the lament of tragedy but a stated happy ending. This conclusion leads us to the obvious question: Is there a lament in *La Numancia*? Yes, but it is not the city's lament but Cipión's. He has failed to achieve a victory. Witnessing the suicide of Bariato, the Roman general states: "Tú con esta caída levantaste / tu fama y mis vitorias derribaste" (vv. 2407–8). Fame restates this Roman defeat:

Alzad, romanos, la inclinada frente,
llevad de aquí este cuerpo, que ha podido
en tan pequeña edad arrebataros
el triunfo que pudiera tanto honraros.

(vv. 2421–4)

The lament of Xerxes in *The Persians* corresponds to the lament of Cipión in *La Numancia*. Thus, the apparent differences presented above have vanished: Aeschylus, an Athenian, writes a tragedy of the defeat of the Persians (the enemy). Cervantes, a Spaniard, composes a tragedy dealing with the defeat of Numantia's enemy, the Romans. Both imperial powers are seen at the brink of disaster, humiliated by small but valiant city or cities.

Once this is clarified, a comparison of the two texts reveals astounding similarities. No one has claimed that Cervantes actually imitated Aeschylus. Lewis-Smith explains: "Cervantes, I suppose, was aware of the existence of Aeschylus' tragedy, but he could not have read it and it is doubtful indeed that it provided him with any inspiration: in the sixteenth century Aeschylus was very much overshadowed by Sophocles, Euripides and Seneca; all three were both better known and more respected" (1987, 25). Even those who have suggested that the episode of the battle of the sheep in *Don Quijote* (1978, 1.18) may be derived from Sophocles' *Ajax* have to contend with the fact that this tragedy "was not translated into Spanish until long after Cervantes' time; the first translation into a modern language was the Italian one published in Venice in 1603" (McGaha 1991, 158). Consequently, a later model for the episode, Apuleius's *Golden Ass*, has seemed to be the more probable subject of imitation (Selig 1983, 286). If there is doubt that Cervantes had read Sophocles, critics feel almost certain that he never read Aeschylus.

Nevertheless, the many similarities between *La Numancia* and *The Persians* claim more than a coincidence in authorial perspective. If Cervantes was acquainted with Aeschylus and modeled his work after him, *La Numancia* would then be the first play in Christian Western Europe based on Aeschylus. John Milton's *Samson Agonistes*, "a pure re-creation of Greek tragedy" based on *Prometheus Bound* (Highet 1949, 295), would then be second.[18] Cervantes could have become acquainted with the Greek text either in Latin translation[19] or through a summary provided by one of the many compendia of the times. Aeschylus's tragedy deals with a situation that is clearly reminiscent of Cervantes's own experiences in the 1570s. It tells of a crucial naval battle, one that changed the history of the times. Salamis was for the Greeks what Lepanto was for Golden Age Spaniards. Both Athenians and Spaniards fought a naval battle to contain the imperial expansion of a culture centered in the Middle East. And both were successful. It is known that Aeschylus was present at the battle in the Strait of Salamis (Aeschylus 1981, 3), and thus many critics have attempted to read *The Persians* as an eyewitness account of the battle, disregarding the fact that it is a literary representation. Cervantes's own participation at the battle of Lepanto, in which the allied forces of Spain, Venice, and the Papal States defeated the Turks, led to its inclusion as an episode in the Captive's tale in *Don Quijote* (1978, 1.39). The tale not only describes the battle of Lepanto but critiques subsequent naval encounters with the Turkish fleet. At Navarino, for example: "Vi y noté la ocasión que allí se perdió de no coger en el puerto toda el armada turquesca" (1978, 1.39.478).

Not only the tale of the *Captive* but also plays such as *El trato de Argel*, *Los baños de Argel*, and *La gran sultana* and the novella "El amante liberal" deal with the relationship between Spaniards and their enemies – the Moors of Algiers and the Turks of Constantinople, both a part of the Ottoman Empire. As Ottmar Hegyi has shown, these works contain not only positive references to Islamic justice but also instances "where he awakens compassion towards his Islamic characters" (1992, 274–5). We have then two writers who took part in naval battles that changed history and were able to present the point of view of the enemy. William Arrowsmith contends that Aeschylus "feels compassion for others in whom he recognizes by his own condition – the common suffering of a common fate. It is this shared suffering, this compassion, that the Greek poet here, with astonishing sympathy of comprehension, extends to the Persian enemy" (1981, x). Cervantes fosters compassion for his fellow human beings through the representation of characters such as Zoraida and Agi Morato.

Although Cervantes may not have developed this sense of understanding and compassion for the Other until after his Algerian captivity, he could have come across Aeschylus' text during his Italian sojourn (1569–75) and only later understood its resonances with his own vision and experience. If Cervantes knew any of Aeschylus's tragedies, the *The*

Persians is the most likely candidate. Not only did it enjoy great popularity in its own time, but during the decline of the Roman Empire it was chosen as one of seven plays of Aeschylus for school reading. As such, it was preserved in medieval manuscripts. Furthermore, *The Persians* was also included in a collection of three of Aeschylus's plays to be read in the schools of the Byzantine Empire (Aeschylus 1981, 16). Greek manuscripts of Aeschylus were brought to Italy with the fall of Constantinople, and the editio princeps of his works was published in 1518 (Sandys 1962, 2.105). Indeed there were several exemplary editions of his plays during the sixteenth century: "High points in this history are the editions of Turnubus (1552), Robortello (1552), Vittori (1557) and Canter (1580)" (Rosenmeyer 1982, 17).

Of the many manuscripts available, one has a curious history that may impinge upon Cervantes. As Janet Lembke explains, the Biblioteca Nacional in Madrid houses a manuscript of *The Persians* and of works by other Greek poets that was once in the possession of Constantine Laskaris. Born in Constantinople, he went into exile when the Turks took the city. In a personal note in the manuscript, Laskaris tells how he lost the manuscript twice and miraculously found it each time in another city. It took him eighteen years to find it the second time, in Messina, Sicily. Laskaris "left his MSS to Messina, then under the rule of Castile. At Messina they remained until 1679, when they were removed, first to Palermo and thence to Spain" (Sandys 1962, 2.77). We know that the soldiers wounded at Lepanto were sent to a hospital in Messina. Cervantes was here on 31 October 1571 and was discharged on 24 April 1572 (Canavaggio 1987, 57–8). Could Cervantes have heard the story of the strange fate of the manuscript which contained *The Persians* while he was recuperating in the Messina hospital? Certainly his obsession with lost manuscripts as evinced by the fictional tale of Cide Hamete Benengeli's text of *Don Quijote* indicates that he would have been particularly interested in such a story. Like the fictional narrator of *Don Quijote*, Cervantes could have paid someone to translate the manuscript. The many months spent in the hospital would have provided him with ample time to contemplate the political and artistic implications of Aeschylus's play.

It would be particularly fitting to have Cervantes discover *The Persians* through Laskaris's tale, since this manuscript collector mourned the loss of his Greek heritage to the Turks. During the Renaissance, the fall of Constantinople to the Ottoman Empire came to be regarded in terms of the ancient battle of the Greeks and the Trojans. The Turks were thought to be descendants of the defeated Trojans, and Constantinople was considered the seat of the Eastern empire, the empire of the Greeks. The fall of Constantinople to the Turks in 1454 was thus interpreted as a "well-deserved punishment for Greek pride" (Hegyi 1992, 21). The Greeks defeat the Persians and the Trojans; the Romans and the Turks defeat the Greeks; and in 1571, Spain defeats the Turks. This never-ending rise and fall of empires, where pride leads to downfall, could have led Cervantes to reach back to Aeschylus in order to once again show compassion for the enemy, the Romans, a proud imperial power that is surprisingly defeated. Just as Aeschylus may have been warning his own people, "already tempted toward its own later imperialistic *hubris* by a *daimon* as deadly as that of Xerxes" (Arrowsmith 1981, x), so Cervantes may be warning the rising Spanish Empire of its *arrogancia*. Although the play represents a vision of the enemy's tragedy, the compassion reaches forward to Spain – with a warning.

But let us leave the tale of Laskaris's manuscript as recovered by Cervantes, a story whose fictionality may be comparable to the discovery of Cide Hamete's manuscript by the "second author,"[20] and turn to other, less interesting yet more likely, possibilities. When Turnubus was preparing his Greek edition of Aeschylus (published in 1552), he also did a translation and commentary in Latin of three of his tragedies: *Prometheus Bound, Seven against Thebes,* and *The Persians.*[21] This first attempt at translation remained in manuscript form. Now housed at the Bibliothèque Nationale in Paris, it was once the property of the abbey of Saint-Germain-des-Prés. What is curious about this manuscript is that it also contains a translation of Sophocles' *Ajax,* the play critics claim Cervantes could not have known when writing of the battle of the sheep in *Don Quijote* (Mund-Dopchie 1984, 57).[22] There is an even more likely, although less interesting, model for Cervantes's imitation. Jean Sanravius (actually the Seigneur Jean de Saint-Ravy from Montpellier) published in 1555 a translation into Latin of six plays by Aeschylus, including a life of the playwright (Mund-Dopchie 1984, 84).

Having determined that Cervantes could have known *The Persians,* let us take a closer look at the links between this Greek tragedy and *La Numancia.* In order for the plot of the "antagonist" to become tragic, it needs far more than a final lament. To the elements of *koros* (excessive prosperity), the tragic flaw (hamartia, hubris), and a catastrophe that results in *ate* (ruin) must be added the notion of a worthy hero, an unusual human being, who is able to confront a tragic fate and its concomitant omens. As Lembke and Herington assert: "The Greek poet consistently strove to set the transient doings of mortals against a permanent universe, a universe of ever-present death and ever-living gods" (1981, p. 5).

From the start, *La Numancia* represents the Roman general in such a way that he is seen as worthy and admirable. When the play opens, Cipión is the first to speak. The *antanaclasis* found in the first three verses (Casalduero 1966, 259) shows the heavy burden that the general has assumed. Noting previous failures, the Roman Senate has sent him to subdue Numantia. His first effort is to strengthen his forces by improving the habits and morale of the soldiers, who have given themselves to the pleasures of Venus and Bacchus. Casalduero states that the *lascivia* and general "immorality" of the Roman troops contrast with the Christian morality and honest love found in the inhabitants of Numantia (1966, 266). Indeed, this is an important dramatic function of the Roman army's debauched state. But another function which may be as important is the testing of Cipión's qualities as a leader. From the first scene the audience emerges admiring the grand figure of Cipión, who is able to rescue the troops from despair and impart new pride in them. There can be little doubt that the work presents an admirable Cipión. The stage directions are clear: "Cipión se sube sobre una peña que estará allí" (p. 41). As he towers over his army (and over the audience), his harangue can be admired as a masterpiece of Roman rhetoric, one whose persuasive powers change the outlook of the army. Just as the description of Xerxes in *The Persians* shows him as a great leader, so does Cipión's role in the first act exhibit heroic qualities.

Yet, worthiness alone does not make a tragic hero. He must emerge from an environment steeped in wealth, so that *koros* (satiety) can lead to wanton insolence. As Winnington-Ingram states, "The divine world is jealous of human success, of human prosperity; the tangible evidence of prosperity is wealth, and the pre-eminent symbol of wealth is gold. . . . So, Atossa leaves the gold-bedecked palace . . . to express her fear not only for the men but for the wealth of the Persians" (1983, 8). Indeed, Atossa exclaims: "Nothing / guards my inmost self / against the fear / that vast Wealth, / kicking up dust / as it pelts headlong, / may overturn / continued joy / in the prosperity" (1981, 46). In Cervantes's tragedy, there are no images of the golden palaces of the Romans, but there is a clear portrayal of prosperity and wealth in Cipión's exhortation. In discussing the concubines, the wine, the gambling, the soft beds, and the soldiers with exotic perfumes, he is pointing to a prosperity that must be curbed if the gods, particularly Mars, the god of war, are to favor the Romans. Cipión, then, seems wiser than Xerxes because he attempts to curb the *koros* that may trigger the tragic. Like Atossa, he fears too much wealth.

Even though Cipión attempts to remove all traces of excessive prosperity from his army, and thus emerges as an ideal leader, he must incur some error in order to become a tragic figure. As pointed out by H. D. F. Kitto (1968), the tragic hero must have a hamartia. In *The Persians*, Xerxes' hamartia is hubris. Darius acknowledges that "[h]eadstrong Xerxes" (1981, 75) has brought forth Zeus's vengeance. The final humiliation and lament contrast with initial arrogance and pride. In this tension of contrast caused by hubris is found the catharsis. Cervantes also presents Cipión as admirable at first and pitiful in the end. Exhortation and lament define the two ends of the tragedy, while in the middle stands his hamartia. Paul Lewis-Smith has argued that if Cipión has a hamartia in *La Numancia* it is "his unshakable assumption that the Numantians will surrender if imprisoned in their city and starved to the point of death" (1987, 17). Even though Cipión does assume this, he does so from his own vantage point as a conquering Roman. Believing that the others are of lesser mettle than the imperial troops, his error is one of imperialist pride. Thus, the tragic flaw in both *The Persians* and *La Numancia* is hubris.[23] The Spanish text refers over and over again to Cipión's pride.[24]

When the ambassadors from Numantia arrive to propose peace and to come to terms with the Romans, Cipión rejects the offer. One of the ambassadors warns: "Advierte lo que haces, / señor, que esa arrogancia" (vv. 278–9). The people of Numantia ask for an honorable settlement, but Cipión's pride demands a conquest. This excessive pride goes counter to his role as a leader. The second ambassador warns Cipión that he is not conducting himself in a manner suitable to his station in life: "correspondiendo mal de ser quien eres" (v. 292). The negation of the famous phrase "soy quien soy" points to the coming disaster.[25] This scene would be sufficient to convince the audience of the existence of a tragic flaw. Cervantes, however, reaffirms Cipión's condition in the third act.

Caravino comes to the Roman camp proposing the end of the war through the battle of a single Spaniard with a Roman. Numantia's goodwill and desire for peace are again disdainfully rejected by Cipión:

Bestias sois, y por tales encerradas
os tengo, donde habéis de ser domadas.
Mía será Numancia a pesar vuestro,
sin que me cueste un mínimo soldado.
(vv. 1190–4)

The river Duero also accuses the Romans of pride. Viewing the future, the Duero predicts the eventual fall of Rome through hubris, a fall that parallels the moral destruction of Cipión within the play:

Y puesto que el feroz romano tiende
el paso agora por tu fértil suelo,
que te oprime aquí, y allí te ofende
con arrogante y ambicioso celo,
tiempo vendrá, segŭn que ansí lo entiende
el saber que a Proteo a dado el cielo
que estos romanos sean oprimidos
por los que agora tienen abatidos.
(vv. 465–72)

Xerxes and Cipión both believe they can control human events. Yet, hubris places them in the hands of fate. This attempt at control, according to Leo Aylen, is viewed in *The Persians* through the image of yoking. Atossa's dream in which Xerxes yokes two women to his cart has been recounted above. The image found in this dream is repeated by Darius when he appears and warns of Xerxes' yoking the Hellespont: "He hoped to dam / the flow of holy Hellespont – / the Bosphoros / that streams from god – / by locking it / in shackles like a slave" (1981, 76–7). Leo Aylen states: "The implications of slavery with the girls is clear, and ties in with the reference to his enslaving the Hellespont" (1964, 49). Thus, Xerxes appears as a leader ready to enslave humans and the elements, whereas the Greeks fight for liberty.

In *La Numancia* the image of yoking appears early in the play. In order to explain to Cipión why they have rebelled against the Romans, the Numantian ambassador states:

Ellos, con duros estatutos fieros,
y con su estraña condición avara,

pusieron tran grande yugo a nuestros cuellos,
que forzados salimos de él y de ellos.

(vv. 245–8)

As Jane Tar has noted, "Numancia's escape from one kind of yoke has resulted in only another — their city under military siege" (1990, 24). We have seen how this new yoke has transformed the Numantians into beasts in the eyes of Cipión. Thus, the duality slavery–freedom is found in both *The Persians* and *La Numancia*. In both, a freedom-loving city or cities fight against the yoke of an imperial power.

Xerxes and Cipión can be viewed as heroes who, through excessive pride, come to believe they can control human events: they will take away the freedom of others. This will to succeed, this relentless force, is exercised for the most part outside the bounds of the play itself. Xerxes is conspicuous for his absence. Cipión, although present at several points in the play, shares the focus of attention with the city of Numantia. This absence may have a dramatic function. As stated before, although the Persian king does not appear until the end, the audience hears about him over and over again. His absence makes us more aware of the power and force he exercises. But all is in vain. Another hidden force, Fate, will bring him down through his hubris. The analogy between Fate and Xerxes based on absence creates a particularly intense drama. Cipión is present at three essential moments in the Spanish play: first, in the beginning, to show his worthiness and create admiration; second, to evince his tragic flaw in rejecting offers from Numantia; and third, in the final lament. The third moment parallels *The Persians*. The other two serve to define Cipión as a tragic hero. Thus, he is presented only at the three essential moments of a tragedy: in his greatness, as he errs, and as he laments his fall. Cipión, like Xerxes, is absent from a large part of the action. Yet, like Xerxes, his power and relentless drive are felt throughout the play. All actions are reactions to his deeds. This absence may serve the same dramatic function in *The Persians* and in *La Numancia*: to relate analogically Fate and tragic hero, thus increasing the dramatic tension.

Indeed, some of the images of Fate in both plays are curiously similar. The figure of the mother in *The Persians* serves to trigger foreboding through a dream and an augury. In *La Numancia*, the river Duero refers to the allegorical figure of Spain as a mother (v. 441). As in Aeschylus's play, she calls forth images of doom. Atossa also describes an omen: "And

I see / an eagle / fleeing toward the altar's god bright flame /. . . / and soon I see a hawk in downstoop" (1981, 48–9). The hawk that vanquishes the eagle is a clear omen of a small state destroying the imperial or aquiline powers. In *La Numancia* birds also fly in an ominous manner above the altar:

¿No ves un escuadron airado y feo
de unas águilas fieras, que pelean
con otras aves en marcial rodeo?
. . . .
¿Águilas imperiales vencedoras?
(vv. 849–51, 856)

The result of the celestial battle is different, however. In Cervantes's play, the imperial eagles (the Romans) seem to be triumphant.[26] As above, so below. Fate is enacting through the birds the actions to be played out by human beings.

Act 2 of *La Numancia* has often been neglected by critics since it presents a series of omens in a most theatrical manner, culminating with a feat of necromancy unparalleled in Golden Age theater. As noted previously, stage effects were minimal during the latter part of the sixteenth century. With the arrival in Spain of Italian set designers in the 1620s and 1630s, sets and stage effects suddenly acquired great sophistication. In Cervantes's stage directions it is interesting to note his desire for visual effects, although these have to be achieved by rudimentary means such as rolling a barrel full of stones to simulate thunder (p. 69). These stage effects, which culminate in Act 2, are akin to those of Aeschylus, who, in spite of being one of the earliest of the tragedians, "was known in antiquity as the most spectacular of tragedians for his use of visual effects" (Spatz 1982, 24). The summoning of the ghost of Darius with its concomitant rituals is perhaps the most striking visual effect of *The Persians.* The many rituals of the Numantians, as well as the raising of one of the dead, are parallel events in Cervantes's play. The theatricality of these events serves to imbue these tragedies with the play of the gods, with the mysteries of Fate.

When Xerxes appears at the *exodos,* or concluding section, of *The Persians,* his first words are an acknowledgment of the power of Fate: "Heartsick have I confronted hateful doom" (1981, 84). Or, as Robert Potters's translation would have it: "Ah me, how sudden have the storms of Fate, / Beyond all thought, all apprehension, burst / On my devoted head"

(Oates and O'Neill 1938, 78). This mournful Xerxes, dressed in rags, emerges from his carriage, or *harmamaxa*. One of the vehicle's functions is to remind the audience of Atossa's original entry in a chariot and her dream of her son's overturned vehicle, thus foregrounding once again "the yoke-image" (Aeschylus 1981, 118). By attempting to yoke Fate and the gods, by attempting to be a force beyond human possibilities, the tragic hero has called upon forces that will destroy him: "Divine wind has shifted. Heaven / blows against me now" (1981, 86). As the chorus and Xerxes engage in a prolonged questioning that echoes the well-known *ubi sunt?* motif ("Where are they now?") (1981, 119), Xerxes' anagnorisis, his recognition of the greater power of Fate, exposes the final *ate*, or ruin (1981, 119–20).

In *La Numancia*, Mario, sent to investigate the events in the city, reveals the death of the inhabitants and the destruction of their valuables, which paradoxically dash all hope of Roman triumph. Aeschylus's image of the divine wind becomes "pues en humo y en viento son tornadas / las ciertas esperanzas de vitoria" (vv. 2261–2). Only the child Bariato lives. His suicidal fall leads Cipión to intone his lament, which is intermingled with anagnorisis:

Tú con esta caída levantaste
tu fama, y mis vitorias derribaste.
. . . .
Tú sólo me has llevado la ganancia
de esta larga contienda, ilustre, y rara.
                    (vv. 2405–6;2411–12)

The valiant actions of a child are enough to bring about Cipión's "moral destruction" (Reichenberger 1970, 168). His overwhelming force is nowhere near the power of Fate, a force that utilizes the life of a child to bring down Roman pride. While *The Persians* ends with the *ubi sunt?* motif, *La Numancia* answers with the power of Fame: the ruined city will become immortal through its reknown. Its memory will lead Spain to imperial *renovatio*.

While Aeschylus's tragedy is triggered by the destruction of the Persian Empire, Cervantes's play may have been conceived as a reaction to the Holy League's triumph over the Ottoman Empire. Both writers participated in naval battles that decided the fate of empires. They also wrote tragedies from the viewpoint of the enemy, pointing to the mysteries of Fate and to the worthiness of those human beings who could stand up under the weight of the heavens. Their view of the enemy's hamartia, though, was not necessarily an indictment of the Other but a warning to their own people not to exceed their humanity. *Koros* should not lead to boastfulness and indifference toward the Other. In their triumphs, Greeks and Spaniards should demonstrate, if not compassion, at least a "sense of natural limit in mortal transience which the Greeks call *sophrosynē*" (Arrowsmith 1981, x).

6

Homer
An epic contest

As early as the eighteenth century, critics envisioned parallels between Cervantes and Homer. Vicente de los Ríos, the first critic to deal extensively with the two writers,[1] begins with biographical similarities: "Ambos fueron poco estimados en sus patrias, anduvieron errantes y miserables toda su vida, y después han sido objeto de la admiración y del aplauso de los hombres sabios en todas las edades, países y naciones" (1819, 14). But he goes well beyond such platitudes to discover compelling comparisons between the Greek epics and *Don Quijote*. Noting that the madness of don Quijote serves a function similar to Achilles' ire in the *Iliad*, he goes on to show that the "miraculous" helmet of Mambrino has an epic precedent in the weapons forged for Achilles and other ancient heroes. In recent years, the comparison of Achilles with don Quijote has been reinforced. For Chester L. Wolford, two qualities of the Homeric hero as typified by Achilles are also present in don Quijote: *areté*, "which demands that he strive ceaselessly for the first prize" (1986, 198), and *menos*, "or the fierce battle-rage into which Homer's warriors whip themselves" (1986, 202). And yet, both "heroes," in typical epic fashion, subvert their salient qualities. In the chapters that follow, subversion will indeed be seen as a key characteristic of Cervantes's *La Numancia*.

Both Wolford and Ríos are proponents of a Homeric subtext in *Don Quijote*, and both foreground the figure of Achilles in their comparisons. Ríos, for example, finds a stronger causality in the gift of weapons in the *Iliad* than in those prepared for the protagonist of Virgil's *Aeneid*: "Homero es superior a Virgilio: Tetis las dió a Aquiles en ocasión que estaba desarmado, y tenía que combatir con Héctor vestido de las armas divinas, que el mismo Aquiles había cedido a su amigo Pátroclo" (1819, 61). Perhaps Ríos's preference for Homer blinds him to the closer kinship between Cervantes's works and Virgil's *Aeneid*. But his careful discussion of many of the episodes in *Don Quijote* should provide a starting point for future studies. Indeed, some of his references to Virgil should also elicit interest, as when he compares don Quijote's vision of the

97

enchanted Dulcinea in the Cave of Montesinos with Aeneas's encounter with Dido in the underworld (1819, 46).[2]

Given Virgil's preeminence as epic poet during the Middle Ages and the Renaissance, and given the fact that Aeneas narrates the fall of Troy in his epic poem, it may be argued that Homeric reminiscences come to Cervantes through his Latin competitor. Indeed, Chapter 9 will show how some aspects of the fall of Troy as refashioned in *La Numancia* are derived from Virgil rather than from Homer. But the question is even more complex. Homer's vision of the fall of Troy is questioned by medieval authors and thinkers, who come to believe that his poem is partial to the Greeks. These writers will turn to the Latin romances by Dictis and Dares in order to gain a more "accurate" picture of what had happened at Troy. Claiming to be translations of lost Greek originals, these works of fiction gained in authority and led to the famous *Roman de Troie* by Benoit de Saint-Maure (ca. 1165). Guido della Colonna translated it into Latin as *Historia destructionis Troiae*. Colonna's text was eventually translated into Spanish. Several versions of the French poem also appeared in Spain, the best known being the *Historia troyana en prosa y verso*. Saint-Maure's poem was also the main source of the chapters on Troy found in Alfonso X's *General estoria*. All these versions and translations eventually lead to the *Crónica troyana*, which enjoyed great popularity during the sixteenth century.[3] The impact of Dictis and Dares is thus felt well into the sixteenth century, inspiring works such as Joaquín Romero de Cepeda's *La antigua, memorable y sangrienta destruicion de Troya; A imitacion de Dares, troyano, y Dictis, cretense* (1583) and Ginés Pérez de Hita's *Los diez y siete libros de Daris del Belo troyano* (1596). Thus, alternate versions of the Troy story were popular at the time Cervantes composed *La Numancia*.[4]

Homer's ascendancy in Spain begins with Juan de Mena's *Omero romançado*, a partial translation made for King Juan II around 1442. Here, Mena praises Homer and attacks the Dictis and Dares tradition through Guido della Colonna. He writes the *proemio* in order to "dañar y destruir si pudiesse los dichos que Guido [della Colonna] escrivio en offensa de Homero: e aun lo mas principal por causar a los lectores nuevo amor y devocion con las altas obras deste autor" (cited in López Férez 1993, 372). In spite of his attacks on Guido, Mena is basing his translation, not on the Greek original, but on a Latin version, *Ilias latina*, made by Pindarus Tebanus. Another early praise of Homer is found in Alonso de Madrigal's *Sobre Eusebio*, published in 1506, but written before 1455 (López Torrijos

1985, 192). Only with Gonzalo Pérez's translation of the *Iliad* in 1556 can Homer be said to have shed his medieval garb in Spanish letters.

This brief outline of the Homeric tradition in early Spanish literature serves to emphasize the difficulty in deciding which "Homer" Cervantes had in mind. No matter how he came to know the Greek bard, whether heavily clothed in medieval attire or having shed most of the borrowed garb, Cervantes often foregrounds the presence of the Greek author in his texts. Juan Antonio López Férez notes that the *Viaje del Parnaso* contains reminiscences of Homer's epics.[5] He hopes for further contributions to the field: "Es un aspecto que requiere la colaboración de helenistas e hispanistas, y, que sin duda, está llamado a dar jugosos frutos" (1993, 378–9). Whatever the end results of these investigations might be, I would like to emphasize the Homeric presence in Cervantes. This Spanish writer continually incorporates reminiscences of the two Greek epics in *Don Quijote*, posing as a reader knowledgeable with the plot and problematics of the Homeric poems. Lorenzo de Mendoza, for example, worries that his son spends too much of his time reading poetry: "Todo el día se le pasa en averiguar si dijo bien o mal Homero en tal verso de la *Ilíada*" (1978, 2.16.154).[6] Don Quijote gives good counsel to the father and tells him to allow his son to pursue his interests. The knight's appreciation of classical poetry is clearly evinced when he recommends the imitation of the ancient heroes: Aeneas, Ulysses, etc. Although don Quijote wants to behave as a prudent Odysseus/Ulysses (1978, 1.25.303), his adventures are failures in imitation. The episode of the corpse may well recall the return of Hector's body in the *Iliad*, but here don Quijote fails to apprehend that the body he encounters has no epic significance.[7] Don Quijote is not alone in his failures. Sansón Carrasco wants to show his knowledge of Horace, but when he cites the *Ars poetica* in praise of Homer, he misquotes the text, saying "aliquando bonus dormitat Homerus" (1978, 2.3.65) instead of "quandoque bonus dormitat Homerus." This failure is typical of the characters in a text that revivifies the ancients through parody. As Michael Gerli points out, Cervantes imitates one of the moments when "good old Homer slept" in his play *El gallardo español*. Evoking Priam's two deaths in Homer, he includes "Alimuzel's double death and double resurrection" (1995, 50).

Cervantes's imitation of Homer, which emerges through parody in *Don Quijote*, is found in a much more "sacramental" manner in *La Numancia*. But even in the pursuit of a "great Original" (Greene 1982, 38–9), Cervantes's tragedy does not succumb to an ahistorical consciousness. He places Homeric motifs in a contemporary context, thus "modernizing" them (Greene 1982, 41), while attempting to retain a certain antique flavor, devoid of many of the medievalizing traits of Guido della Colonna and Benoit de Saint-Maure. In fact, some of his uses of Homer may derive from Aristotle's *Poetics* (or Renaissance commentaries of this work). Although certain events and motifs in the play recall the ancient epic, Homer's presence is always somewhat elusive. In *La Numancia*, the ghostly vision of the ancient bard derives its intangibility from both text and context. Cervantes's Homeric model, as noted above, is not the Greek original but a series of other texts that point to an absent authority. Within the text, the fires of Troy/Numantia consume so many models that the figure of Homer appears only as a fiery specter dancing above the flames. This chapter will develop some of the general Homeric motifs, and Chapter 9, dealing specifically with Act 3 of *La Numancia*, will point to the bard's elusive presence in the elemental fires.

Cervantes's play has often been studied from the point of view of genre.[8] We have seen in the previous chapter how it follows a number of principles of the Aristotelian tragedy and how its structure and vision parallel Aeschylus's *The Persians*. There are, in addition, critics who view the play as neither tragedy nor tragicomedy but as epic. Alfredo Hermenegildo, although conceiving of *La Numancia* as a tragedy, has argued that one of the great merits of the work is to utilize an epic theme so as to infuse new life into the dramatic form (1973, 370). Emilie Bergmann has made a further contribution to this point of view, claiming that *La Numancia* contains a narrative style typical of the epic (1984, 85ff.).[9] In this chapter, I would like to return to the question of genre in Cervantes's play, taking as a point of departure the link between *La Numancia* and the Homeric epic. As noted above, I certainly do not argue here for Cervantes's *direct* knowledge of the Greek poems – he did not know the language. However, certain commonly known structures, motifs, and episodes are inscribed in the work, albeit imitated indirectly. A particular motif from the epic can shed light on the central conflict within the play and on the critical controversy over who is the tragic hero of *La Numancia*.

The link between tragedy and epic had been forged by Aristotle and was well known to the Renaissance.[10] In the *Poetics*, the Greek philosopher states: "Epic poetry, then, has been seen to agree with Tragedy to this extent, that of being an imitation of serious subjects in a grand kind of verse" (1941, 5, 1449b: 9–11).[11] Indeed, Aristotle often refers to the

Iliad and the *Odyssey* in his discussion of tragedy. One particular statement may be of special significance for understanding the nature of the protagonist in *La Numancia.* Having asserted, "The perfect Plot, accordingly, must have a single, and not (as some tell us) a double issue" (1941, 13.1453a), Aristotle goes on to describe the double plot using the *Odyssey* as example: "After this comes the construction of Plot which some rank first, one with a double story (like the *Odyssey*) and an opposite issue for the good and the bad personages" (1941, 13.1453a). He explains that the double story ends with the "salvation" of Odysseus and the death of the suitors (1941, 17.1455b). This type of "tragedy" fails to include the key element necessary for the "finest form of Tragedy" (1941, 13.1452b), which is the *catharsis* of pity and fear caused by the hero's hamartia: "some error of judgement" (1941, 13.1453a).

Cervantes's *La Numancia seems* to belong to the type of tragedy that is not the most treasured by Aristotle, since it has a double story and a double issue like the *Odyssey.* At first glance, the parallels are clear. The city, like Odysseus and his followers, endures great suffering only to be redeemed at the end. On the other hand, the attacking Romans, just like the suitors in the *Odyssey,* fail to achieve their aim through one of the two devices which Aristotle recommends for tragedy and epic: anagnorisis and peripety. However, a careful look at these two stories will reveal that Cervantes adds certain ingredients to the two plots which transform each of them into the ideal tragedy described by Aristotle. Instead of one tragedy of the second rank with one double issue, *La Numancia* combines two tragedies of first rank. However, I will also argue that one of these tragedies (the fall of Numantia) would fall under the rubric *comedia* during the Spanish Golden Age. To accomplish his double tragic task, Cervantes focuses on the central qualities of each of the Homeric heroes and applies one to the city of Numantia and the other to the Roman general.

According to Ernst Curtius, the Middle Ages and the Renaissance witnessed an interminable debate as to what was the highest virtue of the epic hero, *sapientia* or *fortitudo.* This debate had its origins in ancient conceptions of society, such as the caste system of India, where Brahmans had wisdom while the Kshatriyas were the fighters (Curtius 1953, 171). For the Middle Ages and the Renaissance, however, the locus classicus for the debate was the *Iliad,* where "Achilles is not only hot-tempered but he is thoughtless, so that Odysseus is obliged to stop him from rushing ahead with ill-considered military tactics. . . . Odysseus too, the man of many wiles, is older than Achilles and can be compared with Zeus in wisdom" (Curtius 1953, 170–1). The *Iliad*'s "tragedy is wholly comprehensible only as a deviation from an ideal norm, which we may describe as a combination of courage and wisdom" (Curtius 1953, 172). Although medieval and Renaissance treatises debate which one is the highest virtue, most would agree with Isidore of Seville's statement: "For hero is the name given to men who by their wisdom and courage are worthy of heaven" (Curtius 1953, 175).

A version of this debate can also be found in Renaissance painting, and Cervantes's "modern" model could well be, once again, a work by Raphael.[12] The *Vision of a Knight* portrays Scipio Africanus having a dream.[13] In this altered state of consciousness, he is given a choice reminiscent of the one offered to Hercules.[14] The Roman general's options are symbolized by a book, a sword, and a flower. Roger Jones and Nicholas Penny explain: "These attributes in the painting obviously represent the aspirations of the scholar, soldier and lover (or perhaps poet). That a young knight should be all these, but especially the first two, was a commonplace in courtly literature" (1983, 8). They then cite Castiglioni's *The Courtier*, which contains a debate as to "whether arms or letters should have priority in courtly education" (1983, 8).[15] Cervantes turns to this particular version of the topic in *Don Quijote*. The knight's "discurso de las armas y las letras" (1978, 1.38) is certainly reminiscent of Castiglioni's debate on which element should have priority in a knight's education. The notion that arms and letters are the two ways in which a young man may improve his condition is discussed in the very next chapter of the novel, with the difference that a third choice is also available – not poetry, but "mercancía" (1978, 1.39.474).

La Numancia is not so much concerned with the education of a knight or a profitable career. Instead of dealing with arms versus letters it delves into the qualities of the epic hero, a figure who is already a warrior. Should he display as his main virtue valor or wisdom? I would agree, then, with Vicente Gaos's (1976) suggestion that both *Don Quijote* and *La Numancia* reflect a particular dichotomy. While I accept that the novel opposes *cordura–locura*, I see the play as opposing *cordura–valor*, since *cordura* can be seen as a type of wisdom.[16] Raphael's painting can also be seen from this second perspective. Scipio is already a warrior. He has to choose between different ways of approaching his occupation (the book or the sword). A third choice suggests that he could abandon warfare for love (the flower), thus recalling the famous opposition between Mars and Venus foregrounded by Cervantes's Cipión (Scipio) in his speech to the Roman army.

Ambrosio de Morales's *Corónica*, Cervantes's main historical source, tells us that the general was most attracted to the book. Indeed, he is portrayed as a reader of Xenophon's history of Cyrus, the *Ciripedia* (1791, 4.30). Elsewhere, Morales records the very opposition between *sapientia* and *fortitudo* that will be dramatized by Cervantes. Making some concluding remarks on the siege of Numantia, this historian states: "Tito Livio . . . siempre ensalza los Numantinos, y hace muy grande estima de su esfuerzo. Celebra tambien mucho, y con razon, la prudencia y gran destreza de Scipion en enmendar su ejército (1791, 4.46). Even though Homer is the origin of the controversy between wisdom and valor, Cervantes probably derives his version of the opposing virtues from Raphael's *Vision of a Knight*, where Scipio must choose his way of warring, and from Ambrosio de Morales's *Corónica*, where the play's opposition is already stated in terms of Numantia's *esfuerzo* versus Cipión's *prudencia* and *destreza*.

Other models may have also come into play. Virgil, for example, emphasizes the opposition between valor and cunning in the second book of the *Aeneid*, showing how the brave defenders of Troy fell due to the cunning and treachery of the Greeks (particularly Odysseus/Ulysses and Sinon the traitor). Cervantes's readings of Virgil (to be discussed in Chapters 7 and 9) may have been one way through which the Homeric conflict reached him. As noted above, Cervantes would channel the dichotomy into a tragic structure derived from Aristotle's *Poetics*. Cervantes, like Lope de Vega, would know the *Poetics* text through Italian and Spanish translations and commentaries. As noted, Aristotle would have made him aware of the relationship between Homeric epics and tragedy.

Writers and thinkers of the Spanish Golden Age were also well aware of the epic opposition between wisdom and valor.[17] Sebastián de Covarrubias, for example, includes this dichotomy as the subject of one of his *Emblemas morales*, noting that Troy would have never fallen to either Achilles' valor or Ajax's fierceness. Following Virgil, he declares that the city is destroyed by Odysseus's prudence, astuteness, and deceitful arts:

La valentia de Achiles, la fiereza
Para Ganar a Troya, y la destreza
de Ulisses, con prudencia, astucia, y arte
Toda la destruyo pieça por pieça.
                    (1978, 175)

La Numancia incorporates this dichotomy by presenting the city as representative of *fortitudo* and Cipión as an example of *sapientia*. Very much like Odysseus, Cipión is able to bring about the destruction of Troy/Numantia through his prudence and astuteness. The city's actions exemplify, on the other hand, Achilles' valor, an admirable rashness that, even though it kills, preserves the memory of the hero in the annals of Fame. By taking up this conflict, *La Numancia* is able to represent two authoritative views on the character of the hero. Neither Rome nor Numantia is diminished, since each can claim ancient precedents. Fashioning his myth of the Spanish Empire out of a series of authorities beginning with Homer, Cervantes rekindles an ancient conflict in order to explore the qualities that make a hero (and an empire) great. Such was the power of this epic dichotomy and of Cervantes's mythical recreation in his play that, after the decline of the Spanish Empire, thinkers still praised the country's valor against the cunning of the enemy. Benito Jerónimo Feijóo, for example, emphasizes Spain's "esfuerzo" and "gloria militar" (1993, 151) in his *Teatro crítico universal*, asserting that "Milagros hacían los españoles con el valor" (1993, 179). Turning to Numantia, Feijóo follows Cervantes's version of the suicide of the city and rejects Roman valor: "Al fin venció a los numantinos, no el valor romano, sino la hambre" (1993, 163).[18] The Romans, he claims, gained their empire, not through valor, but "usando de la perfidia, del dolo, de la alevosía" (1993, 164). Cervantes's preference for Spanish *fortitudo* over Roman *sapientia* is echoed by Feijóo, who never envisions that the dichotomy invites consideration of both epic virtues. Feijóo also fails to imagine that the infusion of epic into history shows that history is imbued with fiction, that it is constructed by the poet/historian.

La Numancia not only asks which is the higher virtue (valor or wisdom) but prompts a reader/audience to wonder which one is valued by the Spanish Empire that arose (in Cervantes's vision) out of the ashes of Numantia. Furthermore, the play invites an interpretation as to what constitutes heroic valor and wisdom, and which aspects of these qualities can be seen as debased. Is suicide the pinnacle or a debased form of valor? Is cunning a key aspect of a general's wisdom, or is it a faulty application of this virtue? Indeed, the play's emphasis on epic virtue can also extend to encompass all the virtues and even the question of the ethics of empire making. Are the sixteenth-century Spaniards, like the Romans, destroying a series of heroic peoples? The play does not seek so much to answer these questions as to ask them and, in doing so, to heighten the public's awareness of the consequences of empire building. In order to emphasize Cervantine ambiguity, this chapter will tend to side with the enemy (the Romans), since this aspect of the debate has been neglected by critics who, following Feijóo, follow the strict line of patriotism, exalting Spanish valor.

The play begins with a vision of the Roman camp. After sixteen years of siege, Numantia has yet to surrender. For this reason, the Senate sends its most valued general with the difficult charge of ending the war with a new victory for Rome:

Esta difícil y pesada carga,
que el senado romano me ha encargado,
tanto me aprieta, me fatiga y carga.
(vv. 1–3)[19]

The historical Scipio had already fulfilled the Senate's order to destroy Carthage. The play seems to equate the previous charge successfully carried out with a similar mandate for Numantia. The general, then, is an admirable figure who has won the highest admiration from the Roman Senate and has been given yet another difficult task: "Guerra de curso tan extraña y larga" (v. 5). Cipión proposes to fulfill his duty using "[e]l esfuerzo regido con cordura" (v. 13). A learned audience would immediately associate these qualities with the two main traits of the epic hero, *fortitudo* (*esfuerzo*) and *sapientia* (*cordura*). Note how these are the precise terms used by Ambrosio de Morales. Cipión's demand that the army give up the pleasures of Venus and be subjected only to the rigors of Mars further enhances his stature. It also reflects his rejection of the flower as a choice. He would seemingly select both the book and the sword from Raphael's painting.

Two ambassadors from Numantia come to sue for peace. When Cipión dismisses them, the Numantians warn him: "Advierte lo que haces, señor, que esa arrogancia" (vv. 278–9). According to Aristotle, the tragic hero ought to be admirable but not perfect: "a man not preeminently virtuous and just, whose misfortune, however, is brought upon him not by vice and depravity but by some error in judgement" (1941, 13.1453a). It is clear that Cipión is not subject to vice or depravity; he tries to stamp these out from the Roman army. Instead, he is guilty of a tragic error, hubris, which makes him reject all visions of the future except his own.[20] Cipión has a plan to defeat the Numantians: "Pienso de un hondo foso rodeallos, / y por hambre insufrible he de acaballos" (vv. 319–20). For Paul Lewis-Smith, there is a discrepancy between the aims stated in Cipión's exhortation and the way he proposes to win victory. While the exhortation is an exercise in "public bravado," his true intentions – to starve the city into submission – and "his tacit refusal to give his reasons for having misled his men" would lead "the intelligent spectator" to understand "that Scipio is weaving a web of deceit" (1987, 18–19). Consequently, Lewis-Smith views him as a man who deserves to fail, not as a tragic hero. Rey Hazas also contrasts the heroism of the Numantians with Cipión's attitude: "Frente a esta visión del mundo, Cervantes sitúa otra completamente diferente, racional, astuta, más cobarde, menos dispuesta al sacrificio, más pragmática y quizá más efectiva, la de Cipión, el general romano, que cifra todo en el cerco asfixiante sobre la ciudad, para evitar el derramamiento de sangre de sus tropas" (1992, 75).

However, to desire victory with as little cost in human life to his people is more an act of love for his empire than of cowardice. An attentive and informed spectator would realize that Cipión is a hero in the mold of Odysseus. He is not a coward but a wily leader[21] who wishes to win with as few casualties from his own troops as possible. Appian's *Roman History*, which praises Scipio's command, presents his decision as a positive one: "But he showed himself more experienced in war than themselves, by refusing to join in battle with wild beasts when he could reduce them by that invincible army, hunger" (1962, 1.293). In contrast to the wild courage of beasts, Cipión shows civilized *sapientia*. In addition, the type of siege he proposes was well known to the Middle Ages and the Renaissance. An audience of the time would hardly condemn him for his tactics. Odysseus had also participated in an extended siege, that of Troy. He was the one who proposed a clever solution, the wooden horse. In the *Odyssey* it is described as "the horse which once Odysseus led up into the citadel as the thing of guile, when he had filled it with the men who sacked Ilios" (1919, 307–9/8.496–9). Virgil's *Aeneid* further emphasizes the guile that went into this trick. The Trojans of "sounder judgement" request that the Odysseus wooden horse be destroyed: "They thought it was some trick of the Greeks and should be thrown into the sea, or set fire to and burned" (1991, 30/2.35–8).[22] Indeed, the lies of the Greeks are foregrounded through Sinon's invented tale of how the Greeks condemned him to death. Very much like Odysseus, Cipión develops his solution through a type of *sapientia* – cunning or guile. Although he rattles the sword, Cipión follows the book. On hearing the general's plan, Quinto Fabio exclaims, "Valeroso señor y hermano mío, / bien nos muestras en esto tu cordura" (vv. 337–9). While praising his valor, or *fortitudo*, Quinto Fabio understands that Cipión is following *sapientia*, which he here calls *cordura*. In *La Numancia*, wisdom seems to be associated with a cluster of terms with meanings that range from prudence to cunning.

The first act thus presents the admirable qualities of the Roman general through a parallel with Odysseus. At the same time, the Numantians point to a possible tragic flaw in Cipión, his hubris. Tradition holds that the ideal epic hero must combine wisdom with valor. Although Cipión claims both and Quinto Fabio echoes this claim, the audience would understand that the Roman general was relying mainly on *sapientia* for his new conquest. The representation of the enemy as tragic hero is not a strategy created by Cervantes. We have seen in the previous chapter how Aeschylus's *The Persians* depicts the enemy ruler, Xerxes, as the tragic hero. Closer to Cervantes's time, Ercilla's *Araucana* stresses the valor of the Araucanians in their battle against the Spaniards. While pointing to the enemy as heroic, Cervantes does not wish to forget the Numantians. The first act ends with speeches by the allegorical figures of Spain and the river Duero. Their function has been compared to that of the chorus in a Greek tragedy. Their speeches serve both to foreground the element of fate so important to tragedy and to point to the glories of Spain and the misfortunes of Rome in the future:

tiempo vendrá, según que ansí lo entiende
el saber que a Proteo ha dado el cielo
que estos romanos sean oprimidos
por los que agora tienen abatidos.
(vv. 469–72)

However, if the Spanish Empire will oppress Rome in the same manner as Rome has subjected Numantia, what does this parallel say of the glories of the Spanish Empire?[23] Are the modern Spaniards not guilty of the same "arrogante . . . celo" (v. 468), of the same hubris, as their Roman ancestors? The future glory of Spain is predicted by Proteus, a god who is clever at shape shifting, clever in disguise. In the same manner, these laudatory lines can shift in meaning and reveal a disguised critical or ambivalent stance. The god is too slippery to allow those who question him to hear an unambiguous truth. Of his slippery tongue more will be said in the next chapter.

Acts 2 and 3 concentrate on the Numantians. They are the ones who call the Romans cowards (v. 542), but such a charge emerges out of their desperation. They are being conquered without a battle and their only hope is to make the Romans engage them in combat. Instead of cunning, the Numantians embody the epic quality of valor, or *fortitudo*. They want to come out of the city and charge the enemy even though this might

mean defeat and death. Such was the valor exhibited by Achilles in the
Iliad. Furthermore, the Greek hero knew his doom, his Achilles' heel.
The Numantians will also discover their fate in the second act. Indeed,
the whole act involves ritual sacrifices to pagan gods, ending with a spectacular feat of necromancy performed by Marquino. Most of this material derives from yet another classical epic, Lucan's *Pharsalia.* If Cipión
had gained admiration through his words and clever plans, the Numantians in Act 2 partake of *admiratio* through spectacle. According to Aristotle, such stage devices are inferior to words and deeds: "The Spectacle,
though an attraction, is the least artistic of all the parts, and has least to
do with the art of poetics" (1941, 6.1450b). Not only does Numantia suffer from a lesser kind of *admiratio,* but the city is also linked to necromancy, a practice so foul that Lucan states it is only selected by the cowardly. He relates how Sextus, the "unworthy son" (Lucan 1962, 6.420) of
Pompey, disgraced his "pious" father by asking the witch Erichto to bring
back to life the corpse of a soldier so as to learn the outcome of the battle between Pompey and Caesar. So, a learned audience would note that
while the Numantians called the Romans cowards, they themselves
engaged in a most cowardly act, attempting to see the future through
bringing back to life the corpse of a dead Numantian.

Act 3 allows the audience to forget any charge of cowardice that could
be leveled against the city. This act will emphasize the Numantians' *fortitudo* just as Act 1 had stressed the Roman *sapientia.*[24] The city leaders propose to the Romans that the war be decided in single combat between
the two most outstanding warriors from the two camps. The Numantians
acknowledge that their champion could well lose this contest (vv.
1171–6), but they prefer to be defeated in battle than to die of hunger
and disease in the continuing siege. Cipión rejects the proposal. The
Numantians once again accuse the Romans of cowardice, but as Caravino elaborates on the differences between the Numantians and the
Romans, the contrast between the two epic virtues becomes clear:

Mas, como siempre estáis acostumbrados
a vencer con ventajas y con mañas,
estos conciertos, en valor fundados,
no los admiten bien vuestras marañas.
                    (vv. 1225–8)

The Romans, like Odysseus, are linked to terms associated with *sapientia,*
in this case *mañas,* while the Numantians stress their own valor, a *fortitudo*
that they claim is lacking in the Roman camp. The play is careful to show

how each side constructs its own character and that of the enemy. While the Romans regard themselves as showing *cordura*, the Numantians see them as utilizing *mañas*. Although both terms are linked to wisdom, the first has positive connotations while the second is often used in a pejorative manner. The same holds for valor. While the Numantians see themselves as heroic in their behavior, the Romans see them as exhibiting the courage of savage beasts. As such, they must be tamed. Cipión tells the ambassadors: "Bestias sois, y por tales encerradas / os tengo donde habéis de ser domadas" (vv. 1191–2). Cervantes's construction of the character of the Spaniard had such power that the eighteenth century still grappled with the implications of Spanish valor. After citing Livy and Florus (two of Cervantes's own historical models for *La Numancia*), Benito Jerónimo Feijóo warns that Spaniards should not feel complimented when other peoples describe them merely as possessing valor, since this quality also belongs to the animal kingdom: "no es tan propia de los hombres, como de brutos, y más debe llamarse ferocidad que valor" (1993, 153). Instead, rationality should be linked to valor: "hermoseando la parte racional, dan a su valentía todo el lustre de un virtuoso y verdadero valor" (1993, 154). It is thus not surprising that the Numantians fail to perceive Cipión's *cordura*, since it is a quality they do not fully possess.

When the single combat is rejected by Cipión, the men of Numantia express their desire to run out onto the battlefield even though such a sally would mean their death. This desire for swift but deadly combat recalls the *Iliad*. Knowing that fate had decreed that he would perish shortly after killing Hector, Achilles' heroic wrath and desire for revenge are such that he does not even consider the consequences, but sets forth to avenge the death of Patroclus. There is yet another situation in *La Numancia* that parallels the *Iliad*. In the Greek epic, when Agamemnon fears he might lose the war since he does not know the enemies' intentions, he calls a council to decide what ought to be done. Diomedes volunteers to "visit" the enemy camp and see if he can glean their future moves. He adds, however, that he will not go alone, for he believes that the operation will have a greater chance of success if two men go, since this means greater courage and comfort. Although many volunteer to go with him, he chooses Odysseus since he is beloved of Pallas Athena: "If he but follow with me, even out of blazing fire might we both return, for wise above all is he in understanding" (1924, 455/10.245–8). *La Numancia* also depicts a foray into the enemy camp. Cervantes conflates a historical account that told how a few Numantians broke out of the Roman siege with the episode in the *Iliad*.[25] Appian describes the foray thusly:

"But Rhetogenes, surnamed Coraunius, the bravest of all the Numantines, induced five of his friends to take an equal number of servants and horses, and cross the space between the two armies secretly, on a cloudy night, carrying a folding scaling-bridge. Arriving at the wall he and his friends sprang upon it, slew the guards on either side, sent back the servants, drew the horses up the bridge, and rode off to the towns . . . entreating them, as blood relations, to help the Numantines" (1962, 1.287). Ambrosio de Morales repeats Appian's narrative but makes a point of letting the reader know that Appian does not tell how Rhetogenes and his followers fared in the end: "No cuenta Appiano lo que hiciéron Retogenes y los suyos" (1791, 4.41).

The foray in *La Numancia* has a different purpose. Marandro, learning that his beloved Lira is dying of hunger, volunteers to go to the Roman camp to steal food from the enemy (vv. 1506–13). Whereas Diomedes is in search of information concerning the enemy, and Rhetogenes is seeking aid from nearby villages, Marandro does not need to seek knowledge, because the besieged are well aware of the Romans' intentions, nor does he seek aid from other towns. And unlike both Odysseus and Rhetogenes, Marandro does not wish to take a companion in this mission. However, his friend Leoncio insists on accompanying him. At this point, Cervantes's account turns away from the histories and seeks to imitate the epic. The two pairs, Diomedes and Odysseus and Marandro and Leoncio, venture out at night into the enemy camp hoping not to be detected.[26] The classical pair "went their way like two lions through the black night" (1924, 457–9/10.296–7), and the Numantians depart "en el silencio de esta noche escura" (v. 1623). Book 10 of the *Iliad* and Act 4 of *La Numancia* relate the amazing success of the missions. Diomedes kills twelve Thracian soldiers and their king while Odysseus performs some slaughter of his own while stealing a number of horses. Quinto Fabio relates the deeds of the two Numantians:

A las primeras guardas embistieron,
y en medio de mil lanzas se arrojaron,
y con tal furia y rabia arremetieron
que libre paso al campo les dejaron:
Las tiendas de Fabricio acometieron.
Allí su fuerza y su valor mostraron
de modo que en un punto seis soldados
fueron de agudas puntas traspasados.
                         (vv. 1756–63)

The two Greeks not only kill soldiers but their leader. Marandro and Leoncio imitate the epic adventure by slaughtering a number of soldiers and identifying Fabricio. Other important Romans, including Horacio and Olmida, are also killed. Although both episodes show the courage of the two warriors who enter the enemy camp, Cervantes has transformed the Numantian mission to emphasize valor over cunning, *fortitudo* over *sapientia*. Although the plan had been to penetrate the enemy camp with the assistance of darkness, silence, and luck, Quinto Fabio's narration of the episode makes it appear as if all elements of cunning were abandoned by the Numantians, who succeed merely through valor and prowess in arms. The Greek episode provides a different emphasis. Diomedes had asked for Odysseus's aid because he was known for his wisdom and cunning. Indeed, they hide among the dead and surprise an enemy spy, who tells them about the Trojans' plans. He also advises them to cross the Trojan line where the newly arrived Thracians are sleeping. Using this information, the Greeks are able to kill many of the enemy. Although Cervantes may have modeled the Marandro–Leoncio mission after the *Iliad*, he transforms it to underline the Numantians' valor. After all, the cunning of Odysseus belongs to the enemy, the Romans. This enemy acknowledges the valor of the Numantians, although they present it as excessive, as a type of hubris: "Dos numantinos, con soberbia frente, / cuyo valor será razón se alabe" (vv. 1752–3).

In *La Numancia* the representation of valor, the depiction of a courageous wrath so excessive that it may well become hubris, goes far beyond the *Iliad*. In the Spanish epic tragedy, the women ask that they not be left to live if the men decide to burst out of the city in order to die fighting (vv. 1278–1337).[27] Learning of this request, Teógenes, leader of the Numantians, formulates a different plan, one that would preclude a Roman victory. Valor is often associated with wrath, both being qualities of Mars, the god who presides over *La Numancia*. In the *Iliad*, Achilles' wrath is so excessive that it creates both admiration and hamartia. His excess will bring him down. The excessive valor of the inhabitants of Numantia will also lead to a bellicose wrath whereby they will destroy themselves in a collective suicide. Herein lies the greatness and the hamartia of the city. Such a destructive deed is great since it deprives the enemy of a victory. At the same time, it is excessive and suspect. First of all, the priest Marquino is the first to commit suicide. He is the necromancer and as such is a suspect figure. In addition, he kills himself in desperation when he finds out that the city will not prevail. Not only is suicide linked to desperation and necromancy, but a Golden Age audience would be well aware of the very negative view held by the Counter-Reformation church concerning suicide. Third, suicide is accompanied in the play by cannibalism, another abhorrent act:

haréis descuartizar luego a la hora
esos tristes romanos que están presos,
y sin del chico al grande hacer mejora,
repártanse entre todos, que con esos
será nuestra comida celebrada
por España, crüel, necesitada.

(vv. 1436–41)

If the audience had not already distanced themselves from the Numantians when they dealt in necromancy and spoke of suicide, they would certainly have turned away from the inhabitants of the city when they decide to eat the flesh of the captured Romans. The killing of their own women and children, although partaking of a certain degree of *admiratio*, must have also produced further alienation. In representing upon the stage such bloody acts, Cervantes is also transgressing against Aristotle's *Poetics*: "Those, however, who make use of the Spectacle to put before us that which is merely monstrous and not productive of fear, are wholly out of touch with Tragedy; not every kind of pleasure should be required of tragedy, but only its own proper pleasure" (1941, 14.1453b). Rather than allowing a catharsis to emerge out of "the very structure and incidents of the play" (1941, 14.1453b), Cervantes engages in Senecan horror. Numantia, then, transgresses against Christian codes (cannibalism, necromancy, suicide), classical injunctions (necromancy), and Aristotelian poetics (horror).

Two plays are at play in *La Numancia*: one representing Cipión's *sapientia*, the other depicting the city's *fortitudo*. The two epic virtues are shown to become flaws when each exists without the other. Cipión's hubris, his confidence in his own strategy, blinds him to Numantia's own tragic flaw. The city's valor is of such epic proportions that it goes beyond all acceptable behavior. When Cipión first comes to suspect that the Numantians will turn against each other in a suicidal wrath, he explains:

sin duda alguna que recelo y temo
que el bárbaro furor del enemigo
contra su propio pecho no se vuelva.

(vv. 2188–90)

Numantia's valor is thus described as a barbarous frenzy.[28] When the Roman general can confirm that the wrath of the city's inhabitants has turned against them and resulted in mass suicide, he again uses the term "barbarous" ("bárbaro furor suyo" [v. 2238]). The progenitors of the Spaniards have thus become barbarous Others whose excesses make them less than human. In his reconstruction of history, Cervantes's play fails to reject the view of Spain as a country that is much too close to "barbarous" lands such as Africa and Asia. Feijóo, for example, complains that writers of other nations "[r]egulan a España por la vecindad de la Africa. Apenas nos distinguen de aquellos bárbaros sino en idioma y religión" (1993, 151). Cervantes's play revels in this otherness to such an extent that cannibalism, mass suicide, and necromancy – key elements often associated with the African and New World Other – are discovered within Numantia. In contrast to writers such as Feijóo who decry the barbarous nature of the inhabitants of the Iberian Peninsula, the play asks that such "origins" be incorporated into a new myth of empire. At the same time, "civilized" Europe as represented with some irony by Cipión can point to Numantia/Spain as barbarous.

When Cipión discussess the mass suicide of the Numantians, he praises their valor and argues that such *fortitudo* on the part of the enemy forced him to use *sapientia*:

cuyo valor, cuya destreza en armas
me forzó con razón a usar el medio
de encerrallos cual fieras indomables
y triunfar de ellos con industria y maña
pues era con las fuerzas imposible.
                    (vv. 2252–6)[29]

Although accepting the term *maña* that the Numantians once had ascribed to him pejoratively, he adds *industria*, which, when placed next to a somewhat negative term, lends it a certain positivity.[30] At the same time, the Roman general reinforces the characterization of the Numantians as beasts that cannot be tamed. Their valor is perceived as excessive and inhuman. The city's excessive frenzy, then, can be seen as their hubris. While the first "play" (Cipión's) conforms to Aristotle's notions of the ideal tragedy, the second goes against certain precepts, particularly in the use of spectacle and horror. Numantia's tragedy is as imperfect as its barbarous customs.

In this battle between two cultures, Numantia wins from an emotional standpoint. The patriotic feeling of a sixteenth-century audience would give them the laurel of victory. The figure of Spain and of the Duero within the play dictate that this should be so. Such a triumph allows the Spaniards to recognize the self in what some might see as the Other. At the same time, the enemy camp can also be seen to win. It is a triumph brought about by culture and intellect devoid of emotion and passion. It even seems to triumph over the valor of the Numantians/Spaniards when the reader/spectator comes to realize that Cipión has not only wisdom, cleverness, and prudence but also a special kind of valor:

¡Mal, por cierto, tenían conocido
el valor, en Numancia, de mi pecho,
para vencer y perdonar nacido!
              (vv. 2312–14)

Cipión finds the Numantians' death a "grande desvarío" (v. 2304) since he would have had the courage to show clemency once they acknowledged defeat. This new perspective on Cipión's character, his blending of *sapientia* and *fortitudo*, increases his heroic stature at the moment he is about to experience the catastrophe. The final peripety, or change "from one state of things within the play to its opposite" (1941, 11.1452a), is a device praised by Aristotle, who gives as an example the ending of Theodectes' *Lynceus*: "Just as he is being led off for execution, with Danaus at his side to put him to death, the incidents preceding this bring it about that he is saved and Danaus put to death" (1941, 11.1452a). In *La Numancia*, a similar turning around of the action takes place when Cipión's win is turned into a loss. Bariato, the last inhabitant of the city, refuses the Roman general's offer and kills himself. In order to be able to claim victory, the Romans needed at least one survivor. Thus, Cipión's triumph is turned into a defeat. The general's tragic lament recognizes that the peripety has also transformed the city's fate: "Tú con esta caída levantaste / tu fama, y mis vitorias derribaste" (2407–8). If the boy's fall has deprived Cipión of a victory, it will also allow the city to rise out of its ashes through fame. Instead of a lament, Numantia's voice is heard through the happy sounds of eternal fame: "demos feliz remate a nuestra historia" (v. 2448).

Although the "happy" future of the city and Cipión's lament would seem to fit the second-rank tragedies, the ones with a double issue, the fact that each protagonist can be placed under the category of an admirable person or persons who fall due to a hamartia establishes *La Numancia* as a work that transforms the dictates of the *Poetics* and creates

two tragedies of the first rank within one theatrical text. These two stories are structured around the two greatest virtues of the epic hero, *sapientia* and *fortitudo*. Although Cipión is clearly a tragic hero whose fall
comes about through his excessive cunning, the city's role as tragic hero
of the first rank whose downfall comes from an excess of *fortitudo* is subverted through the use of spectacle, through the presentation of codes
of behavior that would alienate a sixteenth-century audience, and
through a final peripety that disallows the tragic lament. And yet, the
ability of a people to stand up as Other and check the forces of civilization, be it in terms of their own tragic form or in terms of their own ethics
of valor, would have given a Spanish spectator a renewed sense of worthiness. The epic contest between *sapientia* and *fortitudo* ends with the
triumph of the latter, since the city will live on through fame. Thus, this
action can fall within the realm of *comedia* or tragicomedy since there is
an "order restored" at the end. The role of tragic hero is to be found in
the second play – it belongs to the defeated Cipión. Indeed, he comes
closest to bringing together the two epic qualities since his cleverness is
also imbued with a type of courage that knows how to show clemency to
a defeated enemy. The play as epic contest points to the transcendence
of contest through the merging of opposites. If both *sapientia* and *fortitudo* must coexist in the ideal hero, it would follow that an ideal empire
must derive its best qualities from both Numantia and Rome. In *La
Numancia*, Spain should be heir to both. In fashioning Rome into an
enemy, Spain could be elaborating its own tragic flaw.

7

Virgil
Prophesying empire

Whereas the Homeric epics are evoked in *La Numancia* in order to question who is the perfect hero, Achilles or Odysseus, the city of Numantia or the Roman general, Virgil's words are resurrected within the play so that his *Aeneid* may provide the prophesying impulse and the imperial vision that are central to Cervantes's politics of imitation. There is in Cervantes's epic tragedy a hidden yet unmistakable construction of origins. By this I mean that *La Numancia* affirms "its own historicity, its own involvement in disorderly historical process," through "constructions of meaning connecting the past to the present" (Greene 1982, 16). Specifically, the play links the classical past, a past replete with authority, to a present that wishes to partake of that *auctoritas*.[1] The classical past is used not only to dignify "but also to evaluate" a historical present (Hamilton 1990, ix). Raphael had attempted such links between Virgil and his own present in the representation of the burning of Troy as found in *The Fire in the Borgo* (Fig. 11). If in the Vatican of his mind Cervantes chose to remember this link, he also preferred to quench the fires of destruction so as to begin his play with the waters of prophecy. Thus, this chapter focuses on the penultimate element.

Although Raphael never attempted to draw the Virgilian prophetic waters, he did compose *Quos ego*, where the god of the waters, Neptune, calls upon the wind, Aeolus, to calm the storm which had been summoned by Juno to destroy Aeneas's ships. As Roger Jones and Nicholas Penny explain: "The print takes its name from the way in which the god begins his furious speech to the winds with two pronouns of a sentence he never completes – the most famous example of the device in literature: *Quos ego*" (1983, 180). Cervantes recalls the events (but not the linguistic device) from Book 1 of the *Aeneid* in the *Viaje del Parnaso*. Describing a ship created by Mercury in order to lead the poets to Parnassus, the poem stresses the safety of the vessel, contrasting it with the destruction of Aeneas's ships by Aeolus, on Juno's orders (1984b, 59). The ship is described as the most beautiful vessel that sails upon Neptune's waves:

"Del más gallardo, y mas vistoso extremo / de cuantos la espalda de Neptuno / oprimieron jamás, y el más extremo" (1984b, 59).

Although referring to the *Quos ego* episode in the *Viaje del Parnaso*, Cervantes will not evoke Neptune in *La Numancia*.[2] Instead, he will imitate the words of yet another sea god. Neptune was far too forthright for Cervantes's purpose. His prophetic and subversive needs demand a substitution. In the *Quos ego* Raphael represents nine moments of Book 1 of the *Aeneid* in an effort to make his visual art compete with the authoritative words of Virgil. Cervantes seeks to reconstruct an ancient epic upon the Spanish stage, providing both visual and verbal instances of his art. He carefully provides stage directions so as to coordinate the two: the personification of a river will attempt to rival Virgil's description of the Tiber, and a sea god will serve his subversive needs.

This chapter will seek to historicize the fluvial rhetoric in *La Numancia* through an examination of the politics of imitation, through an investigation of how the utilization of classical models allows us to perceive Spanish imperial expansionism. Act 1 of *La Numancia* ends with a situational foregrounding that points to a particular myth of origins.[3] At the act's conclusion, all characters leave the stage so that two geographical figures may emerge: Spain and the river Duero. According to William R. Blue, "The way a group describes, depicts, and structures its geography, whether in maps, narratives, poetry, or drama, entails a set of beliefs about how their locale is and thus how the people who inhabit that space are."[4] Consequently, we cannot just dismiss Spain and the Duero as mere allegories. Furthermore, the traditional analogy "between geography and history as the stage and the drama" (East 1967, 2) breaks down in this representation since both figures show the active role played by geography. From ancient times the Spanish peninsula was seen as a specific region, albeit with many rival factions at war. In a book of emblems from 1589, Juan de Horozco y Covarrubias describes ancient Roman coins that depict Spain as a geographical and cultural entity: "La España se pintaba en figura de mujer con unas espigas en la mano y en la otra un manojo de saetas y un escudo" (Fernández Arenas 1982, 83). He chooses one coin in particular to serve as a model for his own emblem on the subject: "Adriano Emperador en una medalla puso a España con un ramo de oliva en la mano y al pie un conejo" (Fernández Arenas 1982, 83). Although Cervantes, following tradition, represents Spain as a woman holding in her hands certain symbolic objects, he also shows her as actively engaged in her own future. A careful look at the objects, however, shows that they differ from traditional representations. In the play, the figure appears "coronada con unas torres y un castillo en la mano que sinifica España" (p. 52). These are the insignias of Castile and not of Spain as a whole.[5] Juan de Caramuel y Lobkowitz, for example, describes Castile with "un castillo de oro en campo carmesí con puertas y ventanas azules, con tres torres y en cada una tres almenas de oro" (Herrero García 1966, 23).[6] The text, then, proposes a geographical site but actually reveals it as being "ruled" by Castile.

The diversity of cultures encountered in the peninsula came to be rewritten as a providential sign of empire. In 1629, Benito de Peñadosa, for example, asserted: "Esta variedad de climas y naciones causó la Providencia Divina en España, para que los españoles que habían de extenderse por todo el mundo, ya predicando la fé católica, ya señoreándolo con sus armas, nada admiraran y no les empeciesen climas contrarios" (cited in Herrero García 1966, 21–2).[7] The Spain of La Numancia does not present the variety of cultures as a positive trait. She represents a single cultural and political identity and asserts that she is constantly threatened by "others." Spain complains of the Phoenicians and the Greeks who stole her treasures and bemoans the fact that she has continuously been "esclava de naciones estranjeras" (v. 370). In this myth of origins the Numantians are viewed as the early "authorized" inhabitants of the region. However, their fight for freedom is about to be lost. In an instance of active involvement by geography, Spain asks the river Duero for help in avoiding the feared outcome. Spain's lament for what is about to happen is positioned early in the play so that a sixteenth-century audience would be able to partake of the happy and triumphal ending proposed by the figure of Fame at the end of the comedia, a paradoxical emotion since all the inhabitants of Numantia meet their destined doom.[8]

The Duero is the second geographical figure that takes an active role in the comedia. Even before Spain's request, the river has already increased its volume so that the Romans would not be able to attack the city from its shores: "he llenado mi seno en tal manera, / que los usados márgenes revientan" (vv. 451–2). But even this feat will not gain a reprieve for Numantia. The river's main function here is, not assistance, but prophecy. Juan Bautista Avalle-Arce claims that this speech is concerned with the question of imperial renovatio: "España, en la profecía del Duero, renueva la idea de Imperio y sojuzga, al hacerlo, a la propia Roma" (1962, 58). Even though Numantia falls to the Roman Empire, a sixteenth-century Spanish Empire will rise from the ashes of the valiant city and will gain its revenge through the sack of Rome in 1527. Avalle-Arce's hints of a Virgilian subtext[9] are taken up by Carroll Johnson, who asserts that "Virgil's poem provides a mythical–heroic underpinning for the glories of Augustus's empire by locating its origins in the disastrous defeat of Troy. Similarly, Cervantes' play posits the beginnings of the Spanish empire in the destruction of Numancia" (1980, 79).[10] It could be argued, then, that the figure of Spain provides a notion of fixity of place that is absent from Virgil's text. While there is a need for *translatio* from Troy to Rome in the *Aeneid*, in *La Numancia* only the passage of time is required, since Spain as an entity was constituted from time immemorial as a site for empire. Cervantes's text thus strives to surpass Virgil's imperial epic by transforming a geographical figure into a cultural and political entity that embodies the destiny of a land and its people. However, the archeology of its reconstruction will betray signs of contamination from other cities, such as Troy and Rome.

In studying the function of the river Duero, critics have failed to take into account not only geography as a historical factor but also the relationship between fluvial rhetoric and prophecy. W. H. Herendeen explains: "As a unique geographical phenomenon, the river embraces the essential mysteries of nature, and so the rhetoric carried in its current relates first of all to the pursuit of wisdom, and as such it passes freely from the realm of geography to that of language" (1981, 108). The wisdom of rivers is often prophetic, and the figure of the river god, as Karl Ludwig Selig demonstrates, appears in Garcilaso's poetry. The *Second Eclogue*, for example, depicts a river god who lives in a cave and has an urn from which the waters flow.[11] "The river-speech is fused to an ekphrastic tradition, as history is revealed on the urn" (Selig 1971, 683). In the case of *La Numancia*, the appearance of a river god to prophesy would thus be accepted as part of this tradition. Furthermore, it was believed that the river Duero had its source in the vicinity of Numantia: "No lexos del nacimiento del río Duero se muestran rastros de aquella ciudad" (Covarrubias 1987, 832). Indeed, the play locates this source close to the city of Soria: "junto a Soria, que en aquel tiempo fue Numancia" (p. 55). As noted in Chapter 1, Cervantes here is following Ambrosio de Morales's *Corónica general de España*, whose historiographical rigor, "which required the careful comparison of written sources and the utilization of such archaeological data as inscriptions, coins, and medals" (King 1979, 202), led Cervantes to reject the identification of Numantia with Zamora.

Although the river Duero points to the site of the city, to the archeology of its reconstruction in Cervantes's text, it also points to a textual place, to the locus classicus of the prophesying river, the eighth book of the *Aeneid*.[12] One night by the Tiber River, "heart sick at the sadness of war" (1991, 190/8.29),[13] Aeneas "saw in his sleep the god of the place, old Tiber himself" (190/8.31). This deity spoke to Aeneas and "lightened his sadness" (190/8.35) with advice and prophecy. This is precisely what the river Duero does for Spain. Spain's "amargo duelo" (v. 357) caused by the siege of Numantia is lightened by the Duero's assurance that the loss will not be in vain: "Tus razones alivio han dado en parte, / famoso Duero, a las passiones mías" (vv. 529–30). In modeling the Duero's speech after the Tiber's, *La Numancia* is building a new site. The city is no longer a Celtiberian locale but one that is constructed after the classics. The river's speech is not only reinforcing a myth of origins but is also establishing yet one more parallel between the birth of imperial Rome and the rise of the Spanish Empire. In turning to Virgil, Cervantes's text is acquiring authority both for itself and for the construction of a new imperial myth, one where geography and archeology are subtly distorted.

In the *Aeneid*, the Tiber as river god can prophesy because he stands at the source of the river and is thus a guardian of the unmanifest and an agent of manifestation. The notion of manifestation from the source is presented in Virgil through the image of the reeds (1991, 190/8.34); in Garcilaso it appears as the urn. Having witnessed the trick by which the power of Castilla came to be embodied in the geographical figure of Spain, a reader/audience may want to scrutinize the Duero's representation in *La Numancia*. Nothing is said of this figure's attire nor is it described as carrying any symbolic objects. The text, however, explains: "Sale el río DUERO con otros tres ríos, que serán muchachos, vestido como que son tres riachuelos que entran en Duero junto a Soria" (p. 55). Why does the text depart from traditional representations? Why does it call upon three tributaries of the river? Imitation, as Donna B. Hamilton reminds us, was "a practice founded on methods for changing (that is, for disassembling, rearranging and redistributing) the precursor text, as well as for concealing those changes; it is a common rule in treatises on imitation that what the imitator is doing should not be made too evident" (1990, 4).[14] But every imitation, no matter how hidden, must advertise its precursor "in such a way as not to remove the pleasure of the reader in discovering the artistry that the concealment itself promoted" (Hamilton 1990, 16). I would argue that the visual representation of four rivers

represents the first veiled hint as to the text that is being imitated. Four
are the rivers that surround Paradise and an equal number form the
boundaries of Hades.[15] These four streams are often associated with the
notion that all rivers on earth have one source.

The portrayal of the Duero in *La Numancia* has a deeper source – a
Virgilian source.[16] In the *Fourth Georgic*, Aristaeus is as much in need of
consolation as Spain in Cervantes's play. The fact that his apiary has
become extinct is not as trivial a matter as it may appear since, as David
Quint suggests, it is related to "mortality, the plague which threatens to
extinguish both the herds and their human masters" at the end of the
Third Georgic (1983, 33). Aristaeus journeys to his mother's abode to seek
a solution to his plight. The sea nymph Cyrene inhabits a cave where all
the rivers of Earth find their origin: "And now, marvelling at his mother's
home, a realm of waters, at the lakes locked in caverns, and the echoing
groves, he went on his way, and, dazed by the mighty rush of waters, he
gazed on all the rivers, as, each in his own place, they glide under the
great earth" (1978, 3.363–7; 1991, 180).[17] According to David Quint,
Virgil is here following "Plato's description of the earth's underground
water system in the final pages of the *Phaedo* (11d ff.). In the Platonic
myth, all the earth's springs, rivers and seas have their source in Tartarus,
through which flows the great river Oceanus. . . . There too are the four
rivers of Hell" (1983, 34). What greater authority for prophecy than the
place of origin? The watery source is but an image for the source of language and history. The river Duero in *La Numancia*, then, through its
fourfold nature seems to be assuming the greatest authority because its
utterances proceed from the one place of origin.

Confirmation of the Virgilian model appears in the Duero's speech:

> tiempo vendrá, según ansí lo entiende
> el saber que a Proteo ha dado el cielo
> que estos romanos sean oprimidos
> por los que agora tienen abatidos.
> (vv. 469–72)

In the *Fourth Georgic*, Cyrene tells her son that he must undergo yet one
more *catabasis*[18] in order to find out why his bees have died: "In Neptune's Carpathian flood there dwells a seer, Proteus, of sea-green hue . . .
for the seer has knowledge of all things" (1978, 4.387–8; 1991, 392).
Aristaeus must journey to Proteus's ocean cavern to find the answer to his
plight. *La Numancia*, like the *Fourth Georgic*, includes two figures in the

quest for an answer. Spain, like Cyrene, is labeled as a mother ("Madre querida" [v. 441]). But the river Duero also shares some of the traits of the sea nymph. Cyrene, like the Duero, points to Proteus as the final authority in questions of prophecy.[19] The Renaissance saw Proteus as a particularly admirable figure. A. Bartlett Giamatti explains: "Not only is Proteus appropriate to figure the multiple glories of man, but man's Protean ability to adapt and to act many roles is the source of the power that enables him to assume the burdens of civilization, to create cities on earth and win citizenship among the immortals. Man is not Protean because he is civilized; he is civilized because he is Protean" (1968, 439).[20] Discussing the hidden meanings in the personification of this sea god, Natale Conti, a sixteenth-century mythographer, asks: "¿quién ignora que no hay nada más necesario en la administración de las ciudades o en la vida cotidiana que la variedad de ingenio. . . ? Así pues, conviene que el hombre prudente . . . se introduzca con diferentes formas en la amistad de los hombres y haga uso de diferentes decisiones en la administración de las ciudades, puesto que unos acontecimientos requieren la clemencia, otros la severidad del juez" (1988, 599). Proteus, then, is not only the god of prophecy but also the deity of culture and civilization. In *La Numancia* he prophesies the rise of a new civilization centered in Spain. Authority has been heaped upon authority, source upon source, so that the Duero's utterances may not be doubted.

And yet, there might be another Cervantine trick hidden in this allusion, another instance of the wiles of imitation.[21] Cyrene clearly explains to Aristaeus that Proteus will not willingly tell the truth. In order to hear what is to be, Aristaeus must hold him "in the grasp of hands and fetters" (1978, 4.408; 1991, 225). When Proteus takes on manifold forms and transforms himself into countless wild beasts, Aristaeus is to tighten his fetters until the Old Man of the Sea eventually regains his original shape. Only then can Aristaeus command him to abandon his wish to deceive (1978, 4.447; 1991, 227).[22] Although Proteus is, on the one hand, a truthful seer, he is also a creature who can change shapes and deceive the eye and the ear. As such, he can be compared to an actor in a play. In Diego Lopez's translation of Alciati's *Emblems*, we encounter two less-than-admirable portrayals of the god.[23] As an actor ("tiene forma de representante" [1670, 621]), the god seems to encourage role-playing, a form of lying. Proteus's transformations are also related to the changeable or mutable nature of the human being: "Para significar aquellos que facilmente mudan el parecer, y son poco constantes" (Lopez 1670, 621).

As a liar and an inconstant god, Proteus is criticized in Plato's *Republic* since Socrates believes divinity should not be capable of deception or mutability. In another dialogue, Socrates describes two Sophists as, "like the Egyptian wizard Proteus, they take different forms and deceive us by their enchantments" (cited in Giamatti 1968, 453). Proteus is also seen by Dionysus of Halicarnassus as the representation of "a clever man who can vary his speech and so beguile the human ear" (cited in Quint 1983, 37). Even in the very positive description of Natale Conti we are warned: "Otros dijeron que fue un hombre muy versado en la palabra, que fácilmente podía empujar a los hombres a cualquier emoción del espíritu, por lo que se dijo que adoptaba muchas formas" (1988, 599). The extremes of Proteus's subversiveness are revealed by Gilles Deleuze (1990), who turns to this deity in his attempt to "reverse Platonism."[24] Renaissance mythographers took up the hints found in Plato and elaborated a second Proteus, no longer the truthful seer but the deceptive magician.[25] Only when bound will Proteus tell the truth; only when "the infinite forms which matter [and language] may assume" (Quint 1983, 36) are held in check will this deity provide a reliable answer. Proteus's forms and language can drift aimlessly unless they are bound – unless "the word installs itself in a culture" (Greene 1982, 15). When bound by Aristaeus, Proteus can reveal a cultural and a personal "truth": how Aristaeus infringed upon his culture's laws and how that culture views atonement and regeneration.

Cervantes's Proteus is a counterfeit. The god is a creature of another culture that is re-created in order to imbue a modern text with the authority of the ancients. Even though Virgil is a figure of *auctoritas* during the Spanish Golden Age, his gods no longer hold the power of prophecy. If the Roman poet is accepted as a prophet, it is because his *Fourth Eclogue*, which prophesies the rebirth of empire, was taken by early Christian writers to refer to the rebirth that is to come about through the Christian religion. The child that is to be born according to Virgil's prophecy is Christ. Only in the sense that *La Numancia* approaches the vatic power of Virgil's *Fourth Eclogue* can it said to be truly prophetic. But curiously, *La Numancia* imitates, not the *renovatio* proposed in the *Fourth Eclogue*, but the one found in the *Fourth Georgic*. It is a Protean character and not a Christianized *vates* that is inscribed in the text.

Furthermore, the power of prophecy does not derive from imitation but is often conferred by the source. The Renaissance (as well as the Spanish Golden Age) participated in a debate "over whether the text's source of meaning and locus of value lie in the literary originality of its author or in an extratextual, authorized origin that subtends its discourse" (Quint 1983, 23). Cervantes both turns to an extratextual origin (Virgil) and points to originality by invoking the river source, or fountainhead, which was the most common figure of origin in the period. Both loci of value are subverted through the figure of Proteus. Counterfeit gods cannot prophesy; and Proteus, the newly forged deity, was seen since ancient times as a most ambiguous figure. More important, only the bound Proteus will speak without deceit the truth of a culture – and nowhere in the Duero's speech are we told that the god is fettered.

Proteus is both poet and prophet, Sophist and seer. By pointing to this deity, *La Numancia* brings into question the truth of both poetry and prophecy. The reader or audience is thus warned not to succumb to the wiles of fluvial rhetoric. Proteus's role is to prophesy the future of Spain – a future often constructed by Golden Age poets as the triumph of empire. In imitation of Virgil, this empire was thought to be providentially decreed in order to bring about universal goodness and peace. The river god (through the words of the Duero) does conclude with the ordained Virgilian vision:

Debajo de este imperio tan dichoso
serán a una corona reducidos,
por bien universal y a tu reposo,
tus reinos hasta entonces divididos.
(vv. 513–16)

This laudatory presentation of the Spanish Empire has led critics such as Stanislav Zimic to assert: "El orgullo nacional se expresa de manera inequívoca en la profecía del Duero" (1992, 84). Indeed, Willard F. King argues: "The eight octaves of the prophecy bridging the long centuries between Celtiberian Numancia and Spain of the 1580's are the basis of all interpretations of the drama as a clarion call to militant expansion of empire" (1979, 213). I would argue instead that the Virgilian vision is subverted by the historical/prophetic account that precedes it. Proteus, through the river Duero, constructs an imperial history for Spain, one where words and shapes are as slippery and unstable as this god. While pretending to praise the new Spain, this lying god is actually subverting this imperial vision. Let us look at this construction of history.

First of all, the trigger for empire as explained by the god is the desire for revenge – not a very lofty ideal: "que estos romanos sean oprimidos /

por los que agora tienen abatidos" (vv. 471–2).[26] The first to revenge what
Rome did to Numantia will be, according to Proteus's prophecy, the "fiero
Atila" (v. 482), who threatened Rome in the same way the Spanish army
threatened this city in 1527. Certainly, a comparison between Spanish soldiers and those of Attila provide us with a sense of martial prowess. But
is Attila's ruthless rule an apt model for Spanish power? In the most important Golden Age depiction of this figure, Cristóbal de Virués's *El fiero Atila*,
Attila is portrayed as a bloody tyrant: "manda quemar la nave con los soldados dentro de ella . . . , ahorcar en una almena al gobernador de Ratis-
bona . . . , descuartizar a tres hermanos . . . , cortar narices, orejas y lengua
al embajador romano" (Hermenegildo 1994, 26). Is this how Spanish
imperial forces are to behave? After Attila's conquest, Proteus expounds
on the 1527 sack of Rome by the Spaniards. There is a notable absence
here of more than seven hundred years of history. If we follow the Duero's
account, Proteus says nothing of the period between Attila's march on
Rome and the rise of the Spanish Empire under Charles V. What of the
Moorish presence in Spain, which lasted more than seven hundred
years?[27] Why not, for example, include the fall of Granada in 1492? This
was a key event in Spanish unification, and one that pointed to the magnanimity of the conquerors, since the Catholic kings gave assurances of
freedom of worship.[28] Alfredo Hermenegildo has pointed to the absence
of Islam in the text, linking it to the 1569 rebellion of the *moriscos* triggered by Philip II's repressive laws.[29] The cruelty and bloodshed with
which this rebellion was put down, I would argue, would certainly merit
the comparison between Attila's troops and Spanish warriors. The
absence of the Moors from the prophecy may simply have to do with the
question of Spanish unity. The presentation of the siege of Numantia
seems to show that the city was able to resist bravely because there was no
diversity or divergence among the inhabitants. Similarly, the Duero points
to the unity of Spain: "católicos serán llamados todos" (v. 503).[30] Moors,
Jews, and *cristianos nuevos* are Others and can have no say in the building
of empire. Proteus does not mention them because they have no status
within the land. To skip seven hundred years of history simply points to
the disempowerment of the Other within the empire.

   If this absence raises a number of questions concerning Spanish unity,
the next event prophesied by Duero/Proteus points to other concerns.
The sack of Rome in 1527 by the imperial forces of Charles V was thought
to be "symptomatic of Christianity's ultimate crisis" (Chastel 1983, 84).
André Chastel documents the myriad predictions that were made around

this time.[31] Proteus's pronouncements in *La Numancia* partake of this prophesying frenzy, which took on apocalyptic proportions and continued well into the seventeenth century. The many unsettling events taking place in Europe pointed to some type of collapse and to an impending *renovatio*. It was left up to the many interpreters to decide its form and meaning. Proteus's prophecy is thus imbued with the myriad of meanings attributed to this event. It has been suggested that the sack of Rome by imperial troops in 1527 became a symbol of "Hispania victrix" whereby "La gran soberbia de Roma / hora España la refrena" (Johnson 1980, 90, 81). And yet, such an interpretation of events was held by a minority. It is true that Reformist pamphlets echoed the German soldiers' cry of "Viva Luther Papa" (Chastel 1983, 36), but this can hardly be used to support the view of one religion, one empire. In Spain, Charles V's secretary, Alfonso de Valdés, composed *Diálogo de las cosas ocurridas en Roma* immediately after the event, claiming the sack as providential punishment for a pope who was too involved in politics. Luis Zapata, whose works Cervantes knew and praised, also echoes this view, according to Márquez Villanueva: "Cuando relata el saco de Roma se acoge en el *Carlo famoso*, aunque muy sobre ascuas, al habitual argumento erasmista [Alfonso de Valdés] de que el verdadero responsable fue el pontífice Clemente VII" (1973, 142). For Stanislav Zimic, the Duero's prophecy echoes the Erasmian point of view: "La profecía del Duero ... hace evocar fuertemente la actitud de algunos humanistas españoles, comúnmente erasmistas, respecto a la guerra de Carlos V contra la Roma papal de Clemente VII ... Alfonso de Valdés justifica el saqueo de la ciudad Eterna, señalando como causas la inmoralidad, la corrupción y la política maquiavélica del Papa" (1992, 85–6). But even Valdés's vehement defense of the emperor had to present the other side of the argument. The work is a dialogue between Lactancio, who defends the sack, and a Roman archdeacon, who condemns it. Although Lactancio's rhetoric wins out, the archdeacon is able to make one important point: "el ejército del emperador ha saqueado la ciudad de Roma, ha cometido sacrilegios y desmanes sin cuento con una impiedad que era de todo punto impropia de un espíritu católico" (1975, 30). Lactancio can only reply that the emperor did not order and had no knowledge of the sack.

The difficulty in transforming the sack into a victory for the empire not only was obvious through the clash within Valdés's text but was also evident in the reaction elicited by the *Dialogue*. Baldassare Castiglione, the papal nuncio, vigorously opposed Valdés's version of the sack. He

complained to Charles V, to the royal council, and even to Alonso Manrique, archbishop of Seville and inquisitor-general. Although Valdés
escaped trouble "because of his position and the support he enjoyed in
high places" (Longhurst 1952, 13), his *Dialogue* was eventually placed in
the index of prohibited books (Longhurst 1952, 15; Bataillon 1925,
404). If Castiglione did not succeed in the immediate ban of the book,
he is said to have convinced Charles V "to erase all memory" of the sack
of Rome (Chastel 1983, 37).[32] Even though the emperor made a point
to forget, and not to include this feat in the triumphs of his rule, many
soldiers remembered that "[l]ess than two months after we occupied
Rome, 5,000 of our men had died of the plague" (Chastel 1983, 91).
Instead of thinking of the sack as providential punishment of the city,
many thought that the plague was divine retribution for desecrating a
city left by Emperor Constantine to the spiritual authorities – a blameless
city. Proteus, a figure known for his clever rhetoric, can easily damn with
faint praise.

    According to André Chastel, the 1520s was a time for a "new religios-
ity" (1983, 12) in Rome, with Pope Clement VII as one of the leaders of
what has been called a "Catholic pre-Reformation" (1983, 10). The
artists that came to Rome were enchanted by the "balance between the
sacred and the profane" (Chastel 1983, 12), a syncretic art that blended
mythological and biblical elements. The battle of 1527 was not so much
one for the soul of Rome but one between empire and papacy, "two kinds
of power that historians have tended to underestimate in their concern
with the 'modernity' of the sixteenth century" (Chastel 1983, 15). Due
to miscalculations (Clement VII discharged his mercenaries thinking he
had reached an agreement with the viceroy, but it had never been rati-
fied by the imperial commander, Charles de Bourbon), bad weather (the
fog made it impossible for the Romans to fire their cannons at the
invaders), and bad tactics (the Romans never destroyed the Ponte S.
Sisto), the city fell to the imperial army virtually without a fight. If Proteus is attempting to praise the valor of the Spanish armies, he certainly
selected a moment lacking in martial glory.

    Although Rome did not endure a siege, "it did fall prey to sustained,
atrocious pillage" (Chastel 1983, 33). The horrors inflicted upon the
inhabitants of the city are narrated in a number of French treatises:
"Relics spat upon, churches burned, nuns raped, matrons debauched,
young people enslaved" (Chastel 1983, 36). Cervantes's own sojourn in
the "eternal" city allowed him to gain firsthand experience of some of the

sacrileges. The Spanish writer's humanist training would have led him to decry not only religious profanation but the defacing of Renaissance art. He would surely have heard of and might have seen the graffiti in the *stanze* decorated by Raphael in the Vatican.[33] Such sacrilegious inscriptions could have also taught the young writer the power of subversion. If reckless soldiers can bring down with a few strokes of the pen an artist's laudatory portrayal of the papacy, what cannot a playwright do in four acts? *La Numancia* then not only aspires to the artistic heights of a Raphael but also aims to cut down its own vision of imperialism through a subtle rewriting of both *laus Hispaniae* and imperium. This criticism is veiled in a net of perspectivism that leads the audience from the Numantians to the Romans, not knowing which faction is to represent the "blessings" of empire.

Treatises on the sack of Rome not only decry sacrilege but also the greed, lewdness, and cruelty of the imperial army. José Luis Abellán asserts that the Spanish soldiers were the worst offenders: "Según el testimonio de casi todos los historiadores, gozaban más en derramar sangre, en profanar con ella los templos y en perseguir a los obispos y sacerdotes" (Valdés 1975, 28). Such actions are at odds with Cipión's designs on the city in *La Numancia*:

¿Es de mi condición, por dicha, ajeno
usar benignidad con el rendido,
como conviene al vencedor que es bueno?
¡Mal, por cierto, tenían conocido
el valor, en Numancia, de mi pecho,
para vencer y perdonar nacido!
(vv. 2309–14)

In contrast to Cipión's benign intent to pardon a defeated city, the imperial army subjects Rome to every horror. Reference to the sack of Rome serves not to praise imperial troops, but to show Cipión's moderation. The Roman general, like a new civilizing Proteus as described by Conti, knows when to show clemency. Indeed, Cipión is one of the figures praised by Anchises in his prophetic speech to Aeneas when the epic hero comes to hear his dead father's counsel in the underworld. Anchises tells of the founding of Rome, a city "whose empire shall cover the earth and whose spirit shall rise to the heights of Olympus" (1991, 157/6.782). Both Scipios are called as "thunderbolts of war" (1991, 159/6.842) and are among those heroes who will help to bring about the Augustan Golden Age in Rome. But in order to "crown Peace with Law," Aeneas and his heirs must learn "to pardon the defeated and war down the proud" (1991, 159/6.853).[34] As Avalle-Arce has noted (1962, 69), Cipión sees his task as warring down the proud Numantians: "se tiene que poner la industria nuestra / que de domar soberbios es maestra!" (vv. 1794–5). But he is also very conscious of the first part of Anchises' command, "to pardon the defeated." He thus claims that his task is both to vanquish and to pardon (*perdonar*). The brief description of the sack of Rome in the Duero's speech makes it clear that the new Spanish Empire does not seem to have learned one of the lessons of its predecessors, and one of the two foremost commands given by Anchises to the Romans: "to spare the humbled."

The wily Proteus gives us yet another clue as to the hidden meaning of the events he foretells: the 1527 sack of Rome immediately follows the reference to Attila. From the Vatican of his mind, Cervantes projects the image of Raphael's *Leo I Stops Attila's Invasion* (Fig. 8) onto a Virgilian prophecy. This is most fitting since Raphael, in the Vatican *stanze*, invokes more than once the power of this epic poet. Whether portraying him next to Homer in *Parnassus* or evoking the burning of Troy and Aeneas's deliverance of his father, Virgil's authority is used to buttress the agenda of papal power in Raphael's frescoes. Through careful but clever recollection, Raphael's art is inscribed into the play for the same reason the graffiti appear in the *stanze*: to subvert the power that is praised. *Leo I Stops Attila's Invasion* shows how the barbarous Attila refrained from an attack on the Holy City.[35] This miraculous event was brought up at a council of the church in 1536 when Jacopo Sadoleto reminded his listeners with this reference that "the pontiff stands above temporal powers" (Chastel 1983, 222). The evocation of Attila serves Proteus's purposes: to praise the Spanish Empire while showing its faults. The imperial armies committed a sacrilege that not even a barbarian was prepared to perpetrate. Proteus/Duero explains:

Y portillos abriendo en Vaticano
tus bravos hijos, y otros estranjeros
harán que para huir vuelva la planta
el gran piloto de la nave santa.
(vv. 485–9)

The brave Spaniards are portrayed as fighting with "otros estranjeros." It was well known that many Lutheran mercenaries fought in this army, desiring the end of the papacy. Proteus thus points to the strange company being kept by the Catholic Spaniards. The image of the pope fleeing is certainly problematic, pointing both to the emperor's power and to the sacrilege just committed. It also detracts from the pope's aura of spiritual authority so convincingly portrayed in Raphael's frescoes in the Vatican. In the double vision of Cervantes's Protean language, neither pope nor emperor attains to exemplarity. Both partake of ancient error.[36] Cervantes's fleeing pope may have even triggered an Erasmian smile.[37] In writing these lines Cervantes could have been reminded once again of Luis Zapata, who, on hearing of Clement VII's demise in 1534, wrote "con nuevas de que ydo era a la gloria / si allá fue) el papa séptimo Clemente" (Márquez Villanueva 1973, 142). If Cervantes knew the line, he also remembered Zapata's fate – to be imprisoned by Philip II.[38]

Whatever Erasmian echoes can be found here,[39] by evoking the "nave santa" the text is mirroring the most common symbolic image used to represent the sack.[40] Chastel explains: "There is nothing more familiar than the *navicula Petri*, the mosaic placed by Giotto in the façade of St. Peter's, referred to by everyone and made familiar by innumerable paintings and drawings" (1983, 41). The events of 1527 were often represented in this manner, as in a French *tableau* in which France and England come to the rescue of Saint Peter, whose ship is ready to capsize. In evoking the *navicula Petri*, Proteus recalls a key image of the papacy and thus grants authority to the fleeing pope. Proteus could have picked from numerous other triumphs by Charles V, triumphs that would have been much less problematic, such as the victory over the French at Pavia only two years before. Through his selection, and through the link established with Attila, imperial rule is seen in a troublesome light, one that contrasts with the vision of Philip II propounded by Titian in his famous allegory *Spain Coming to the Aid of Religion* (ca. 1570).

And it is with Philip II that the Duero ends Proteus's prophecy. The first event of his reign that is narrated is yet a second imperial invasion which threatens Rome. As the duke of Alba approaches Rome and Pope Paul IV calls on the French for assistance, apocalyptic prophecies and dreams of *renovatio* are once again in the air. But Alba, in spite of his victory, prevents a second sack of Rome (Chastel 1983, 227). Once again, the events portrayed are problematic. As Willard F. King perceptively argues: "The memory of Alba's clemency in 1557 had long been obscured by the uncompromising brutality and terror of his government of the

Netherlands in 1567–73, marked by the infamous Council of Troubles, the execution of the Counts of Horn and Egmont . . . and the bitter siege of the city of Haarlem" (1979, 214). There is also the question of selection and absence.[41] While Proteus's prophecy speaks again of a threat to the center of Catholicism, it says nothing of what Fernand Braudel has labeled "the most spectacular military event in the Mediterranean during the entire sixteenth century" (1973, 2.1088). The great naval battle at Lepanto, a "dazzling triumph of courage and military technique" (Braudel 1973, 2.1088), was an event often utilized to praise Philip II's reign. This was the battle that led Fernando de Herrera to compose his famous poem and Titian to paint *The Allegory of Lepanto* (Fig. 10). Here, Philip II lifts his newborn child up to the heavens. The motto *maiora tibi* suggests even greater triumphs for Philip's son, Prince Fernando (Wethey 1969, 2.132). Cervantes was quite aware of the importance of this battle, in which he had fought valiantly. Braudel states that with this battle "the spell of Turkish supremacy had been broken" (1973, 2.1088). Cervantes, in the tale of the Captive interpolated in the first part of *Don Quijote*, made a similar assertion.[42] If Proteus's intentions are laudatory, if the god truly wants to prophesy the creation of a new empire forged by "el segundo Felipo sin segundo" (v. 512) whose purpose is universal harmony, why choose a problematic threat to Rome while omitting one of Philip's (and Cervantes's) greatest triumphs?

By praising Philip II through the use of such a prosaic pun, "sin segundo," the speech may be debasing the figure of the Spanish king. This should come as no surprise. In the *Viaje del Parnaso*, Cervantes proudly proclaims that his sonnet "Al túmulo de Felipe II en Sevilla" was composed "por honra principal de mis escritos" (1984b, 103).[43] The sonnet is directed to the gigantic simulacrum of a tomb that was built in Seville at the death of Philip II. Showing how the poem deals with the complexities of representation, Mary Gaylord (in press) notes the emptiness of words and tomb: "Rather than promising to carry celebrative discourse into a glorious future, the poem moves abruptly from silence to silence." The poem, which pokes fun at the enterprise and at the dead king, became enormously popular. Adrienne Martín asserts: "The sonnet spread like wildfire, circulating across Spain in manuscript copies and broadsheets. . . . The poem's great popularity also suggests an attitude toward Philip II that is difficult to reconcile with the 'official' one" (1991, 105). This was not Cervantes's only criticism of the monarch. Américo

Castro has pointed to some lines in the *Galatea* and the *quintillas* written by Cervantes at Philip's demise in order to show a continuous current of criticism (1974, 83–5).[44]

Proteus's foretelling frenzies, which culminate in this faint praise of Philip II, can also mirror the many prophecies that circulated throughout Spain during the last twenty years of the sixteenth century and that were commonly uttered in the marketplace. Although the history of street prophets in Spain is yet to be written, Richard L. Kagan has made an auspicious start. His description of the political dreams of Lucrecia de León, who dreamed of (and announced) the defeat of the Spanish Armada less than a year before it occurred,[45] provides a detailed study of a popular seer who prophesied the decline of Spain and blamed Philip II for the state of affairs. In 1588, her predictions of doom led her followers to "transform several caves into a survivalists' bunker . . . stocked with stores of wheat, oil, and wine, even some firearms" (1990, 124). As for the attacks on Philip, they are particularly forceful and bitter. She asserts that the king "is responsible for the evil and ruin of Spain" (1990, 80). On 12 March 1590, Philip is again reminded of his failures: "The worst thing that can happen to a king is to discover that no one wishes to write his history, either because they do not wish to uncover the faults or to lie" (1990, 83). But Cervantes's Proteus is not bound by truth. He can lie. His slipperiness can include both praise and criticism.

The Duero's speech and Proteus's prophecy include as the final triumph of empire Philip II's annexation of Portugal, an event that was decried by another seer, Sor María de la Visitación (Kagan 1990, 7). Although Proteus's narrative is celebratory on the surface, it also contains a veiled criticism. According to Alfredo Hermenegildo, the prophecy simply serves to foreground "la situación conflictiva creada con motivo de la anexión" (1976, 47). Spanish rule over Portugal, which lasted some sixty years, came in spite of the fact that the "mass of the country was violently opposed to Spanish domination. The urban population and the lower clergy hated the Spaniard with a vehemence which made the rich and powerful shudder" (Braudel 1973, 2.1181). But it was the rich and powerful who needed the Spanish. Braudel explains: "The rallying to the Spanish cause of the rich and powerful men of Lisbon was firmly linked with the desperate need for the Portuguese Empire, already embarrassed by Protestant privateers on the ocean and shortage of specie, above all not to quarrel with her powerful neighbor" (1973, 2.1182). It was also a need for American silver, which the Spanish navy helped them to bring to Europe. But the Duero's speech does more than present another problematic situation:

el girón lusitano tan famoso,
que un tiempo se cortó de los vestidos
de la ilustre Castilla, ha de zurcirse
de nuevo.
                    (vv. 517–20)[46]

The image of Castile's torn dress which is now mended debases the endeavor and brings into question its heroic nature. The invasion, which was completed in four months, was "little more than a military exercise" (Braudel 1973, 2.1183) since the Portuguese had not sought to strengthen their army. Philip's policy had relied more on cunning than on force – he acted more like Cipión in *La Numancia*. The verb "çurcir," according to Sebastián de Covarrubias, means "cierta manera de coser tan sutil que no se echa de ver la costura" (1987, 430). Philip, through certain members of the Portuguese nobility and the clergy, had woven such a web of deceit that Portugal had easily become part of his rule. Instead of the tales of the gods which are woven by Cyrene's nymphs (*Fourth Georgic*, 1978, 4.334–5; 1991, 221), the Duero's nymph, Spain, deals merely with mending. In addition, the Duero clearly states that it is not Spain but Castile who owns the dress, who has the power. Both Spain and the river Duero, although pretending to speak for all of Spain, see Castile as the power – all else is adornment, a dress, an object to be owned. Portugal is but a torn piece from Castile's garment. Castile's arrogance can be linked to the Roman general's hubris in Cervantes's *comedia*. If Cipión falls due to his tragic flaw, Castile's empire could well be in danger.

While *divinatio* arose from the ability to read the signs of the world, *eruditio* dealt with understanding the signs of the ancients. Michel Foucault explains: "The heritage of Antiquity, like nature itself, is a vast space requiring interpretation; in both cases there are signs to be discovered and then, little by little, made to speak. In other words, *divinatio* and *eruditio* are both part of the same hermeneutics" (1973, 33–4). In *La Numancia*, these two forms of knowledge come together in Proteus. This figure practices *divinatio* but emerges from *eruditio*. This way of knowing came to an end at the beginning of the seventeenth century. Foucault points to Cervantes's *Don Quijote* as an example of this transformation. He is a madman because he is alienated in analogy, because "for him the crown makes the king." *La Numancia*, I would argue, foreshadows this break.[47] Proteus's poetry seems to destabilize the world of resemblances since *divinatio* comes to include the art of weaving deceitful words.[48] As for *eruditio*, it not only concerns itself with *aemulatio*[49] and the unveiling of the wisdom of the past. It also seeks to reveal Proteus as a false god. Proteus as god of origins is transformed into Protean originality. Paradoxically, a new wisdom emerges from deceit and originality. It could even be argued that these traits derive, in reality, from a historicized imitation of the ancients.[50]

Although Proteus adopts a pose of consolation, constructing a history that appears, on the surface, to praise Spanish imperialism, to bring *alivio* to Spain's distress, in reality Proteus uses his powers of metamorphosis, the power of language and of rhetoric to shift, conceal, and transform meanings through myriad contexts, in order to reveal the fissures found in the myth of empire. Through problematic confrontations, questionable absences, troubling allusions, and a rhetoric that revels in indeterminacy, the fluvial prophecy delves into the muddy rivers of sacrilege and political cunning. The strong providential streak evoked by the fall of Numantia is subverted through the sack of Rome while the unity and the universal harmony of empire are questioned through the absence of the Other. Although the text points to a Virgilian origin for the myth of empire and to a deeper source for the authority of prophecy, *La Numancia* resists these models, and by turning away from origin, the play exploits a new originality based on Proteus's freedom. Through the meanderings of meaning, the god's mendacity comes to be, paradoxically, a way of revealing deeper secrets.

At the same time, the text renders homage to Virgil through fluvial rhetoric and through the representation of sacrifice. Numantia, as the sacrificial phoenix that will be reborn from its own ashes (v. 392), as a force that through *renovatio* will become the Spanish Empire, parallels the sacrifice that Aristaeus must perform in the *Fourth Georgic*: "Anon, when the ninth Dawn displays her rising beams, thou shalt send unto Orpheus funeral dues of Lethe's poppies, shalt slay a black ewe and revisit the grove. Then to Eurydice, now appeased, thou shalt do worship with the slaughter of a calf" (1978, 4.544–51; 1991, 235) Once this is done, Aristaeus witnesses "a portent, sudden and wondrous to tell – through the paunch, amid the molten flesh of the oxen, bees buzzing and swarming forth from the ruptured sides" (1978, 4.554–6; 1991, 235). Since Aristaeus's swarm of bees is compared to a human kingdom, the parallel with Numantia and Spain is clear. Sacrifice has led to *renova-*

tio. But Aristaeus has followed the prescribed practice of sacrifice. He has atoned for his faults.[51] Numantia's sacrifice, although modeled to an extent on Virgil's apiarian metaphor, is not one that follows the will of the gods. The sacrificial rites within Numantia will explain why the city's sacrifice was not altogether pleasing to the divinity – why the *renovatio* brings about, not the perfect universal empire, but a mere simulacrum.

8

Lucan
The necromancy of imitation

In *Don Quijote* (1978, 1.6.115), the priest, as he examines the books in the knight's library, tells the barber how Alexander the Great kept Homer's *Iliad* in a richly ornamented casket captured from the defeated Darius. In contrast with the epic's great value, most of the romances of chivalry found in don Quijote's library will be sent to "inquisitional" fires. The priest's drastic censorship of the romances extends the humanists' and the clergy's dislike for the romances to a fanatical extreme. While the humanists who favor the narrative unity of the classical epic are represented by an inquisitorial figure, the proponents of the episodic open-endedness of romance are left with don Quijote, a madman, as their exponent. But the epic tradition as represented by Homer and Virgil also has a "romance" counterpart in Lucan. His *Pharsalia*, although an epic, is episodic in nature like the chivalric romances. Lucan's poem breaks the body of narrative into pieces in much the same way as it revels in the representation of broken and mutilated bodies of soldiers and generals within its text (Quint 1993, 140ff.). In *Don Quijote*, both types of mutilation are included within the romance tradition and are decried by the canon of Toledo. While a child "da una cuchillada a un gigante," the chivalric romances themselves are considered giants or monsters with many limbs: "No he visto ningún libro de caballerías que haga un cuerpo de fábula entero con todos sus miembros . . . sino que los componen con tantos miembros, que más parece que llevan intención a formar una quimera o un monstruo" (1978, 1.47.565). The canon's praise of the classical and well-ordered textual body and his attack on new monstrosities continue in his discussion of Spanish Golden Age plays. He contrasts those that follow classical principles with the new and monstrous theater "que no llevan pies ni cabeza" (1978, 1.48.568). One example given of the well-constructed classical play is *La Numancia* (1978, 1.48.569). It would thus seem odd to search for Lucan's monstrosities in a text heralded as part of the classical aesthetics set forth in Plato's *Phaedrus*.[1] And yet, this chapter will argue that *La Numancia* imitates some of the monstrous qualities of the *Pharsalia*, while also striving for some of the more "classical" features of Homeric and Virgilian epic.

Both types of epic serve to represent power. In some ways *Don Quijote*'s (con)fusion between history and fiction is derived from the epic's re-creation of history in order to extol a particular power. In the *Life of Alexander*, Plutarch tells the anecdote concerning Alexander's venera-tion of Homer's *Iliad*. He shows how Achilles' valor became a model for Alexander's prowess. Bemoaning the fact that he had no Homer to immortalize his victories, Alexander came to picture himself "as an epic hero, competing for fame with the hero of an earlier poem" (Quint 1993, 4). Epic poetry, then, contains heroic models of behavior that affect the struggles for power and the representations of history. Such an agenda extends to the chivalric romances. Emperor Charles V, for exam-ple, was devoted to the romances, attempting to turn fiction into reality. He wished to be considered the foremost of knights, engaged in the fashioning of a universal empire. This type of quest was later satirized in Cervantes's *Don Quijote*, where the mad knight's attempts to restore a golden age serve in many cases to deepen the chaos of the iron age. Dur-ing the scrutiny of the knight's library in *Don Quijote*, the priest orders that the chivalric romance *Palmerín de Inglaterra* be saved "porque es fama que le compuso un discreto rey de Portugal" (1978, 1.6.115). Although the book was actually authored by Francisco de Moraes Cabral,[2] the priest's comment exemplifies how, in the first half of the six-teenth century, the chivalric romance, like the epic, was associated with the discourse of power.

The political agenda of the epic and the ruler's desire to control it are clearly exemplified in another of Plutarch's anecdotes. He tells how Julius Caesar cried when he thought that "Alexander at my age had con-quered so many nations, and I have all this time done nothing that is memorable" (1902, 4.99). In alluding to Alexander, Caesar was also recalling the *Iliad*, treasured by the conqueror of Darius. While Alexan-der sought to emulate the Greek Achilles in the Homeric poem, Caesar turned to Hector. After all, it was claimed that Rome was built by the sur-vivors of Troy, and Aeneas's son Iulius could be claimed as an ancestor of the Julian line. Thus, the Homeric epic is appropriated by different rulers in order to authorize opposite political genealogies. Caesar was also aware of Alexander's lament for a lack of an appropriate poet to sing his deeds. He thus wrote his own *Commentarii* on the *Gallic War* and the

Civil War, a tradition that might be at the root of the legendary royal authorship of the *Palmerín de Inglaterra.*[3]

Virgil's *Aeneid,* like Caesar's genealogy of imitation, begins with Hector. His "political appropriation of Homeric epic" (Quint 1993, 7) turns the Trojan defeat into a foundation myth of Rome. Thus, when Homer and Virgil are depicted in two separate scenes under Raphael's *Parnassus,* the Renaissance may have perceived them not only as complementary epic authors but also as literary and political competitors. Juan Luis Vives, for example, discusses this *aemulatio,* or competition: "En la *Eneida* lucha con Homero empeñando todas sus fuerzas . . . y, aun a veces, le supera, bien venciendo las gracias griegas con la gravedad romana o con una más moderna invención, la rudeza primitiva" (1947, 1.547). *Aemulatio,* then, includes the (re)vision of an ancient model through a more modern perspective. This is precisely what Cervantes attempts to do in *La Numancia.* He reenvisions the epics of Homer, Virgil, and Lucan through the perspective of sixteenth-century imperial conquest. The opposition between Greece (Homer) and Rome (Virgil) portrayed by Raphael and explained by Vives did not create a major rift in epic continuity. Rather, it preserved "the conservative tendency of the epic genre, which inclines to perpetuate – through imitation – its formal structures of narrative and diction, its motifs and commonplaces of plot: the same story told over and over."[4] Lucan's *Pharsalia,* on the other hand, became the model for discontinuity. It has been called an anti-*Aeneid,* embodying what David Quint has called the epic of the defeated: "The victors experience history as a coherent, end-directed story told by their own power; the losers experience a contingency that they are powerless to shape to their own ends" (1993, 9). In the *Pharsalia,* Caesar becomes the enemy, although he triumphs and becomes heir to empire.[5] The poem glorifies instead the republicanism of Pompey. The sixteenth century was very much aware of the conflict between the two epic visions. Juan Luis Vives, for example, composed *La fuga de Pompeyo* as a lament by Pompey at the loss of the Republic and the advent of Caesarean tyranny. In opposition to imperial conquest, the *Pharsalia* stands as a narrative of resistance and focuses on the struggle for *libertas* (Quint 1993, 11).

Cervantes's *La Numancia,* as seen in the preceding two chapters, reflects the continuity between the Homeric and the Virgilian epic through *aemulatio.* This chapter will show how it incorporates Lucan's *Pharsalia* very much as an anti-*Aeneid,* in order to disrupt the glorious prophetic vision of empire.[6] In the *Viaje del Parnaso* a poet is enjoined to move away from Lucan and contemplate for a while the solar figure of Apollo:

Aunque Lucano por tu voz respira,
déjale un rato y, con piadosos ojos,
a la necesidad de Apolo mira.
(1984b, 69)

This movement is reversed in *La Numancia*. Act 2 turns away from the brilliancy of empire and canonicity and looks at the shadows of the losers. Cervantes problematizes the opposition between the *Aeneid* and the *Pharsalia* by representing an action where imperial power belongs to the heirs of the defeated Numantia. Thus, it seems as if the Roman "losers" utilize the language of Virgil's imperialism. But Cervantes conflates two languages and visions since Lucan's epic of the defeated is also part of the vanquished city's rhetoric. Since it is difficult to resolve who wins and who loses in *Numancia*, neither epic program can have total mastery over Cervantes's text. Indeed, this ambiguity serves to foreground Cervantes's original achievement, which borrows from, but is not controlled by, either type of epic.

The notion of *libertas*, central to Lucan's epic, is brought out in the first act of Cervantes's play by the allegorical figure of Spain:

¿Será posible que contino sea
esclava de naciones estranjeras,
y que un pequeño tiempo yo no vea
de libertad tendidas mis banderas?
(vv. 369–72)

Cipión is seen as the representative of a mighty empire that is the last in a series of nations that desire to enslave Numantia. Imperial exploitation is made clear when Spain complains that "a mil tiranos mil riquezas diste" (v. 365). The inhabitants of Numantia oppose the imperial and colonizing agendas with cries of liberty: "¡Numantinos libertad. . . ! (v. 1357). They counter imperial/colonial exploitation by burning all their riches. This opposition between imperialism and liberty is borrowed from Lucan's *Pharsalia*. W. R. Johnson explains that "Lucan cannot bring himself to think that freedom is incompatible with empire, but this underground thought . . . haunts the poem" (1987, 88). Cervantes's text also toys with the idea of freedom as incompatible with empire, but seems to dismiss it. While the Numantians' freedom is exalted against

Roman imperialism, it is left up to the reader/spectator to decide if the new Spanish imperialism represented by Charles V and Philip II takes away the freedom of others. While the Duero's prophecy follows Virgil's *Aeneid* and the *Fourth Georgic*, we have seen in the previous chapter how the historical narrative included in the prophecy subverts some of the imperialist ideals. The seeming randomness of Proteus's historical narrative recalls the "vision of history-as-chance and a corollary sense of narrative aimlessness" that are key to the *Pharsalia* (Quint 1993, 136). This apparent aimlessness in Cervantes aims at disrupting the well-ordered imperialist Virgilian vision.[7]

We have seen how Xerxes' yoking of the Hellespont in *The Persians* is an indication of his hubris and his imperial desire for enslavement of others. Cipión's yoking of Numantia derives not only from Aeschylus's tragedy but also from Lucan's *Pharsalia*, where Caesar attempts to yoke the port of Brindisi: "But unwilling, on the other hand, that the enemy should range freely over the deep, he blocks the sea" (1962, 2.661–2).[8] Lucan compares Caesar's feat with Xerxes' bridging of the Hellespont: "Such, by the report of fame, was the road built over the sea by the proud Persian" (1962, 2.672–3). Since Xerxes is described as overly proud in Aeschylus and Lucan, comparison with Caesar in the *Pharsalia* points to Julius's hubris. The yoke of the proud is a "demonic" weapon that will lead only to disaster.[9] In *La Numancia* and in the *Pharsalia* the proud enemy seems to win (Cipión and Caesar) while the forces of liberty appear to be defeated (Numantia and Pompey). But the attempts at yoking bring some kind of reversal or retribution in the future (Caesar will be assassinated, and the Spanish Empire will rise to sack Rome). The *libertas* for which Numantia perishes seems to be forgotten in its imperial resurrection. Thus, the *Pharsalia* is used by Cervantes in this instance both to praise the Numantians in their defeat and to stir doubts concerning their imperial inheritors.

Another example of the struggle between the Virgilian epic and Lucan's narrative of the defeated can be found in the topos of the prophetic curse issued by the losers so as to prevent the imperial victors total control of the future. David Quint (1993) has noted how this curse is found throughout sixteenth- and seventeenth-century epic poems, including Ercilla's *La Araucana*, Gaspar Pérez de Villagra's *Historia de la Nueva Mexico*, and Camoes's *Os Lusíadas*. Cervantes's *La Numancia* follows this tradition. Inscribed within the Virgilian prophecy of the river Duero is the curse of the defeated. In this brilliant conflation of two traditions

Cervantes proclaims both the origins and the originality of his prophetic discourse. He can utilize both Virgil and Lucan in one speech since Numantia is both the winner and the loser: although it is destroyed by Cipión, it will rise from its ashes to create a new empire. The curse against the Romans is clear:

y puesto que el feroz romano tiende
el paso agora por tu fértil suelo,
que te oprime aquí, y allí te ofende
con arrogante y ambicioso celo,
tiempo vendrá, según que ansí lo entiende
el saber que a Proteo ha dado el cielo
que estos romanos sean oprimidos
por los que agora tienen abatidos.

(vv. 465–72)

Although the Virgilian Proteus is called upon to issue a statement of imperialist victory, he intones the traditional curse of the defeated. Many of the curses in narratives of the defeated are contingent, partial, or reversible.[10] They attempt to open up a space for the loser in a world ruled by the victor. But Cervantes knows that Spain will eventually rise victorious. His curse can be complete. It can turn the table on the Romans.

Although in Lucan the curse is voiced by Erichto,[11] most of the epic curses are intoned by a defeated warrior who is on the point of death: an Acoman who is about to hang himself in Pérez de Villagrá's *Historia de la Nueva Mexico*; Adamastor, the defeated Titan in Camões's *Os Lusíadas*.[12] These characters can most effectively express their bitterness toward the victors. The curse in *La Numancia*, however, is uttered by a Virgilian god, Proteus. His authority makes it clear that the vengeance of the defeated will be effected. The god's words also share a number of characteristics with the *Aeneid*, when this epic is studied in terms of the defeated. Virgil's epic poem contains its own curse of the vanquished. It is uttered by the lovesick Dido on seeing her beloved Aeneas departing Carthage.[13] In a dream, Aeneas learns that he must quit the city and abandon his love-making in order to turn to his true destiny, the founding of Rome. Not knowing how to confront the Carthaginian ruler, he begins his preparations for departure in secret. Virgil's text explains: "But the queen – who can deceive a lover? – knew in advance some scheme was afoot" (1991, 90/4.296–7). She confronts Aeneas: "You traitor, did you imagine you could do this and keep it secret? Do you think you could slip away from this land of mine and say nothing?" (1991, 90/4.305–6). Her words, which have stirred the imagination and the emotion of thinkers such as Augustine and Juan Luis Vives,[14] fail to persuade Aeneas.

When she observes from her "high tower . . . the fleet moving out to sea" (1991, 99/4.586–7), she curses her former lover: "If that monster of wickedness must reach harbor, if he must come to shore and that is what the Fates of Jupiter demand, if the boundary stone is set and may not be moved, then let him be harried in war by a people bold in arms; may he be driven from his own land and torn from the embrace of Iulus; may he have to beg for help and see his innocent people dying . . . let him fall before his time and lie unburied on the broad sand" (1991, 100/4.612–20). In contrast to the Duero's triumphal curse, Dido's is contingent. The "if" clause limits her power to affect the victor's future. And yet, she can bring about havoc and woe before the Romans' final triumph.

But how is Dido's contingent curse imitated by Cervantes in *La Numancia?* I believe that the Spanish play imitates the second part of the curse and the circumstances of Dido's tragic death as described by Virgil. Upon her beloved Aeneas's departure, the queen of Carthage commits suicide, throwing herself upon a funeral pyre. Virgil repeatedly calls her Phoenissa (1991, 25/1.670; 91/4.348,),[15] a word whose sound recalls the phoenix. This mythical creature, like Dido, immolates itself in a fiery pyre. Legend has it that the phoenix rises from its own ashes, and the city of Carthage will rise over and over again to combat the Romans.[16] Dido asks her compatriots to "pursue with hatred the whole line of his [Aeneas's] descendants. Make that your offering to my shade" (1991, 101/4.622–4). West's translation should be amended here to read "my ashes" or "my dust" instead of "my shade,"[17] since it is out of her ashes (like a phoenix) that her avengers will arise. This is the Virgilian background to Cervantes's curse. Numantia, like Dido, will burn in the flames of destruction. The allegorical figure of Spain compares this fire to the one that consumes the mythical phoenix:

llegada ya la hora postrimera,
do acabará su vida y no su fama,
cual fénix, renovándose en la llama.
(vv. 390–2)

Like the Carthaginians, who will rise again to combat Rome even after their city has been destroyed over and over again, the descendants of

Numantia will form an empire that will sack the Eternal City in 1527 and threaten it again in 1556 (vv. 485–96). Both Numantia and Carthage are cities akin to the phoenix since they can renew themselves after destruction. But there may be a touch of *contaminatio* in this image. Lucan also mentions the phoenix. In his text, the ashes from this mythical bird are added to the foul potion that Erichto brews in order to bring a dead soldier back to life (1962, 6.680). Is Numantia's resuscitation as an imperial power a heroic Virgilian myth or a necromantic event that should arouse suspicion?

In the *Aeneid*, Dido calls for a champion: "Arise from my dead bones, O my unknown avenger, and harry the race of Dardanus with fire and sword" (1991, 101/4.625–6). The Roman readers of Virgil's poem would have known that this first avenger would be Hannibal. Together with Attila the Hun, this Carthaginian conqueror was remembered through medieval and Renaissance times as a fierce warrior who threatened Rome. It is thus no coincidence that the Duero's prophecy singles out Attila as the one who will carry out the prophesied revenge: "Estas injurias vengará la mano / del fiero Atila en tiempos venideros" (vv. 481–2). But Cervantes veers away from the Virgilian model at this juncture and portrays a different avenger and a different result. In Bloomian terms, we have a kind of swerve, a Lucretian *clinamen*, which brings about an unexpected creation (Bloom 1973, 44). We have seen how in Raphael's fresco *Leo I Stops Attila's Invasion*, the "barbarian" warrior is prevented from sacking "civilized" Rome by the spiritual powers of the pope. Numantia's curse, which had seemed to be triumphal and absolute, is thus mitigated and subverted by reminiscences from the fresco and the legend it evokes. Once again, Cervantes's originality derives from the struggle between the political agendas represented by different Renaissance and classical models.

In Lucan's *Pharsalia*, Caesar comes to the same place in Africa where Scipio was victorious over Hannibal.[18] Here, the text indulges in a narrative of how in this very place, long before Scipio or Caesar, the giant Anteus fought with Alcides (Hercules). Anteus seems to stand for Africa. He is a monstrous Other who, like Carthage, rises over and over again in spite of civilization's attempts to tame or destroy him. Even Hercules is amazed at how the giant regains his strength. His secret is that on falling to the ground, he gains the support of his mother, Earth (1962, 4.593–660). In *La Numancia*, when the city is destroyed, it returns to the bosom of Mother Spain. Like Anteus, Numantia comes back to life revi-

talized and stronger in the guise of the Spanish Empire. While Act 1 of
La Numancia foregrounds the Virgilian prophecies through the element
of water, the second act emphasizes a lower element, earth, and turns to
Lucan's predictions. Like the giant Anteus in the *Pharsalia*, the Numantians will appear as inhuman. They will be depicted as the monstrous or
barbarian Other that is being subdued by civilized Rome. A second Scipio must come to destroy a second Carthage.

Critics have often ignored the second act of *La Numancia* since most
of it revolves around pagan rites. The representation on stage of elaborate sacrifices with sacred fires, incense, wine, priests dressed in exotic
garb, and a sacrificial ram that is stolen by a demon would certainly
impress an audience that thrives on stage effects and exoticism. The second act culminates with a feat of necromancy unparalleled in Spanish
Golden Age theater. Although critics have pointed to the importance of
the omens in this act for heightening the tragic destiny of the inhabitants
of the city,[19] few have thought them worthy of extended commentary.
Alfredo Hermenegildo complains that the entire second act is devoted to
predictions thus "se da importancia excesiva a algo que no debe ser sino
un puro instrumento" (1973, 375). Jean Canavaggio, for example, calls
the stage effects "impressionant" but adds that they rely on a "technique
très simple" (1977, 317).

However, this act of theatrical exhibitionism serves to lead a learned
audience away from Virgilian contexts and toward a subtext of resistance
and anti-imperialism. In opposition to the fluvial prophecy of the previous act, this most theatrical of acts presents a series of prophetic scenes.
The several prophetic frenzies evoked by Cervantes in this act,[20] and particularly the feat of necromancy, point to a specific classical text and its
mythical background. M. P. O. Morford has shown how Lucan's *Pharsalia*
contains "a careful account of the practice of necromancy, the fullest in
Latin literature" (1967, 67). James Nicolopulos (forthcoming) asserts:
"But it is Lucan himself who brings the *locus* to its apogee . . . , glorying
first in the exploits of the witches of Thessaly (*Pharsalia* 6.434–506), then
outdoing himself with the bizarrely hyperbolic excesses of the arch-
necromanceress Erichto (*Pharsalia* 6.507–68)."[21] Necromantic prophecy
is achieved through the invocation of the gods of the underworld.

Nicolopulos goes on to explain that this locus classicus flourished during the Middle Ages and on into the Renaissance and was used by Spanish writers such as Juan de Mena and Ercilla. *La Numancia* follows this

lead. The audience is alerted to the classical subtexts by the amazing exhibition of pagan rites and prophetic frenzies. Most of Act 2 must be seen as a refashioning of Books 1 and 6 of the *Pharsalia*. The few critics who have noted a possible parallel between the two works have dismissed it as unimportant. María Rosa Lida de Malkiel exclaims, "¡tan poco cuadraba a Cervantes el efectismo declamatorio de la Farsalia!" (1950, 520). Canavaggio (1977), on the other hand, asserts that although there are many classical reminiscences in *La Numancia*, none of them play a key role in the text.[22]

Contrary to these opinions, I would argue that the *Pharsalia* plays a central role in the elaboration of Act 2. In his epic poem, Lucan contrasts the "heretical" act of necromancy to previous prophecies which are part of the official religion of Rome. Cervantes follows suit. Both texts begin with the religious rites. In the *Pharsalia*, Arruns, a soothsayer from Ethuria, calls for a procession which will culminate in an animal sacrifice: "He gives sanctity to the spot, and next brings near to the holy altar a bull with neck chosen for the sacrifice" (1962, 1.608–9). A horned animal is also key to the sacrifice in *La Numancia*. Two priests bring in a *carnero* (p. 67), its horns crowned with olives and flowers. Both texts refer to wine and purifying water (Lucan 1962, 1.609–10; Cervantes 1984a, v. 798); and both sacrifices are directed to Jupiter (Lucan 1962, l.633; Cervantes 1984a, v. 829). As god of the thunderbolt, Jupiter's presence is felt in both texts. While Arruns "collects the scattered fires of the thunderbolt and hides them in the earth with doleful muttering" (1962, 1.606–7), the priests in *La Numancia* see a lightning bolt and consider it a bad omen (vv. 843–5). Both sacrifices have ominous conclusions, which predict disaster. In *La fuga de Pompeyo*, Juan Luis Vives imitates the *Pharsalia* and fashions a lament by the defeated Pompey. Recalling the ominous presence of the thunderbolt in Lucan's epic, Vives's leader asks: "¿Que hace ahora ¡oh Júpiter! tu rayo? ¿Por qué no le arrojas? . . . Y permites que viva César, pestilencia universal del mundo" (1947, 1.587). Jupiter thus withholds his thunderbolt and allows Caesar to conquer. Vives's imaginative essay thus contains a lament for the fall of the Republic. As in the epic, Caesar, the imperial winner, is criticized. In Cervantes's play, Cipión, as representative of the Roman Empire, also triumphs. And yet, criticism of this figure is partially muted since Cipión's imperialism is anachronistic. Although the Rome of his time was engaged in imperial conquest, the government had not as yet moved to Caesarian rule. Indeed, the lament of Scipio Africanus in the *Pharsalia* precedes the rise of empire. Once again, the Spanish text sets up a series of dichotomies that cannot be easily resolved, in order to trigger meditations on the nature of empire.

There are other evil omens in the *Pharsalia* which are imitated in *La Numancia*. Arruns claims that "the infernal gods have entered into the body of the slaughtered bull" (1962, 1.633–4). In Cervantes's play, a *demonio* steals the sacrificial victim: "Sale por el güeco del tablado un demonio hasta el medio cuerpo y ha de arrebatar el carnero" (p. 71).[23] In addition to the Etruscan *haruspex*, Lucan's text includes two more official prophecies, one by the astrologer Nigidius Figulus and a second by a matron inspired by the god.[24] After passing in review all the planets, Nigidius points to Mars's power and desire for mischief since it is situated in the constellation Scorpio, which it rules. The astrologer concludes that "Mars alone lords in heaven" (1962, 1.663). Cervantes's text seems to refer to Lucan's predictions in the emphasis that is placed on the stars (vv. 446, 627) and in the focusing on Mars (vv. 89, 154, 713).

In contrast to the "official" readings of disaster, Book 6 of the *Pharsalia* presents the necromantic findings of the witch Erichto. Cervantes follows Lucan's lead by presenting Marquino's necromancy after the official readings. If a learned audience had failed to apprehend the parallels between the previous scenes in the *comedia* and the *Pharsalia*, the structure and language of Marquino's deeds would serve to awaken Lucan's memory. Both writers follow the same pattern. The first element in the necromancy scenes in Lucan and Cervantes involves the choosing of a corpse. Both Marquino and Erichto prefer a recently deceased young male belonging to the side of the conflict which wants to know the future: a soldier from Pompey's army in Lucan and a Numantian youth in Cervantes.[25] Second, the witch or necromancer uses a potion or potions to bring the body back to life. While Marquino makes use of three different vials,[26] Erichto concentrates on one brew. She "poured in lavishly the poison that the moon supplies. With this was blended all that nature inauspiciously conceives and brings forth" (1962, 6.669–71). A second model may have been available to Cervantes for the brew. While preparing a potion to bring back old Aeson's youth, Medea, in Ovid's *Metamorphoses*, "thrice sprinkled water caught up from a flowing stream upon her head" (1921, 1.355/7.189–90).[27]

The third element shared by Cervantes and Lucan is the use of voice. Once the witch has perfected her brew, Lucan explains that "Erichto began to use her voice, which had more power over the rulers of the

Underworld than any drug" (Graves's translation, p. 145).[28] In *La Numancia*, Marquino reminds the powers of Hades that "sabéis que mi voz es poderosa / de doblaros la rabia y el tormento" (vv. 995–6). Fourth, both Marquino and Erichto call upon many of the same inhabitants of Hades: Cerberus, Charon, Proserpina, and the ruler of the underworld, Pluto. Fifth, both texts evince the vacillation or reluctance of the soul of the dead to come back into its mutilated corpse. On seeing the ghost of the soldier, who "shrank from entering the gaping bosom, the vital parts and the flesh divided by mortal wound," Erichto marvels that he "had power to linger thus" (1962, 6.722–2). In Cervantes, Marquino asks the corpse: "¿No respondes? ¿No revives?" (v. 1033). Sixth, both necromancers must utilize threats, insults, and blackmail to bring about the appropriate results. Erichto's threats are very specific. For example, she warns Pluto, "And on you, the worst of the world's Rulers, I shall launch the sun's light, bursting open your den; and the sudden light shall blast you" (1962, 6.742–4). Marquino, on the other hand, simply threatens: "¿Buscáis con deteneros, vuestros males . . . ?" (v. 989) and "Pues no esperéis que más os amenace" (v. 1014). Erichto insultingly describes Hecate as "wasted and pale of aspect." She must put on her makeup to visit the gods above. Erichto threatens her thusly: "I shall show you to them as you are" (1962, 6.737–8). The witch professes to know some unlawful bond between Pluto and Proserpina, which she will reveal (1962, 6.740–2). Although Marquino in *La Numancia* knows not of such bonds, he does claim that Pluto's wife "está, sin duda, haciéndote cornudo" (v. 999). The seventh element is, of course, the prophecy uttered by the corpse.

In both *La Numancia* and the *Pharsalia*, necromancy proves to be a much more accurate and specific means of learning the future than the more traditional or accepted means. These texts first evoke the "official" religion, in which Jupiter is the object of sacrifice. Once these sacrifices are rejected and even desecrated (a demon steals the sacrificial animal in *La Numancia*), the key myth that controls the prophetic frenzy becomes evident. The gods of the underworld preside over this act and are called through an act of necromancy. Since ancient times this practice had been considered one of the foulest and most loathsome means of divination. Lucan makes it clear that no respectable Roman would utilize such methods. In the *Pharsalia*, it is Sextus, the "unworthy son" (1962, 6.420) of Pompey, who turns to Erichto: "Fear urged him on to learn beforehand the course of destiny" (1962, 6.423). Like Sextus, Marquino must be viewed as unworthy and unclean. The Numantians once again are portrayed as barbarous Others who must succumb to the civilizing powers of empire. Their witchcraft (a term charged with meaning in Cervantes's world, where the *Malleus Maleficarum* and the persecution of those supposedly involved in a demonic plot against Christianity were very much on the minds of the people) must be annihilated by the more "rational" Romans.[29] While attempting to fashion an imperial (albeit somewhat subversive) discourse for Spain, Cervantes seems to be representing Numantia through the rhetoric of the conquered – they are monsters akin to the phoenix and the giants, and necromancers akin to sixteenth-century witches and magicians. In this veering away from the Numantians, the text may be providing space for the reader/audience to look at both Romans and Numantians and decide which one is the best ancestor, which one deserves a greater place in the myth of origins of the Spanish Empire.

In *La Numancia*, necromancy is not as far removed from official fortune-telling as it is in the *Pharsalia*. During the sacrifice to Jupiter, one of the priests utilizes an invocation reminiscent of Marquino's and Erichto's. Very much like these necromancers, he calls on Pluto and Proserpina (vv. 864, 868). Furthermore, he includes in his prayer entities that Marquino neglects to invoke but that are central to Erichto's magic: the Furies (v. 874; Lucan 1962, 6.703, 730). This is *contaminatio* in a negative sense, a sacrificial contamination that makes all of the rites of Act 2 particularly suspect since sacrifice and prophecy, although ostensibly directed at Jupiter, in reality cluster around figures from the underworld. An audience of the period may have well felt *admiratio* when witnessing these spectacular events, but the rites and, more important, their connection to the underworld (often related to the Christian Hell) would have distanced them from the Numantians. This distance from the Numantians allows the reader/spectator to reconsider questions of origin.

Act 1 had ended with the prophecy of the river Duero, one of imperial *renovatio* reminiscent of Virgil's *Aeneid*.[30] In the *Aeneid*, the destruction of Troy by the Greeks leads to the foundation of Rome. In Cervantes's *comedia*, the destruction of Numantia serves to create the Spanish Empire. Through this parallel, Spain, in Cervantes's text, becomes imbued with the Virgilian spirit of empire. As noted above, Lucan's *Pharsalia* is in many ways a response to the *Aeneid*. In this "neo-epic," imperialism gives way to republicanism,[31] legend to history, elegance to sensationalism, and religion to witchcraft.[32] The *Pharsalia*, then, is the ideal text with which to bring down Virgil's imperialist vision. By placing his imitation of Lucan immediately after a Virgilian imperialist evocation, Cervantes's text subverts the heroic tone and the triumphant message. Awareness of this imitation undercuts the arguments of those who view the play as an unambiguous celebration of a Spanish empire. By using Lucan, Cervantes is pointing to a "Spaniard" who became successful under the Roman Empire. The author of the *Pharsalia* was born in Cordoba in A.D. 39, and went on to Rome, where he wrote under Nero. Cervantes is also pointing to a writer who, although part of the greatest empire of his time, was able to criticize it. This might also be one of the functions of the imitation of Lucan in the play. The *Pharsalia* as a subtext for *La Numancia* serves to foreground and problematize the question of empire.

The imitation of Lucan brings into question the heroic nature of the Numantians and consequently the status of the city as tragic/epic protagonist. It also sheds light upon the heroic qualities of the Roman general. The corpse revived by Erichto tells how ancient heroes are weeping for Rome. Scipio Africanus is one of those melancholy shades who laments the future. The *Pharsalia*, then, portrays the ancestor of the general of *La Numancia* as a hero who cares for his land. Furthermore, while Cervantes creates a feeling of *admiratio* for the Roman general through his exemplary harangue to the soldiers, the city is surrounded with a negative *admiratio* through pagan ceremonies and deeds of necromancy. When viewing the end of the play from the perspective of tragedy, the collective suicide has been seen by critics as an ideal catastrophe that leads an audience to the appropriate tragic catharsis. But the ending can also be viewed from the epic tradition. The suicide of the vanquished is found in Lucan's *Pharsalia* (1962, 4.474–581), in Ercilla's *Araucana* (Canto 26), and in Pérez de Villagra's *Historia de la Nueva Mexico*. It is regarded by Quint and other critics as part of the "Stoic contempt for the body" (1993, 144) and stands as an exercise in stoic morality: "It is no arduous feat of virtue to escape slavery by one's own hand" (Lucan 1962, 4.576–7).

On the question of suicide, Cervantes's text may be alluding to Lucan's death as described in Ambrosio de Morales's *Corónica*. After all, Morales was Cervantes's main source for the history of Numantia. The Spanish historian foregrounds the *Pharsalia*: "Dexónos Lucano su Farsalia, donde escribe la guerra civil de César y Pompeyo" (1791, 4.433). Aware of the dispute as to who is the better epic poet, Virgil or Lucan, Morales opts for the former: "mas yo por mejor y mas cierto tengo el juicio del mismo Lucano, que hablando de sus poesías en comparacion de las de Virgilio dicen, que dixo: ¡O quánto me falta para llegar al Culice de Virgilio! El Culice es una obra pequeña que Virgilio hizo de un mosquito" (1791, 4.433). Morales not only emphasizes the minuscule value of Lucan's poetry when perceived in terms of Virgil's but also contrasts Lucan's suicide with Seneca's. Both writers were ordered to kill themselves by Emperor Nero for their alleged participation in a plot to murder him. Nero had by this time departed from Seneca's teachings and become a most cruel ruler. This suicide would place Lucan among the upholders of Stoicism as described in his *Pharsalia*. Like them, Lucan would shine with virtue as he attempted to escape tyranny "by one's own hand." However, Morales, following Tacitus, prefers to stress Lucan's cowardice: "Nerón con mucha astucia le prometió la vida si descubria los conjurados, estuvo Lucano tan desatinado, y vencido de la codicia de vivir, que nombró entre otros á su madre Acila" (1791, 4.433). This cowardly deed failed to prevent his death. Nero "solamente le guardó para matarle en los postreros" (1791, 4.433). Lucan's suicide, then, is tinged with cowardice in Morales's account. Instead of exemplifying Stoic virtue, it shows a covetousness for life that goes against the principles of this philosophy. Thus, Lucan's death recalls Marquino's suicide in *La Numancia* since the priest's cowardly attitude makes it impossible for him to face the events foretold.

Although the suicide of a whole city can be traced back to Renaissance epics which borrow from Lucan, Cervantes once again takes up a model and veers away from it, creating a Bloomian *clinamen*. This time, he does not set up a Virgilian counterpart, although Dido's desperate suicide cannot be forgotten. Instead, he fractures the classical meanings by bringing together two moments from Lucan: "Stoic" suicide and foul necromancy. Edward H. Friedman rightly points out that once the corpse has prophesied in veiled terms the collective suicide of the Numantians: "The foreshadowing device received further amplification as Marquino himself converts words into deed by committing suicide" (1977, 83). Thus, Stoic suicide has been contaminated with foul necromancy and with desperation. *Desesperación* is condemned by religious doctrine of the Counter-Reformation. This act is said to bring about eternal damnation. In *Don Quijote*, Cervantes is careful to veil Grisóstomo's suicide, although allowing for his "Canción desesperada" to be sung.[33] Grisóstomo's poem, as Marasso has pointed out, contains verbal reminiscences from Lucan's *Pharsalia* (1954, 86–99). It would be difficult, then, to see suicide as an event that would inspire catharsis in a religious audience of Cervantes's

time. From the point of view of epic, Stoicism is rendered suspect by Marquino's desperation. Thus, *La Numancia* presents an ambiguous praise of
suicide. Even though, on the surface, the city triumphs through this
device, the notion of heroic suicide is subverted (1) by its unsuitability
for catharsis; (2) by the association with Lucan's cowardly behavior before
his suicide; and (3) by the link created between necromancy (a practice
associated with the foulest witchcraft), Marquino's suicide, and the suicide of the city.

According to Thomas M. Greene, the concept of imitation can be
related to necromancy. When faced with *imitatio*, the critic must ask of a
text that imitates a classical model "whether the necromantic disinterment is brought off, whether the Latin text emerges still mummified
from the tomb, or shrunken and thin, or merely ornamented, or whether
rather an authentic resurrection has occurred" (1982, 37–8). In order to
answer this question, Greene proposes four types of imitation. The first
two, sacramental and eclectic imitations, are "failed" necromancies
where the text/corpse is mummified, shrunken, or ornamented.[34] Only
the final two types, the heuristic and the dialectical, are truly necromantic according to Greene since they revive the dead and make it sing
new things. Although critics such as Canavaggio and Lida de Malkiel
have argued that *La Numancia* utilizes a type of imitation that would
correspond to the eclectic or exploitative, this analysis of the two works
shows a much more thorough pattern of necromantic imitation. In *La
Numancia*, Lucan's text emerges as neither mummified, shrunken, nor
ornamented.

In his heuristic imitation of the ancients, Cervantes brings forth a fluid,
expansive, and vital resurrection that establishes a dialogue between
ancient and modern and even between two ancients: Virgil and Lucan.
The battle between the two ancients is picked up by Cervantes
in the contrastive views of empire presented in the first two acts. While
the first shows Spain as heir to empire through a Virgilian *renovatio*, the
second brings in Lucan's critical text. Although there is dependence on
the models, there is also a "declaration of conditional independence"
(Greene 1982, 41), which comes when the Golden Age text shows how a
new context can transform and problematize even further the ancient
models. In order to enliven the classical material, Cervantes changes the
historical context to give immediacy to the past. *La Numancia* invites the
reader/spectator to establish a series of parallels between ancient and
modern history, parallels that are not without paradox. If Numantia is to

be seen as the origin of the Spanish Empire, how are the spectators to view imperial Rome in this genesis? Is Spain born out of the ashes of Numantia or out of the destruction of pagan Rome? If Numantia is the "myth of origins" (Greene 1982, 41) of Spain, why are its gods those of the underworld? On the other hand, if Rome is the origin, is Scipio's hubris a cause for concern for the modern heirs? Thus, the ancient model has been given immediacy through a new historical context. This context frees the exhumed textual body from a mummified state, granting it the fluidity of parallel and paradox. Nor is the ancient text shrunken. Cervantes revels in prophetic exhibitionism. The battle between Virgilian *renovatio* and the necromantic doom predicted by Lucan expands into a universal vision of history which projects Spain into the pattern of the rise and fall of empires. What the ancients had to say is then vital to what Spain has become. Who is to be heeded, Virgil or Lucan? Will the empire survive or be threatened by internal rivalries? Is the glorification of empire a symptom of hubris or simply the acceptance of *renovatio*? These and other questions create a bridge between the two worlds, ancient and modern. But they also allow the modern text to displace the old by giving a new voice to the corpse of the ancients.

Finally, we should address the literary reasons why Cervantes chose to foreground necromancy. Beyond the desire to clearly exhibit his model so that Lucan's critical stance would be perceived within *La Numancia*'s celebratory text, Cervantes may have foregrounded necromancy as a metaphor for the very process of imitation. The Spanish play is an exercise in archeology, bringing back from ruin and oblivion the city of Numantia. Such archeological designs were often applied to Rome during the Renaissance (Greene 1982, 222). Indeed, Cervantes's tragedy "resurrects" not only a small ruined city in Spain but also the seat of an ancient empire, through the valor and hubris of Cipión and the Roman soldiers. But, very much like Du Bellay in the *Antiquitez de Rome*, Cervantes's work is "not so much about the Roman ruins, as about an individual responding to the ruins" (Greene 1982, 223). The Spanish author responds through necromancy, a practice that brings the dead back to life. *La Numancia* is, on one level, an archeological text, but it also engages in forbidden practices. The reader or audience, through an act of metaphorical necromancy, is presented with an illusion of Numantia and of Rome.

The poet as deceiver is a figure that commonly appears in Cervantes's works. According to Alban K. Forcione, "any supernatural connections which they may have are infernal; and their abode is not the city, but some underworld kingdom which is opposed to all conventional values" (1970, 306). In *La Numancia*, Marquino's underworld is the abode of the Cervantine poet. The necromancer calls forth a vision that commingles the past, present, and future. Afraid of what he sees, Marquino (the poet) commits suicide. His illusion has proven to be fatal to the illusion of empire. However, his suicide will be followed by a revivification of the poet. The new bard will turn away from a heroic and imperialist vision to the critical and comic stance of the writer of *Don Quijote*.

Through the techniques of conflation, *clinamen*, and conflictive fragmentation, through the medium of prophetic frenzies, Lucan comes alive in Cervantes's imitation, presenting his ancient critical vision of empire. In *La Numancia*, the myth of the underworld not only questions the heroic qualities of the inhabitants of the city but points to the poet–necromancer, a suspect figure who opposes conventional values and deals in illusion. His successful necromancy creates a bridge between ancient text and modern play, one that allows the revivified textual corpse to become fluid, expanded, and vital through parallels and paradoxes based on the relationship between ancient prophecies and modern history. The illusion created shatters imperial illusions and impels the poet to suicide. Out of the ashes of empire will rise a new Cervantine poetics, a literary *renovatio* that will transform a tragic/epic vision into a Quixotic enterprise.

9

Contaminatio
Epic flames/textual ashes

From the waters of prophecy of Act 1 and the earthen necromancy of Act 2, the reader or spectator turns to the fires of destruction in Act 3 and most of Act 4. Here, we are told how the Numantians erect a large bonfire at the very center of the city, a fire that covets all their riches and that destroys all the booty desired by the Romans:

En la plaza mayor, ya levantada
queda un a ardiente y cudiciosa hoguera,
que de nuestras riquezas menistrada,
sus llamas sube a la cuarta esfera.
(vv. 1548–51)

These destructive flames ascend to the fourth sphere, the solar realm, ruled by Apollo. It is fitting that he welcome these flames. As the god who presides over *Parnassus* (as seen in Raphael's fresco and in Cervantes's own *Viaje del Parnaso*),[1] he witnesses how Numantia has transformed itself from a little-known Celtiberian town into a place to be remembered in histories, tragedies, and epics. The inhabitants, through their valor, have forged for themselves a destiny that will be sung by the poets. Cicero's dictum that history must be entrusted to the orator and Vasari's desire to imitate ancient histories where exemplarity has led to fame (Rubin 1995, 153) combine in Cervantes's play by giving the city a poetic voice and thus immortalizing the Numantians. The city's sacred offering to the gods will consume not only all the riches of the city but even the inhabitants themselves, who kill each other and throw the bodies into the flames. Both glory and the voracity of time (the flames of Numantia) are topics found in the introduction to Vasari's *Lives of the Artists* and in Cervantes's play. But in this mythical Numantia constructed by Cervantes, the Apollo who rules Raphael's *Parnassus* and Vasari's *Lives* is metamorphosed into a very different god. The action is far from having an Apollonian character. The Bacchic frenzy of the Numantians centers on the fire:

Mas vamos a la plaza adonde yace
la hoguera a nuestras vidas importuna,
porque el que allí venciere pueda luego
entregar al vencido al duro fuego.

(vv. 2176–9)

The covetous fire has become a funeral pyre. Indeed, the whole city is soon engulfed in flames, becoming one great sacrificial altar that destroys all: "y las casas y templos más preciados / en polvo y en ceniza son tornados" (vv. 2054–5). In the flame, nobles and plebeians, men and women, humans and precious objects, turn to ashes and become one with each other. This merging of differences into one final sacrificial ash recalls Cervantes's own imitative strategies at this point. *Contaminatio* is here taken to such an extreme that it comes close to what Thomas Greene calls eclectic or exploitative imitation, where "echoes, phrases, and images from a large number of authors jostle each other indifferently" (1982, 39).[2] Such is the power of Cervantes's creative sparks in Act 3 and most of Act 4, that Empedocles, Homer, Virgil, Seneca, other classical writers, Neoplatonists, and mythographers coalesce in the preparation for the destruction of the city. But the result is far from being a "stockpile" of "ahistorical citations" (Greene 1982, 39). Out of the ashes of destructive imitation arises an elusive, allusive, alluring, and altogether brilliant phoenix-like creation, which attempts to soar above the classical and Renaissance models. Reveling in anachronism, different traditions are rewoven into a tapestry that seeks to surpass the ancient sieges, to melt into one final work of art all the epic deeds and horrors of war. The ashes will also hide carefully hidden imitations of specific models. As a key figure in the Pythagorean tetractys of Raphael's *School of Athens*, Empedocles can be seen not only as a structuring force in Cervantes's elemental text but as a person who is associated with both the waters of poetry and philosophy and the fires of destruction. He is part of the fires of *contaminatio* since legend has it that this poet and philosopher committed suicide by plunging himself into the fires of Mount Etna. Thus, the elemental roots of writing and suicide in Cervantes's text can be traced to a figure in one of Raphael's frescoes.

I have already discussed the Homeric epics in Chapter 6, and will only allude briefly to them here. But Virgil's *Aeneid* will be rekindled – the burning cinders of Dido's funeral pyre will be evoked one more time. The flames invoked and evoked in *La Numancia* are not just those of war,

fury, and destruction. The flames of passion also merge with those of bellicose fury in yet one more fusion. For these two fires to burn brightly,
they must be tended to and fed from their inception. Images of fire are
present from the beginning of the play, building to a crescendo in the
later pages. Indeed, the very first fire to be evoked is the flame of lust.
When Cipión examines the Roman army he is to command, he immediately discovers that they are being consumed by lust and other vices:

Si este daño común no se previene
y se deja arraigar su ardiente llama,
el vicio solo puede hacernos guerra
más que los enemigos de esta tierra.
                    (vv. 45–8)

Realizing that the destructive power of vice is a stronger enemy than
the Numantians, he determines to quench its flame. His *allocutio*, or
harangue, is then a call to a new way of life, one that paradoxically
emerges from the placid verses on country life penned by Virgil. The
Spanish play chooses some verses from the *Fourth Georgic* which follow
those devoted to Proteus, thus creating a link with the prophesying utterances of Act 1. In Virgil's bucolic poem, the same Cyrene who had advised
her son to bind the sea god in order to find out the truth about the dying
bees now watches as her nymphs spin "fleeces of Miletus, dyed with rich
glassy hue." On some of these tapestries, Clymene "was telling of Vulcan's
baffled care, of the wiles and stolen joys of Mars, and from Chaos on was
rehearsing the countless loves of the gods" (1978, 221/1.344–6). In the
myth, the wily Mars seeks to trick Vulcan so that the god of war can pay
lustful attention to Vulcan's bride, Venus. In *La Numancia*, Cipión
becomes a wily Mars/Odysseus whose tricks are directed at a very different conquest and deception. Through the strategies of siege warfare, he
seeks to conquer a city, not a goddess. While Helen and Troy stand
together as the conquering aim of the Greeks, Cipión centers his gaze
only on Numantia. Within it, the women do not seem to render homage
to the goddess of love, represented by Helen. Rather, they align themselves with the warring males and pray to Diana, the goddess of the warlike hunt (v. 2105). Only Lira seems to evoke Venus in Numantia. Her
beauty, like that of Helen, inspires warlike deeds. The love of Marandro
for Lira is very different from the lustful and illicit union of Venus and
Mars. It inspires great deeds. Thus, the *Fourth Georgic* provides the figures
of the two deities to Cervantes's text, but *La Numancia* rejects Virgil's tone

of amorous deceit and banter. The countless loves of the gods will be replaced by Fortune's turns and Mars's bellicose and cunning temper. And yet, Cipión's conquest of Numantia, like Mars's affair with Venus, ends in humiliation. The collective suicide and the burning of all possessions leave the Roman general without humans and goods to exhibit in a triumphal march. Like the Mars who is made fun of by the gods when caught in Venus's arms through Vulcan's subtle net, Cipión can be perceived as a laughingstock of Fortune. At the moment of victory, the golden net of fiery self-immolation exhibits him as embracing a fading goddess of victory. Only his generous recognition of Numantia's memorable deeds allows him to regain heroic status. As opposed to the comic and lustful Mars, Cipión's final embrace of the city exhibits a tragic grandeur.

Virgil's reference to the love affair between Venus and Mars, which causes Vulcan's baffled care and leads to the lovers' humiliation, is but one of the threads of classical imitation woven by Cervantes into the Mars–Venus references in *La Numancia*. The tradition of the forbidden love between these two deities is such a complex one that Cervantes's text seems to surrender to an eclectic banquet of classical models. Although it is difficult to determine Cervantes's antique models for the Venus–Mars relationship in *La Numancia*, we know from Chapter 4 that Giulio Romano's *Apparition of the Cross to Constantine* is the visual trigger for such recollections. A brief history of the Venus–Mars affair in classical antiquity will underscore some of the many other possibilities available to Cervantes. Homer, in the eighth book of the *Odyssey* (1919, 291–9/8.266–369), has Demodocus sing of Aphrodite/Venus's infidelity. He tells how she lies with Ares/Mars when the lame Hephaestus/Vulcan, her husband, is absent. But he, informed by Phoebus/Apollo of this adulterous affair, creates a fine net of bronze in which he traps the lovers and exposes them to the laughter of the other deities.[3] While Homer combines humor with the joy of narration, other classical authors imbue the tale with symbolic meanings. In Empedocles these gods are examples of the two forces that rule the universe: love and contrariety; in Lucretius, the image of Mars resting in the arms of Venus is iconic in nature, based on paintings or sculptures of his time. Ovid adds to the story that Harmony was the offspring of this love affair;[4] while Plutarch sees this birth as symbolizing the harmony that arises when opposites are tempered.[5] The myth was prized during the Middle Ages and the Renaissance, when mythographers like Fulgentius, Neoplatonists like Marsilio Ficino, and artists like Botticelli made use of the antique tale.

Indeed, Cervantes was not only aware of the many permutations of this tale but also fashioned several versions of this forbidden love in his works. The classical couple can be found not only in *La Numancia* but also in other plays, such as *El gallardo español,* where the Neoplatonic notion of *discordia concors* is discussed through the love of the two gods, and *La casa de los celos,* where the action is ruled by the opposition between the two deities.[6] These deities appear even in Cervantes's poetry. In the *Viaje del Parnaso* the narrator explains that the two main subjects of poetry are love and war: "Llorando guerras o cantando amores" (1984b, 56). He also includes the customary opposition between the softness of Venus and the harshness of Mars:

pintando en la palestra rigurosa
las acciones de Marte, o entre (las) flores,
las de Venus, más blanda y amorosa.
(1984b, 56)

These words echo Cipión's harangue in *La Numancia.* In Cervantes's sonnet "Al *Romancero* de Pedro de Padilla," there is a Venus–Mars conjunction. The poetic voice praises Padilla because he sings of Venus's child, Cupid, with "dulce fuerza y arte." The oppositions sweetness and force in this verse relate to the harmony between Venus and Mars. But Padilla's verse is particularly admirable because, having sung of love, the poet can turn to the "duro Marte" and write of "las fieras armas y el valor sobrado" (1981, 2.350; see also Schevill and Bonilla 1922, 6.36). There is thus a double conjunction of these deities, first in the harmony between sweetness and valor and second in the ability to compose works of love and texts of war.

These two pagan deities also appear in at least two of the *Novelas ejemplares.* In *El celoso extremeño,* Peter Dunn explains that even though Carrizales's discovery of Leonora and Loaysa embracing repeats the iconography of Vulcan's discovery of Venus and Mars, Cervantes fails to follow the Renaissance mythographers' interpretations: "Cervantes, al revés que los mitógrafos renacentistas como Cartari, Conti o Ripa, no tiene interés en resucitar al mito pagano como un esquema coherente de la experiencia" (1973, 103). Here, life surpasses myth. *La española inglesa,* on the other hand, establishes a close link between the mythographers, the Neoplatonic thinkers, and the myth, according to Karl Ludwig Selig (1967). The same can be said for Cervantes's last work, *Persiles y Sigismunda.* In the novel as in the works of the mythographers, Venus and Mars personify lustful love and war.[7] There are other oppositions here that are also found in *La Numancia*: the opposition between Mars and a Christian Mars, as well as the rift between "las blanduras de Venus" and chaste love.

Don Quijote is hardly an exception to the proliferation of the tale. When the knight becomes embroiled in a net of green thread, he exclaims: "Pues mándoles yo que aunque estas redes, si como son hechas de hilo verde, fueran de durísimos diamantes, o mas fuertes que aquella con que el celoso dios de los herreros enredó a Venus y a Marte, así las rompiera como si fueran de juncos marinos, o de hilachas de algodón" (1978, 2.58.476). Helmut Hatzfeld argues that the humanization of myth found in this passage is similar to what appears in Velázquez's paintings (1952, 277–8).[8] And yet, Cervantes is not superimposing humanity on myth but adding a mythical ambience to Don Quijote's adventures. I would thus argue that the reference elevates the adventure not only in the knight's own eyes but also in the minds of his listeners. This raising of expectations through mythical means, however, often serves to bring down Cervantes's comic hero. In the very same chapter in which Don Quijote alludes to the Mars–Venus affair, he also refers to Cipión. Telling how the Roman general can transform a bad omen into a spur for battle, the knight shows how the hero can surpass his fate (1978, 2.58.274). But Don Quijote does not follow his own advice not to heed omens. He is particularly vainglorious in this chapter, having received a good omen ("buen agüero" [1978, 2.58.473]). He thus tells the inhabitants of this feigned Arcadia that he will defend them against any "threats" coming down the road toward them for the next two days. The knight and the squire are soon trampled by a "tropel de los toros bravos" (1978, 2.58.481).

In the fifteenth chapter of Part 1, don Quijote accepts defeat, claiming that because he fought against those who were not knights, the god of war, Mars, punished him (1978, 1.15.192). Sancho is designated by don Quijote to fight *villanos*. But the squire, chastened by many blows, claims he is an "hombre pacífico, manso, sosegado" (1978, 1.15.193). Against the harshness of war, he fashions an image of softness derived from Venus. Don Quijote warns him against such an attitude, arguing that if the winds of fortune lead him to acquire an island, Sancho must learn to do battle if he is to rule there. Newly conquered kingdoms or provinces ("reinos y provincias nuevamente conquistados" [1978, 1.15.193]) require forceful rulers.

In *La Numancia*, the Romans have been unable to conquer precisely because they have given themselves to the soft influence of Venus. Cipión's exhortation foregrounds the opposition between Venus and Mars and leads his troops to understand that the winds of fortune, the winds of war, will only be propitious if the army embraces the god of war alone. Cipión's lines "La blanda Venus con el duro Marte / jamás hacen durable ayuntamiento" (vv. 89–90) would lead a learned audience to ponder a veritable catalogue of possibilities. However, most models could be rejected from the start. The passage lacks the humor of Homer's *Odyssey*. It also goes counter to Ovid's and Plutarch's tales of the birth of Harmony, since Cipión is rejecting the union of Venus and Mars. For the same reason, astrological explanations of conjunctions and the Neoplatonists' notion of *discordia concors* would have to be excluded from the interpretation. Empedocles' notion that these two forces rule the cosmos would lead to an allegorization of Cipión's words, something that Renaissance mythographers were particularly fond of. It is certainly plausible to see the siege of Numantia as the triumph of the principle of discord. After all, the elemental imagery of the play owes its first impulse to Empedocles' classification of the four elements. A more didactic approach would envision the Roman army as representing contrariety and the Numantians as proto-Christians embodying the principle of love. But Cervantine ambiguity as to the ethics of each camp would break down such a construction.

It may be that the apparent eclecticism of the Mars–Venus scene disguises a particular model. To write is to conceal, claims Johannes Sturm in *Nobilitas liberata* (1549): "For he ought to be a hider of his Arte which would be a good imitator" (Hamilton 1990, 14). This concealment provides the reader with the joy of discovery. As noted above, the *Fourth Georgic* includes both the portrayal of Proteus and the tapestry of the love of Venus and Mars. This juxtaposition alerts the reader/audience to a Virgilian connection. We have seen how Act 1 of *La Numancia* blends both the *Aeneid* and the *Fourth Georgic* in order to create Proteus's prophecy. The Venus–Mars imagery in Cipión's allocution also has a double Virgilian model. While Aristaeus is astonished at the tapestries depicting the Mars–Venus affair in the *Georgics*, Aeneas is "lost in amazement" (1991, 19/1.495) as he gazes at the depiction of the Trojan War in Juno's temple. So great is his astonishment that he fails to notice Dido's entrance. Whereas he is in awe at the depictions of war, the queen is amazed at his presence: "Dido of Sidon was amazed at her first sight of him" (1991, 23/1.613). While Aeneas gazes at scenes of war, she gazes at a human figure. The scene is set for a collision between the cares of love and the constraints of war, between Venus and Mars.

Cipión's entrance into his new army's camp also triggers such a conflict. The Roman general expounds on the Venus–Mars opposition:

ella regalos sigue, él sigue el arte
que incita a daños y furor sangriento.
La cipria diosa estése agora aparte,
deje su hijo nuestro alojamiento
que mal se aloja en las marciales tiendas
quien gusta de banquetes y meriendas.
(vv. 91–6)

The gifts, banquets, and festivities of Venus are as evident in Dido's palace as in Cipión's Roman camp. The Phoenician queen wishes to welcome Aeneas in opulence and style: "Meanwhile the inside of her palace was being prepared with all royal luxury and splendor. They were laying out a banquet in the central hall and the draperies were of proud purple, richly worked" (1991, 24/1.637–9). Although the Carthaginians were renowned for their martial deeds, Dido's banquet leads her away from the cares of Mars and into the arms of Venus. All that remains of the mettle of war is the silverware: "The silver was massive on the tables, with the brave deeds of their ancestors embossed in gold, a long tradition of feats of arms traced through many heroes from the ancient origins of the race" (1991, 24/1.640–2).

When she first enters and before she sees Aeneas, Dido is described as a figure akin to the goddess Diana, known for her warlike hunting: "She carries her quiver on her shoulder, and as she walks, she is the tallest of all the goddesses. . . . Dido was like Diana, and like Diana she bore herself joyfully among her people, urging on their work for the kingdom that was to be" (1991, 19/1.500, 503–4). Thus, Dido and her followers are very much like the women of Numantia, who toil for their city and imitate the goddess of the hunt (v. 2105). But the wiles of Venus soon transform Dido's temperament. In order for the influence of passion to conquer the Diana-like queen, Venus disguises her son Cupid to look like Ascanius, Aeneas's child. Each time Dido caresses the boy, she is fingering the fires of passion (1991, 25/1.673). As the "fire within her grew" (1991, 26/1.713), so did the Venus-like feasting. In the *Aeneid*, like in *La Numancia*, the goddess of love is accompanied by the god of drink and revelry. Toasting to Aeneas and his men with a bowl filled with wine, the Phoenician queen commands: "Let Bacchus, giver of good cheer, be among us" (1991, 27/1.734). Whereas Dido calls for the god to assist Venus, Cipión warns that martial prowess cannot coexist with either deity:

Vosotros os vencéis, que estáis vencidos
del bajo antojo y femenil, liviano,
con Venus y con Baco entretenidos,
sin que a las armas estendáis la mano.
(vv. 121–4)[9]

Dido's Bacchic feast will eventually turn into a Bacchic furor, once she discovers that her loved one is false: "Driven to distraction and burning with passion, she raged and raved round the whole city like a Bacchant" (1991, 90/4.300–2). Her passion will then have both a constructive and a destructive aspect. The latter recalls the frenzied dismemberment of Bacchic orgies.

Cipión represses the Venus instincts in himself and in his army so as to concentrate solely on masculine aggressiveness and power. He must destroy Dido/Venus in order to accomplish his heroic task. In the second act, one of the Numantians, Leoncio (whose very name suggests lion-like power), questions his friend Marandro using words that recall Cipión's harangue to his army:

¿No es ir contra la razón,
siendo tü tan buen soldado,
andar tan enamorado
en tan estraña ocasión?
Al tiempo que del dios Marte
has de pedir el favor
¿te entretienes con amor
que mil blanduras reparte?
(vv. 709–16)

But Marandro responds with another question: "¿hizo el amor, por ventura, / a ningún pecho cobarde?" (vv. 723–4). Through Marandro, the inhabitants of Numantia will embody the ideal of the Renaissance courtier, as Karl Ludwig Selig has noted.[10] Contrary to Aeneas/Cipión, who must destroy Dido/Venus in order to succeed, Marandro can embrace the goddess in the belief that through the reconciliation of opposites a final harmony can be achieved. What we have, then, in *La Numan-cia* is a love that transforms war from a destructive pursuit into a desire for harmony. In this Neoplatonic and Christianized version of the myth, self-sacrifice is stressed. The Homeric sally into the enemy camp, planned by Marandro in Act 3 and executed by him and his friend at the beginning of Act 4,[11] exemplifies the power that comes from joining Venus and Mars. To bring bread to Marandro's beloved, Marandro and Leoncio accomplish a deed so astonishing that it arouses admiration in their Roman enemy. Thus, love (Venus) is a trigger for heroic actions (Mars).

This conjoining of Venus and Mars is present even in the fires of destruction. Teógenes calls the flames that consume the Numantians' possessions a "dulce juego" (v. 1430). Thus, the martial destructive pow-ers are combined with the sweetness and play of Venus. Even the flames carry the licentious ("licenciosa" [v. 1427]) feel of the goddess of love. Toward the end of the third act, one of the Numantians describes all the precious materials that are being consumed in the flames:

Allí las perlas del rosado Oriente,
y el oro en mil vasijas fabricado,
y el diamante y rubí más escelente,
y la estimada púrpura y brocado
en medio del rigor fogoso ardiente
de la encendida llama se ha arrojado.
                    (vv. 1656–61)

Although the flames are now described as rigorous rather than licen-tious, the presence of Venus entwined with Mars is felt in the objects offered to the fire. The first precious object mentioned is the pearl. Let us recall that in Botticelli's *Birth of Venus* the goddess rises from the ocean in a shell, which makes her the embodiment of the pearl.

In his *Venus Vanquishing Mars*, Botticelli shows the goddess wearing a ruby, the fiery red gem of Mars, encircled by pearls. Among the stones tossed into the fire in the third act of *La Numancia* are rubies and dia-monds. The latter creates a kind of *coincidentia oppositorum* since it par-takes of the qualities of both Venus and Mars. Its hardness is often asso-ciated with the god of war and contrasted with the *blanduras* of Venus. On the other hand, it is a gem that symbolizes constancy in love, thus belong-ing to the celestial Venus. These three objects, then, emphasize a Neo-platonic harmony that in Renaissance syncretism was often associated with a Christian vision. Destruction arises from a harmonious union of all the inhabitants of the city and is based on a vision of wholeness. Golden receptacles and purple cloth are also burned in order to connote that the inhabitants of Numantia will not be subjected to foreign rulership or kingship. The Mars–Venus love affair has thus ceased to be an image of the flames of lustful passion and has become a foreshadowing of the collective and loving suicide of the men and women of the Celtiberian city, who together wish to fend off foreign domination. The description of the flames of conjunction prepares the reader/audience for Marandro's heroic feat, his martial endeavors incited by his love for Lira/Venus. Sacrificing himself for his beloved, bringing her bread and his own blood, Marandro symbolizes the Christian Eucharist.

Marandro and Cipión thus have very different ideas of Venus. The Roman general perceives only what Ficino would call the bestial Venus, the deity that rules over concubines, wantonness, lust, and luxury; the Numantian envisions a higher goddess. In turning away from epic and toward the mysteries of mythology, the Numantian sacrifice of Marandro for his beloved Lira will open up numerous textualities based on the mythographers, the Neoplatonists, and even Renaissance art. The ashes that remain from the destruction of Numantia point to the textual ashes of a multitude of artistic and literary models. Two manners of imitation thus vie with one another through the Mars–Venus interlude. On the one hand, the imitation of two Virgilian poems (the *Aeneid* and the *Fourth Georgic*) together with Homer's *Iliad* provides the substance of the episodes; on the other, eclectic reminiscences of a series of texts (con)-fused within the ashes of Numantia add sparkles of contextual creativity to *La Numancia.*

Love and war coalesce in the flames of destruction. Although banishing Venus and Bacchus from his camp, Cipión is still possessed by desire. His new Venus is the city of Numantia.[12] His martial spirit strives to conquer her. But she longs for a different Aeneas, for a leader who will not use his guile to lead her into surrender. The Numantians believe that the Romans, the sons of Dardanius, do not have a pious and honorable leader with whom they can deal. The Romans are, in Caravino's words:

¡Pérfidos, desleales, fementidos,
crueles, revoltosos y tiranos,
ingratos, codiciosos, mal nacidos,
pertinaces, feroces y villanos,

adúlteros, infames, conocidos
por de industriosas, mas cobardes manos!
(vv. 1206–14)

Numantia's damnation of the Romans recalls Dido's cursing of Aeneas. She shouts at him: "You are a traitor. You are not the son of a goddess and Dardanus was not the first founder of your family" (1991, 92/4.365–6). She perceives him as a liar[13] who won her love and is now leaving her. In her bitterness she exclaims: "So much for his pledge" (1991, 100/ 4.597–8). She calls him crueler and harder than the Hycarnian tigers (1991, 92/4.367) and a "monster of wickedness" (1991, 100/4.613) who came to her land shipwrecked and impoverished only to take all her love and riches and flee her land.

Having lost all, Dido has a funeral pyre built in which she will sacrifice herself. Numantia, like Dido, will transform itself into a funeral pyre and perish. Both Dido and Numantia are victims of a foreign hero whose cunning, covetousness, cruelties, and lies bring about their downfall. Both will damn their destroyers, bringing upon them future miseries: Numantia's curse will trigger successive sacks of Rome, and Dido's malediction will bring about the Carthaginian Wars. While the first invokes Attila, the second evokes Hannibal. And, as explained in Chapter 8, both Numantia and Dido, through the image of the phoenix, point to the resurrection that will follow their deaths. Dido as Phoenissa, a term akin to the phoenix, will have an avenger rise from her dead bones (1991, 101/4.625), while the figure of Spain envisions its own *renovatio*: "cual fénix renovándose en la llama" (v. 392).

The fires of war and destruction rage in the Numantian camp during much of Acts 3 and 4. In their Bacchic orgy of destruction, the inhabitants of the Celtiberian city emulate the excesses of the queen of Carthage, who, like "a Bacchant," is "roused to frenzy" (1991, 90/4.300). Both Dido and the inhabitants of the city will end their frenzies when they plunge into the final fire. The fires within Numantia serve to construct the metaphorical funeral pyre that will lead to the city's immolation. They also recall the burning of Troy. In a Homeric/Virgilian manner, the male inhabitants decide to rush out of the city, meet the enemy, and be killed. In Virgil's re-creation of the fall of Troy, Aeneas pronounces a short harangue to some of the soldiers he encounters as the city is being destroyed by the Greeks: "You are the bravest of all our warriors, and your bravery is in vain. If your desire is fixed to follow a man who fights to the end, you see how things stand with us. . . . You are rushing to defend a burning city. Let us die. Let us rush into the thick of the fighting. The one safety for the defeated is to have no hope of safety" (1991, 40/2.348–50, 352–4). In a similar manner, Teógenes exhorts the male inhabitants in the doomed Numantia to go out and fight, knowing that death will come:

Esta noche se muestre el ardimiento
del numantino acelerado pecho,
y póngase por obra nuestro intento,
el enemigo muro sea deshecho,
salgamos a morir a la campaña,
y no como cobardes en estrecho.
Bien sé que sólo sirve esta hazaña
de que a nuestro morir se mude el modo,
que con ella la muerte se acompaña.
                    (vv. 1242–50)

But this Virgilian and martial contest would exclude the feminine. The women would be left behind. To underline the need for a Venus–Mars concordance in the Numantian camp, four women with their babies arrive: "Entran cuatro mujeres de Numancia, cada una de ellas con un niño en brazos y otros de las manos" [p. 87]). The quaternity created is a symbol of harmony. Lira, whose musical name also underlines harmony, accompanies them. The women of Numantia refuse to be left behind:

¿Resolvéis aun todavía
en la triste fantasía
de dejarnos y ausentaros?
¿Queréis dejar, por ventura,
a la romana arrogancia
las vírgenes de Numancia
para mayor desventura?
¿Y a los libres hijos vuestros
queréis esclavos dejallos?
                    (vv. 1307–15)

The women's lament may well derive from classical plays that, like Aeschylus's *Persians,* show a siege from the perspective of the vanquished.[14] Euripides' *Trojan Women* evokes the burning and destruction of the city from the captive women's perspective. According to Angela Belli (1979), the structure of this Greek tragedy and many of its motifs

served as models for Cervantes's play. Euripides' tragedy was later imitated by Seneca in his *Troades*. In spite of repeated rejections of Senecan
influence on Golden Age theater, Flavia Marín (1994) has shown striking parallels between Seneca's tragedy and *La Numancia*. Indeed, Seneca
would have been much more accessible to Cervantes than Euripides.[15]
However, it must be emphasized that in both classical tragedies, the
women are made captive. In *La Numancia*, the women speak to prevent
such an occurrence. It is the women's perspective that leads Teógenes to
come up with a new plan: the death and suicide of all the inhabitants of
the city. In Seneca's *Troades*: "The flames check not the victor's greedy
hands; Troy is plundered even as she burns" (1979, 1.18–19); but in *La
Numancia*, the burning of all possessions will preclude the final looting.
Both the death of the inhabitants of the city and the destruction of their
possessions will prevent the Romans from triumphing over them. No
slaves and no gold will remain to take back to Rome in a triumphal
parade. The fires of destruction are prepared:

En medio de la plaza se haga un fuego,
en cuya ardiente llama licenciosa
nuestras riquezas todas se hechen luego,
desde la pobre a la más rica cosa.
(vv.1426–9)

At the beginning of Act 4, Quinto Fabio describes the feats of Marandro and Leoncio in terms of fire:

No con tanta presteza el rayo ardiente
pasa, rompiendo el aire en presto vuelo,
ni tanto la cometa reluciente
se muestra ir presurosa por el cielo
como estos dos por medio de tu gente
pasaron. . . .
(vv. 1764–9)

Their sally into the Roman camp is like the lightning bolt that ruptures
the air or the comet that splits the heavens. Marandro and Leoncio pre-
figure the Numantians' moral victory over the Romans since the lightning bolt is the weapon used by the father of the gods, Jupiter, to destroy
those who offend him. By wielding it metaphorically, Marandro acquires
authority for his people. The comet, on the other hand, is often considered an evil omen and appears thusly in Seneca's tragedies.[16]

In a *contaminatio* filled with irony, the Marandro and Leoncio sally (an episode modeled after the exploit of two Greek heroes, Odysseus and Diomedes) is incorporated within a Virgilian–Senecan action that laments the fall of Troy. In Seneca's *Troades* the Homeric heroes are described as "the crafty Ithacan" and "the night-prowling comrade" and compared to the "lying Sinon" (1979, 1.38–9), but in *La Numancia* Marandro and Leoncio are the heroic but vanquished warriors whose valor is exemplary. Through this seemingly senseless joining of opposites, the play strives toward a vision of harmony, which can only be found in the absence of war. By mingling within the fires of Numantia the countless wars that have been fought and the countless heroes who through valor or cunning have made a name for themselves, the text is illuminating both the epic nature of the pursuit and its ultimate futility. Against the backdrop of the rise and fall of empires, the Spanish vision of imperial domination both acquires a myth of origins and becomes one more episode in a seemingly endless succession of violence.

The horrors of war are evinced through the appearance of three allegorical figures: "sale una mujer, armada con una lanza en la mano y un escudo, que significa la guerra, y trae consigo La Enfermedad y La Hambre" (p. 111). For Fernando Cantalapiedra, these figures invite reflection: "De este modo, Cervantes está obligando a su (posible) espectador a una doble reflexión sobre las consecuencias de la Guerra" (1994, 388).[17] Indeed, the figure of war acknowledges that others criticize her endeavor: "Que yo, que soy la poderosa Guerra, / de tantas madres detestada en vano" (vv. 1992–3). Given that a series of mothers carrying their threatened children have been portrayed upon the stage, this criticism becomes particularly poignant. War proceeds to extol the "sweetness" of Spanish bellicose valor: "en la dulce ocasión que estén reinando / un Carlos, y un Filipo y un Fernando" (vv. 1198–9). War's laudatory evocation of three Spanish kings is made while this figure is surrounded by personifications of hunger and disease. War is also responsible for the mothers' laments over their children. Thus, the "sweetness" of imperial expansionism has been tainted with the horrors of war.

As Brian Stiegler has pointed out, the allegorical figures of War, Hunger, and Disease constitute, together with Death, the four horsemen of the Apocalypse, lending *La Numancia* a texture of the end of time (1996, 571). These allusions point once again to a doubling of history within the play. Cervantes's tragedy, written sometime in the 1580s, reflects the numerous predictions and astrological forecasts that centered on the ominous year of 1588. Michel Nostradamus predicted in 1566 that "in the year five hundred fourscore more or less there shall be a strange age" (Kagan 1990, 94). Richard L. Kagan adds: "Astrologers were more precise, predicting that 1588 would be a year of cataclysm because of one solar eclipse, two lunar eclipses and a grand conjunction, a rare astronomical alignment of Saturn, Jupiter and Mars . . . Throughout the continent, therefore, 1588 was anticipated as the 'wonder year,' a time of great changes, perhaps even the end of the world" (1990, 94). It is no coincidence that the three pagan deities named in the astronomical alignment used to prophesy the ocurrences of 1588 influence the action of *La Numancia.*[18] In the years when Cervantes was composing his play, clairvoyants and street prophets in Madrid announced impending doom. Miguel de Piedrola, for example, announced that the "great events of 1588" would lead to the "imminent destruction of Spain" (Kagan 1990, 96). As mentioned before, Lucrecia de León dreamed of the destruction of the Spanish Armada a year before the actual event. But she went beyond this dire prophecy to claim that all of Spain would be lost to foreign invaders: "Moors take up residence in the royal palace, churches are looted, and their contents destroyed. . . . she sees a seven-headed dragon – the seven deadly sins – breathing fire across Spain" (Kagan 1990, 76–7). Those who believed her dream visions prepared "survivalist bunkers" in caves along the Tagus River (Kagan 1990, 78).

But *La Numancia* not only mirrors the apocalyptic events predicted for 1588 but also incorporates in its doubling of history another moment that triggered visions of the end of the world. The sack of Rome in 1527, prophesied by the river Duero, brought about a series of apocalyptic predictions. After all, the desecration of the Vatican, a fleeing pope, the destruction of religious relics, and the very sack of the "Eternal" City were unthinkable events. The apocalyptic figures that accompany the destruction of Numantia also accompany the sack of Rome and the prophesied fall of Madrid. Although Cervantes's play foretells the rise of a great Spanish Empire, it accompanies such predictions with threats of its downfall. That Rome and Madrid would fall just like Numantia recalls the cyclical theory of empires. Authors like Tommasso Campanella, Pedro Salazar de Mendoza, and José Pellicer asserted that Spain had become a universal monarchy, following the Assyrians, the Persians, the Greeks, and the Romans (Jover 1949, 362–3).[19] But if this was the case, would not Spain suffer the fate of the other empires?

Virgil's triumphant *Fourth Eclogue* as well as the prophecies within his *Aeneid* had declared that Rome would have a dominion without end; the city would not fall but would renew itself over and over again. This prophecy not only redeemed Rome from the cyclical theory of empires but also linked the city to the conception of *ekpyrosis*, the periodic generation and destruction of the universe. Against Seneca and the Stoic philosophers, who believed that the universe (and universal empires) had to be periodically purified by fire (or water), Virgil claimed spontaneous *renovatio*. The fires of *La Numancia* evoke an *ekpyrosis* and the destruction and purification of a land so that a new universal empire could arise. Against Virgil's vision, Cervantes's play presents the need for the flames of purification. By opting for this cyclical vision, *La Numancia* also includes the seeds for the destruction of the future Spanish Empire. Cervantes's play emphasizes the cycles through the sack of Rome in 1527. If Spain is to take over from Rome, the *translatio* of power from Rome during Charles V's and Philip II's rule could only mean that Madrid was the next city to suffer siege and destruction by fire. And 1588 was seen by many as the year of the decline and fall of Spain. Indeed, the *plomos de Granada* were discovered in the 1580s. These mysterious parchments found in boxes of lead included an Arabic version of John's Apocalypse, scheduling the end of the world for around the year 1600 (Kagan 1990, 94). Arturo Marasso believes that Cervantes may have alluded to these counterfeit prophecies in *Don Quijote* (1954, 19). The parchments may also be part of the play's palimpsest. *La Numancia* is then both a vision of empire and a warning of possible apocalyptic fall.

By conflating an imperialist Virgilian vision with a Senecan foreshadowing of destruction, Cervantes once again provides the audience with a double vision of history and empire. Such is the artistry of this play that at times the visions are (con)fused in the ashes of destruction. We have seen how it was Virgil who helped to shape images of the fall of Numantia through the tragic episode of Dido's funeral pyre. As Phoenissa, Dido could become an avenging phoenix. In Cervantes's *Numancia*, as in Virgil's *Aeneid*, the avengers would threaten Rome. Seneca's *Troades* also provides Cervantes with a vision of destruction. Although the episode of Bariato in the Spanish play is directly derived from ballads on the subject, it may also mirror the Astyanax tragedy in the *Troades*. Much of the action of Seneca's tragedy centers on Andromache's concern for her child Astyanax. As the son of Hector (the slain Trojan hero) and as the grandson of Priam and Hecuba (the rulers of Troy), he represents the only hope for the rebirth of the city now that the Greeks have destroyed it and killed Hector and Priam. But Andromache dreams of Hector, who warns her to hide the child – the Greeks seek his death. Hiding him in her husband's tomb, Andromache must match her wits against Ulysses/Odysseus's guile. She tries to convince the Greek fighter that the child died in the siege, while he uses his skill with words to discover the truth. In the end, Andromache reveals where Astyanax is hidden but asks for Ulysses' mercy: "learn ye the merciful wrath of Hercules" (1979, 1.730). She thus reminds him that Hercules once took the city of Troy but spared the child Priam, setting him on the throne. Andromache thus praises Ulysses as a new Hercules and "teaches" him to spare her son, just like Hercules spared Priam.

But Hercules has long been dead. Consumed in a funeral pyre much in the same way as Dido, he inhabits the starry firmament. Seneca's *Hercules Oetaeus* describes his death: "The whole forest was piled into a heap; and the logs, starward in layers rising, made all too small a pyre for Hercules. . . . But he, like some huge, suffering lion, which in Libyan forest lying, roars out his pain, hurried along – who would suppose him hasting to the flames?" (1979, 2.1637–8, 1642–4). There may even be a spark of eclectic imitation taken from this play. After all, Numantia as funeral pyre should contain the remains of Hercules since legend ascribed to him the origin of Spanish monarchy.[20] The apocalyptic images of *Hercules Oetaeus* envisioning how "the southern skies shall fall upon Libya's plains" (1979, 2.1104–5), how the sun itself shall fall, and how even the gods will find death suggest the *ekpyrosis* that brings about the end of a universal cycle.[21] In *La Numancia* a city that imitates the valor of Hercules is also engulfed in an apocalyptic and fiery destruction. But there is a chance that not all the Numantians will die in this conflagration. The child Bariato runs to a tower accompanied by his friend Servio. The latter drops to the ground, overcome by starvation. Bariato warns him: "ahí te habrá de acabar / la hambre, la espada o miedo" (vv. 2134–5). But he continues to run toward the tower:

Yo voyme, que ya temo
lo que el vivir desbarata,
o que la espada me mata,
o que en el fuego me quemo.
　　　(vv. 2136–9)

Bariato has escaped the sword of the Numantian soldiers, the flames of destruction, and the apocalyptic horsemen of famine, war, and pestilence. As he climbs the tower of survival, the Romans gain a captive, one they can parade through Rome as a signal of their triumph.

In the *Troades*, the opposite movement occurs.[22] Ulysses will not act like a merciful Hercules. His craftiness overcomes generosity as he considers that a survivor from the Trojan royal family could reignite the conflict in the distant future. He thus acquiesces to the child's murder. Cipión's cleverness has the opposite result since he sees in the survival of the child Bariato a chance for Rome to triumph. While Bariato rushes to the tower in fear of death, Astyanax is led up to the one high tower remaining in Troy so that he can be thrown to his death: "with stately steps the Ithacan makes his way, leading by the hand the little grandson of Priam; and with no lagging step does the boy approach the lofty walls" (1979, 1.1089–91). These two actions, so contrary in movement, coalesce as the two boys, Bariato and Astyanax, stand atop the tower. About to be hurled down by Ulysses, Astyanax exhibits his "undaunted spirit" (1979, 1.1092). Although in the enemy's grasp, the boy "was proudly bold" (1979, 1.1096). Bariato, surrounded now by Roman troops as he stands upon the tower, comes to terms with his own fear of death and is imbued with the spirit of Numantia: "Yo heredé de Numantia todo el brío" (v. 2367). Just as Astyanax "of his own will leaped" from Troy's highest tower (1979, 2.1102) and in sight of all the Greek warriors, so Bariato leaps to his death as Cipión and the Romans witness the fall of the last Numantian. As opposed to Virgil's version of the destruction of Troy, where Aeneas is seen to carry on the spirit of the city, the *Troades* ends in a lament of total defeat. The captive Hecuba laments: "A maiden and a boy have fallen; the war is done. But I, whither shall I betake my tears? . . . Daughter or grandson, husband or country – which shall I lament?" (1979, 2.1166–7, 1169).

No one is left to lament in *La Numancia* since there are no captive women or children. The lament comes from the enemy camp, from Cipión, the proud Roman general who has been denied a great victory by the valiant actions of the Numantians. In his last words, Bariato explains why he and the city have been able to defeat the mighty enemy: "el amor perfeto y puro / que yo tuve a mi patria tan querida" (vv. 2398–9). Numantia's martial deeds arise out of a pure love for the homeland, out of the celestial Venus, who has joined Mars in a union so perfect that it will bring about the birth of a new empire. Harmonia, the daughter of Venus and Mars, is thus reborn as the Spanish Empire.

And yet, victory has come about through suicide. In the conjoining of Dido's desperate death with the valiant actions of a heroic child, Astyanax, Cervantes's text exhibits the scattering of the sparks of war. Heroism and futility, passion and covetousness, vengeance and celestial love, all mix in this funeral pyre where tragic and epic flames commingle in the textual ashes of Homer, Virgil, and Seneca. Out of these textual remains arises the phoenix of fame. By assigning the last words in the play to this figure, the text points to the construction of history, to the fabrication of myths of empire as the worthy deeds of the poets/ prophets – fame is spread through their voices. But the text also warns that the poetic voices of fame are just that, an edifice of words, a false archeology of lost cities. From the ashes of ancient grandeur, *La Numancia* constructs fabled visions of passion, lies, harmony, and horror with which to warn, console, and even praise the possessors of a new empire.

10

Cicero/Macrobius
Intimations of immortality

From the textual ashes of the ancients, scattered through the fires of Numantia, rises a new phoenix, the figure of Fame. She embodies the last of the four elements, air, and conforms to the typical Renaissance representation: a winged figure who travels through this element carrying her news. In *La Numancia*, she speaks of her "presuroso vuelo" (v. 2430). Like other representations of the figure, Cervantes also endows her with a trumpet, a wind instrument, and a clear voice with which to announce great deeds to the world. Fame's first words in the play further emphasize sound/air:

Vaya mi clara voz de gente en gente
y en dulce y suavísimo sonido
llene las almas de un deseo ardiente
de eternizar un hecho tan subido.

(vv. 2417–20)

The result of her trumpet call and her words is to create a fiery wish in the souls of the listeners. The flames that have consumed the city produce a desire to render eternal the tragic events. The upper elements (air and fire) will construct an "eternal" tale out of destruction. What survives, then, are not the deeds of the past but the poet's words that reconstruct these events.

In the first act, Cipión had hoped, "Vuestras promesas no se lleve el viento" (v. 205) – that his soldiers' promises to reform themselves and conquer Numantia, would not be dispelled by the wind. But fire has conspired with air to do just that, since the Numantians can exceed the upper elements. For example, the raid by Marandro and Leoncio shows that they are faster than fire: "No con tanta presteza el rayo ardiente / pasa, rompiendo el aire en presto vuelo" (vv. 1764–5). Nor are the Numantians afraid of the elements. By destroying their own city with fire, they preclude a Roman victory. The Numantians win through the use of the upper elements, and these very forces become an emblem for the Romans' loss. Witnessing the destruction of the city, the Roman Mario concludes: "pues en humo y viento son tornadas / las ciertas esperanzas de vitoria" (vv. 2261–2). While their victory becomes insubstantial smoke and wind, the admirable deeds of Numantia are carried through the air by Fame: "el valor de Numancia, único, solo, / de Batro a Tile, de uno a el otro polo" (vv. 2431–2).[1] With these two exotic locations, Fame grounds air and fire and allows the other elements and the people of the world to partake of Numantia's "immortality." Tile (Tule) is an archipelago and represents water; the Bactrians from Asia stand for earth. Indeed, the mention of Bactria may trigger remembrance of Lucan's *Pharsalia* since both Bactra and the river Bactros have an important role in the epic poem.[2] And we have seen how Lucan's verses denote earth through necromancy.

Fame, then, appears in *La Numancia* as a figure of closure, summarizing the elemental struggle and pointing to the victors and the losers. This closure, however, is paradoxically dependent on the future:

Indicio ha dado esta no vista hazaña
del valor que en los siglos venideros
tendrán los hijos de la fuerte España,
hijos de tales padres herederos.

(vv. 2433–6)

The valor of Numantia will be inherited by an empire that will exude strength. The growth of Spain out of the ashes of the destroyed city will be fostered by the words of Fame. Cervantes included a similar figure in a poem written shortly after rumors of the defeat of the Spanish Armada by the English reached Spain in the summer of 1588.[3] Here, Fame is ordered to fly to the commanders of the Armada ("Bate fama veloz, las prestas alas" [1981, 2.359]) and infuse them with new valor. Countering the foretellings of disaster, the poem envisions a happy ending:

Canción, si vas despacio do te envío,
en todo el cielo fío
que has de cambiar por nuevas de alegría
el nombre de canción en prophecía.

(2.364)[4]

As in *La Numancia*, Fame strives to transform a tragic event into a happy one, using her words to accomplish this purpose. But while the poem wishes Fame to change the course of the naval battle and thus make the poem into a triumphal prophecy, in *Numancia* the outcome cannot be changed. Although closure is partially dependent on the future, on the prophetic powers of the river Duero and of Fame, the latter categorically asserts: "demos feliz remate a nuestra historia" (v. 2448). This happiness arises out of the knowledge spread by the winged allegory that the Roman enemy has been weakened by Numantia's valor and will be eventually brought down as Spain emerges as the heir of universal empire. Fame's prophetic powers fail in Cervantes's poem because the Armada is lost. In *La Numancia*, the river Duero's prophecies are at best ambiguous. What about Fame's words? Should the reader/spectator be moved to accept her closing statement as the final "message" of the action and leave the text or theater with an acceptance of this optimistic vision?

There is yet another representation of Fame in Cervantes's writing, one that would lead us to scrutinize with even more care the allegorical figure that ends the play. In the sixth chapter of the *Viaje del Parnaso*, the poetic voice, the fictional Miguel de Cervantes, narrates a dream he experiences. In it, a gigantic yet beautiful damsel sits on a throne attended by two nymphs. She has inspired the construction, Cervantes is told, of many of the great edifices of the past:

¿No has oído decir los memorables
arcos, anfiteatros, templos, baños,
termas, pórticos, muros admirables,
que, a pesar y despecho de los años,
haciendo al tiempo y a la muerte engaños?
                    (1984b, 141)

This passage not only reflects Cervantes's interest in the archeological recovery of ancient ruins but also testifies to the enduring character of these antique buildings and monuments.

When the fictional Cervantes cannot guess who this woman might be, the guide calls him an "ingenio lego" (1984b, 142), prompting future critics to accept this self-created legend of his lack of learning. The guide then provides him with yet another hint, telling Cervantes that she has also motivated the heroic actions of men such as Mucius Scaevola and Marcus Curcius.[5] Finally, the guide reveals to the dreamer that the mysterious woman is Vanagloria (1984b, 143). The "nymphs" who attend her are False Praise (Adulación) and Lies (Mentira) (1984b, 143). According to Elias Rivers, she serves to "satirize in a very general way the presumptuousness of Spanish poets" (1991, 220). She can also be viewed as a figure akin to Fame. The fame achieved by poets, then, may be nothing but vainglory.[6] A similar judgment can be leveled against classical heroes. If ancient deeds of valor partake of falseness and lies, what is the reader/spectator to make of the Fame that closes *Numancia?*

Although seeming to demand a joyful closure, the words of Fame in Cervantes's play may be seen in a different light when studied in terms of *aemulatio.* There is, I will contend, a contest here between this allegorical figure and the concept of fame as depicted in Cicero's *Dream of Scipio.* Indeed, the oneiric passage in the *Viaje del Parnaso* could well be inspired by Cicero's text and the main commentary on it. Canto 6 of Cervantes's poem begins with a description of the causes of dreams. Macrobius's commentary on *The Dream of Scipio* was one of the most important sources for the classification of oneiric phenomena during the Middle Ages and the Renaissance. Macrobius separates the nightmare and the apparition from dreams that have prophetic significance. The former, he notes, are caused by "mental or physical distress, or anxiety about the future" (1952, 88). Cervantes's examples of nonprophetic dreams in the *Viaje del Parnaso* include all of these categories. The person who is ill and dreams of a cure is reflecting physical distress. The warrior who battles in his sleep, the lover who meets his beloved, and the miser who dreams of treasure are not only reflecting mental distress but also anxiety over the future. Like Macrobius, Cervantes admits that dreams can also be prophetic: "toca en revelaciones" (1984b, 136).[7]

While Macrobius creates a classification for dreams and discusses many of their causes, Cicero says only that "it frequently happens that our thoughts and conversations react upon us in dreams" (1952, 70).[8] He gives as an example Ennius's oneiric experience. Juan Luis Vives provides an explanation for this reference: "Y así aconteció que, como por algún tiempo no tenía en sus labios ni tenía en su mente más que la continua obsesión con Homero, soñó una vez que alternaba con Homero en el Parnaso . . . Fruto y consecuencia de aquel sueño fue que al día siguiente empezó a escribir los *Anales* y aquellos poemas venerables que andan en manos de todos" (1947, 1.638).[9] In the *Viaje del Parnaso* the fictional Cervantes also dreams. As in Cicero, his dream is triggered by his obsessive thoughts on poetry. And, like Ennius, Cervantes's dream is related to Parnassus. While Cicero's and Macrobius's oneiric works discuss at length the notion of fame, Cervantes also uses the dream in order to present a specific trigger for fame, vainglory. Consequently, fame in Cervantes's dreamworld is tinged with a negative motivation. It remains to be seen if Fame in *La Numancia* can also be related to vainglory.

The Dream of Scipio is actually part of Book 6 of Cicero's *Republic*. This work, which is an imitation of Plato's *Republic*, is structured in the form of a dialogue. Scipio gathers in his garden with a group of friends to discuss government and the duties of the statesman. Set in 129 B.C., a year before Scipio's demise, the dialogue has much to say about life after death. Like Plato's *Republic*, where the vision of Er expands the concept of justice to the realms beyond death, Cicero's dialogue includes a dream vision where fame and immortality are discussed. Cicero's *Dream of Scipio* was treated as a separate work throughout the Middle Ages because the oneiric portion of the *Republic* was chosen by Macrobius as the subject of an extended commentary. Replete with Platonic and Neoplatonic materials, including Pythagorean doctrines and many elements from ancient Greek and Roman thought, the *Commentary on the Dream of Scipio* became, according to William Harris Stahl, one of the two most important sources of Platonism "in the Latin West in the Middle Ages" (Macrobius 1952, 10; Bernardo 1962, 9). The book was also a key authority on the interpretation of dreams (as noted above) and an important source for "astronomical and geographical conceptions" (1952, 42, 46).

Macrobius's impact was felt well into the Renaissance. Since Cicero was regarded as one of the major classical writers, Macrobius was often featured as one of his interpreters. In Spain, Juan Luis Vives included in his works a version of Cicero's Latin text along with his own commentary: "No dudo que serán muchos los que, así que vieren u oyeren que voy a comentar el *Sueño de Escipión*, que constituye una parte del libro sexto de *La República*, de Cicerón, pensarán luego al punto que voy a hacer una cosa ya hecha y a tocar un asunto manido, puesto que Macrobio, escritor erudito y no inelegante, escribió dos discretos tratados acerca de este mismo *Sueño*" (1947, 1.630). Knowing that others would immediately compare his text with Macrobius's *Commentary*, Vives chose to avoid direct competition or imitation. He prepared a different type of commentary. Rather than writing a series of short essays on specific lines from Cicero (as Macrobius had done), Vives's *Vigilia al margen del Sueño de Escipión* is a continuous narrative that follows Cicero, expanding and explaining a series of topics. The Spanish humanist underlines two other differences between the commentaries: "Hablaré pues, yo de aquellos pasajes que omitió Macrobio. Lo que él estudió, yo lo estudiaré de otra manera" (1947, 1.631). The Christian vision provided by Vives is part of his innovative response to Cicero. Macrobius, who lived at the end of the fourth and beginning of the fifth century, fails to refer to Christianity in his works and evinces instead a "fondness for pagan antiquities."[10] While Vives sought Christian ideas in Cicero, Macrobius also misread *The Dream of Scipio*. Stahl claims that "Cicero would have been amused at Macrobius' ingenuity in twisting his plain and simple meaning to fit some precise Neoplatonic doctrine" (Macrobius 1952, 12). Vives's reading, however, betrays his knowledge of Macrobius through a series of Neoplatonic interpretations. All three authors, Cicero, Macrobius, and Vives, will impinge upon Cervantes's representation of Fame. It is not my purpose here to disentangle the threads of imitation. I will attempt to explain how, through the *contaminatio* of these three authors, the last soliloquy in *La Numancia* acquires different textures and ranges.

Renaissance thinkers often perceived Scipio in the light of Cicero's text and the commentaries on it. Cicero's *Dream* tells how Scipio goes to Africa to meet with King Masinissa, who had once assisted Scipio the Elder in defeating Hannibal. Indeed, "the aged king could talk of nothing but Scipio Africanus" (1952, 69). Having conversed with him on this subject "far into the night" (1952, 69), the young Scipio dreamed that night that his grandfather Scipio Africanus appeared before him. In a prophetic dream, he is told that he will destroy Carthage and that he "will bring to a close a great war, destroying Numantia" (1952, 70). Or, as we find in Vives' more detailed text: "y luego que hubieres destruído a Cartago . . . harás una dura campaña contra la ciudad de Numancia, destruyéndola y arrasándola del suelo de raíz y cimiento" (1947, 1.596). In the works of Cicero, Macrobius, and even Vives, Scipio attains fame through the destruction of Numantia. Cervantes's text seems to be in competition with this vision. Through *aemulatio*, the Spanish writer transforms an event that brings fame to the Roman general into a tragedy that singles out a small city's valiant struggle with a great empire. Fame will spread the news of Numantia's unique response to Roman power: "con justo intento y presuroso vuelo / el valor de Numancia, único, solo" (vv. 2430–1).

The winged goddess also asserts that she speaks with "lengua verdadera" (v. 2429). And yet, her version of history contradicts the accounts by Appian of Alexandria, Ambrosio de Morales, and Cicero. It follows instead the variant narrated by Anneus Florus. Predictably, Vives's *Vigilia al margen del Sueño de Escipión*, although praising Scipio, also gives the alternate account of Numantia's fall, the one that flatters Spain. According to Vives, Scipio, on entering Numantia, will find "no ninguno prisionero, ni oro, ni plata, ni labrados ni sin labrar, ni género alguno de botín, ni nada en absoluto más que un simulacro vano de la heróica ciudad vencida" (1947, 1.641).

It becomes clear then that *aemulatio* is not just a competition based on poetic technique and inspiration but also a way of constructing new histories and political myths. Events will be presented in a different light, and even changed, in order to favor the Romans or the Spaniards. In contrast to Macrobius's *Commentary*, where Scipio is hailed as the conqueror of Numantia, Juan Luis Vives portrays a city that does not yield triumphal elements to the conqueror. Furthermore, Vives emphasizes Numantia's valor by comparing the city to Sparta: "Esta Numancia . . . no desemejante, ni por sus moradores, ni por sus defensas de Esparta, ciudad de Lacedemonia, sino que Esparta es algún tanto mayor; pero en una y otra sus hombres son de una pasmosa reciedumbre" (1947, 1.641). In contradistinction to Greek and Roman cunning,[11] Numantia and Sparta possess fierceness. *La Numancia* also utilizes a series of comparisons to foreground the city's valor. Very much like the *Aeneid*'s reconstruction of Troy through the myth of Rome, *La Numancia* reconstructs Numantia in order to create a new myth of empire. Fame's veracity has turned out to be a type of fictional mendacity. Different writers compete to spread a particular version of history through the voice of Fame. In the *Viaje del Parnaso*, Vainglory is attended by Lies and Adulation. Could the figure of Fame in *La Numancia* be nothing more than a way to resurrect Spanish vainglory through historical "lies" and the adulation of those who believe in the wars of empire? But is this to be criticized? Must poetry be faithful to history?[12] Today we know that such faithfulness is virtually impossible since history itself partakes of fictionality. Any selection of events or points of view misreads what actually happened. Historical texts also partake of the rhetorical devices utilized in the creation of fiction. Cervantes was well aware of the fluid boundaries not only between poetry and history but also between these pursuits and painting: "La historia, la poesía y la pintura simbolizan entre sí y se parecen tanto, que cuando escribes historia, pintas, y cuando pintas, compones" (1969, 371). Thus, *La Numancia* brings together all three modes, utilizing the paintings of Raphael, the epics of antiquity, and the histories of Rome.

In a fictional re-vision of Numantia from the point of view of Scipio, Carlos Fuentes takes up the relationship between poetry and history,[13] asserting: "la poesía es la luz que descubre la relación existente entre todas las cosas y las religa entre sí. La retórica crea la historia, pero la literatura la salva del olvido. Y, a veces, la eterniza" (1993, 141–2). When envisioning the events that transpired in Numantia, most will remember them not as narrated by Appian but as dramatized by Cervantes. The "eternity" of the city has come about through a fiction. We do not remember the "historical" accounts of the siege of the city (however biased), but what Cervantes envisioned as happening there – his false archeology and his fictional reconstruction of several historical constructions (Appian, Florus, Morales). Analogical thinking imparts a cohesive and compelling meaning to random historical events. Through an elemental play that views the cosmos in terms of a particular siege, *La Numancia* claims a greater authority than history since the play, as Fuentes has argued, "descrubre la relación existente entre todas las cosas y las religa entre sí." *La Numancia* also stands as a poetic work that moves the reader/spectator through a cunning yet wise imitation of the ancients, through a knowledge of how to arouse the appropriate emotions for tragedy and through the grandeur of action and style typical of the ancient epic. These and other elements imbue the text with the spirit of Poetry,[14] an allegorical figure who, in the *Viaje del Parnaso*, can bring about amazing transformations:

Puede pintar en la mitad del día
la noche, y en la noche más escura
el alba bella que las perlas cría.
                    (1984b, 109)

This is one of the great feats of *La Numancia*. In the day of victory, the play can reveal Cipión's dark night of the soul, his tragic lament in failing to find objects or humans with which to triumph. In the tragic night of despair which covers Numantia, the text discovers the dawn of a new age for Spain.

The *Viaje del Parnaso* asserts that, in addition to an "estilo más puro y la elegancia" (1984b, 109), poetry must also be possessed of "divina y moral filosofía" (1984b, 109). How can this be found in a work that partakes of historical mendacity as it attempts to build a new imperial myth? We have seen how, in his construction of a new myth of empire, Cervantes utilizes building blocks from a series of classical writers. Their debate as to the meaning of historical and legendary events is thus replicated within the text of the play. The imperial vision of Virgil is contrasted with the republican leanings of Lucan. Even when voicing the prophecies of empire through a Virgilian deity, the play reveals the meanderings of meaning that inform Proteus's prophecies. Through the theologies and philosophies of Raphael's frescoes, Cervantes points out that only through constant Socratic inquiry can a simulacrum of truth be apprehended.[15] And only through a Vatican of memory and the silences that emerge from a completed journey can the contemplation of the architecture of the ancients yield a more comprehensive structure. The placement of Fame at the end of a text which dramatizes Scipio's famous conquest allows for one more classical context. Cicero, Macrobius, and Vives summarize many of the issues and constructs that emerge from the play. A recapitulation of some of these will serve as a conclusion for this study.

Plato stands at the center of Raphael's *School of Athens* (Fig. 1), holding the *Timaeus* in one hand. Pythagoras's tetractys, in the lower left of the fresco, further emphasizes the numerology of Plato's treatise. According to Stahl, Macrobius's extended discussion on numerology is absent from Cicero's original: "A meager statement about Scipio's life span, couched in prophetic language, starts the author off on one of his most protracted investigations, a study of number lore" (Macrobius 1952, 13). When dealing with numerology, Macrobius's *Commentary* cites profusely both from the *Timaeus* and from Pythagoras's arithmetical investigations.[16] Indeed, the number 4, which is key to Raphael's design and which points to the elemental structure of the *stanze,* is also foregrounded by Macrobius. Alluding to Plato, Macrobius's *Commentary* notes that "the number four is the first of all numbers to have two means" (1952, 104). This led the Creator to bind "the elements together with an unbreakable chain, as was affirmed in Plato's *Timaeus:* in no other way could the elements earth and fire, so opposed and repugnant to each other and spurning any communion of their natures, be mingled together and joined in so binding a union unless they were held together by the two means of air and water" (1952, 105).[17] In a similar fashion, *La Numancia* establishes an "unbreakable chain" through the conjunction of water and earth in the first two acts and fire and air in the latter two. The destruction of the city becomes a universal paroxysm through the juxtaposition of earth (Act 2) and fire (Act 3). Plato had asserted that these two could not be juxtaposed. They must be buffered by one of the two means (air and water). Rather than following a harmonious progression upward, the play brings into contact contrary elements so as to break the harmony and unleash Empedoclean strife, the forces of destruction.[18]

The figure of Philosophy (Fig. 3), allied to *The School of Athens,* preserves the "knowledge of the causes of things." One such cause is discerned in the depiction of Astronomy. The *Commentary on the Dream of Sci-*

pio turns to Plato for astronomical knowledge: "Plato, when speaking in
the *Timaeus* of the eight spheres . . ." (1952, 168). Thus the heavens are
composed of a double quaternity. The "heavenly" ceiling of the Stanza
della Segnatura incorporates two double quaternities, two sets of four
pictures, reflecting the structure of the cosmos. In the theatrical microcosm of *La Numancia*, micro-elemental structures reinforce the double
quaternity of the heavens. As for the causes of war, *La Numancia* points to
the planetary influences found in the "alto, sereno y espacioso cielo" (v.
353). Cipión's repeated invocations to Mars and the Numantians' desire
to propitiate Jupiter are derived, in part, from Cicero and his annotator.
We read in the *Commentary*: "When he [Cicero] calls Jupiter *that brilliant
orb, so propitious and helpful to the human race,* and Mars *the ruddy one,
dreaded on earth,* the words *brilliant* and *ruddy* are appropriate, for Jupiter
glistens and Mars has a ruddy glow; the words are taken from treatises of
those who believe that good and evil come to mortals from the planets,
the evil coming generally from Mars and the good from Jupiter" (1952,
166). *La Numancia* portrays the "celestial" causes of the conflict in terms
of Jupiter and Mars. While Mars was the god that protected the warring
Romans and the deity that had since time immemorial presided over the
city, Jupiter was invoked by the Numantians and later became an image
of Spanish imperial rule. In a doubling of history, the conflict between
these two deities represents the battle between the Roman Vatican and
the Spaniards led by Philip II.

As we have seen previously, Philip II is often viewed critically by Cervantes. As "el segundo Felipo sin segundo" (v. 512), he is numerologically
inauspicious. Macrobius asserts that the number 2 is "separated . . . from
that which is called immovable" (1952, 103). As a number of division and
separation, it is easy to break it apart. It lacks the "mean between two
extremes" (1952, 104) of the number 3 and the double mean of 4.
Indeed, the Pythagoreans, as S. K. Heninger has amply documented, see
it as a number of defectiveness and physicality (1974, 87), relating it to
evil and corruptiveness (1974, 89). Far from being the omnipotent
Jupiter, Philip II becomes, in a numerological scheme, the breaker of
unity, the dissolver of empire, the evil corrupter. The Duero's prophecy
concerning Spain's universal empire is thus not without irony when
placed in the context of Cicero, Macrobius, Pythagoras, and ancient
astronomy/numerology.

Macrobius also takes from Plato, Cicero, and the Neoplatonists the
view of how a soul becomes incarnated. Descending through the planetary spheres the individual acquires those attributes he or she will have

on Earth. Gazing at the wonders of the heavens, Scipio the Younger
yearns to be reunited with his grandfather. But the latter warns: "you and
all other dutiful men must keep your souls in the custody of your bodies
and must not leave this life of men except at the command of the One
who gave it to you" (1952, 72). Macrobius expounds on this section condemning suicide. This lengthy discussion, according to Stahl, "was particularly attractive to readers of the Middle Ages" (1952, 15). Macrobius
shows, among other things: "The difference between death by nature
and by volition is an important one" (1952, 141). The latter breaks
bonds that should be released naturally: "the very compulsion becomes
the occasion of passion, and it is tainted with evil even while it is break-
ing the bonds" (1952, 141). It is clear from Cervantes's play that the
Numantians kill themselves in a Bacchic frenzy of passion. While this
unique action (v. 1431) elicits admiration and propels Fame to sing of
the valor of Numantia, the suicide of these Celtiberians is an evil thing
not only in Christian terms but also in terms of the philosophy of the
ancients.[19] In competing with his ancient models, Cervantes represents
an apparently valorous action that is fraught with theological and philosophical danger. Text and contexts jostle with each other for authority.

The virtuous or evil nature of collective suicide leads us to recall
another fresco from the Stanza della Segnatura, *The Cardinal Virtues* (Fig.
6). Prudence, Temperance, and Fortitude are depicted here. The fourth
cardinal virtue, Justice, appears on the ceiling above. Chapter 8 of the
Commentary on the Dream of Scipio contains a lengthy discussion on these
four virtues. The next six chapters (chapters 9–14) deal with the descent
of the soul to Earth. These chapters include a section condemning suicide (chapter 13). Stahl asserts that "his classification of the virtues, was
one of the most popular portions of Macrobius' work" (1952, 14). Thus,
it may have had an impact both on Raphael and on Cervantes. Plato's
Timaeus, with its cosmology, numerology, and elemental structures, enters
La Numancia through Cicero, Macrobius, and Vives; the same can be said
for the second book that is central to *The School of Athens*. Aristotle stands
next to Plato with the *Ethics* in hand, a work that includes an extended
discussion of the virtues, including prudence, or "practical wisdom." Macrobius's *Commentary* attempts to reconcile a strict definition of these
virtues with Cicero's notion that a statesman can attain to blessedness
through virtue. If virtue belongs to the wise "who search for heavenly
truth" (1952, 120) and thus prudence is nothing more than "to despise
the world and all that is in the world in contemplation of what is divine"

(1952, 121), how can a statesman practice the virtues? Turning to Plotinus and Porphyry, Macrobius explains that each virtue has four levels (a second quaternity): political, cleansing, purified, and exemplary. Defined as "political virtues," the four cardinal principles are at their lowest point. Political prudence, then, encompasses "reason, understanding, circumspection, foresight, willingness to learn, and caution" (1952, 122). In *La Numancia*, Cipión is described in similar terms, but with elements of Greek cunning added: *cordura* (v. 337), *industria* (vv. 1794, 2255), *maña* (v. 2255), and *prudencia* (vv. 2258, 2318). He believes in caution and has learned from Rome's previous encounters with the Numantians that he must not engage them directly.[20] If he lacks foresight, it is only because what the Numantians propose to do goes beyond prudence, understanding, or reason. The Numantians' courage, however, corresponds to the political definition of this virtue as found in Macrobius: "one must exalt his mind above all dread of danger, fear nothing except disgrace, and bear manfully both adversity and prosperity" (1952, 122). Although neither magnanimity nor composure are endowments of courage held by the Numantians, they do exemplify other traits listed by Macrobius, such as "nobleness, constancy, endurance and steadfastness" (1952, 122).

We have seen how this opposition between prudence and courage is at the heart of the definition of what constitutes the central motivation of the epic hero. Juan Luis Vives assigns prudence to the Romans and valor to the Numantians in his *Vigilia al margen del Sueño de Escipión*. The elder Scipio tells his grandson: "y demostrarás que la República Romana está mejor asentada en la ciencia y en el tacto de los caudillos que en la valentía de los soldados" (1947, 1.641). As noted above, Vives describes the Numantians as strong and warlike like the Spartans. They do not share in the Romans' prudence. Macrobius's *Commentary* differs from Vives's *Vigilia* in that it depicts Scipio as combining within the self both *sapientiae* and *fortitudo*: "Since our younger Scipio Africanus, who has just been receiving instructions from his grandfather, belongs to the group of men who both mold their lives according to the precepts of philosophy and support their commonwealths with deeds of valor, he is charged with upholding the highest standards of both modes of life" (1952, 245). Macrobius reflects here the notion that the exemplary hero of the epic ought to combine both of these qualities. In Cervantes's play, Cipión, although leaning toward wisdom, is still at the lowest rung of the ladder. He is attempting to display political wisdom. And yet, his final anagnorisis, when Bariato jumps to his death, may yet lead him to higher realms of virtue. Thus, the play does not end with closure. Neither Cipión's character nor the Fame of the city frames the work.

Let us end with Fame. In *La Numancia* this figure favors the inhabitants of the city, but in Cicero, Macrobius, and Vives she sides with Scipio. The three writers who link Fame with the Roman general expose the fleeting nature of this goddess. Macrobius explains that "in the quest for glory there are two things which may be sought above all others: that the fame reach as far as possible, and that it last as long as possible" (1952, 216). The Romans cannot count on much of a space for fame: "the men of our race occupy only a minute portion of the whole earth, which in comparison with the sky is but a point. . . . Rome herself has not been able to pass the Ganges or cross the Caucasus" (1952, 216).[21] The Duero speech in *La Numancia* attempts to extend the notion of space for the Spanish Empire, claiming for Philip II a universal rule: "siendo suyo el mundo" (v. 511). This statement contradicts sixteenth-century historical realities, evoking a deeply ironic resonance at a time when Spain was surrounded by rival powers, particularly England. It also contrasts with a more accurate (yet still inflated) statement also pronounced by the Duero: "¿Qué envidia, qué temor, España amada / te tendrán mil naciones extranjeras" (vv. 521–2). Through the discovery and conquest of the New World, Spain could claim a larger portion of the world than the Roman Empire, but was still battling other nations close to home, and it still had no knowledge of many of the lands beyond the Caucasus and the Ganges.

As for time, both Cicero and Macrobius describe the constant rise and fall of nations due to floods and conflagrations (1952, 75, 216–19). Vives explains the result of nature's elemental destruction: "La Naturaleza . . . no sufre jamás que las naciones y los reinos tengan estabilidad indefinida. . . . Ello hace que las memorias de las cosas pasadas, no sólo no pueda ser eterna, pero ni siquiera permanente" (1947, 1.668). Indeed, no hero or empire has fame lasting even one year – by which Cicero and Macrobius mean a Great Year. This cosmic year is based on either the precession of the equinoxes (Hipparchus) or "when all the stars and constellations in the celestial sphere have gone from a definite place and returned to it" (Plato, Cicero, Macrobius [Macrobius 1952, 221]). It was computed to last either 15,000 or 36,000 solar years. The Stoics claimed that the universe was periodically destroyed by earth and fire in order to be reconstituted again. In *La Numancia*, the apocalyptic figures and the prevalence of fire point to *ekpyrosis*, to the destruction of a civilization and of the cosmos. Although the figure of Fame says that it will spread knowledge of the city's feats, the Ciceronian contexts lead any learned reader or audience to question how long this fame will last. Granted that it will last close to eighteen hundred years (from the fall of Numantia to the flowering of the Spanish Empire at the end of the sixteenth century), this is but one-twentieth of a precessional year. Curiously, Cicero uses this fraction of the Great Year in his text, claiming that "not a twentieth part of that year has yet elapsed" since Romulus founded Rome and ascended to heavens (1952, 75).[22]

Cicero concludes that earthly fame pales in relation to the eternal: "How insignificant will be that human glory which can scarcely endure for a fraction of a year? . . . Let Virtue, as is fitting, draw you with her own attractions to the true glory" (1952, 76). Juan Luis Vives echoes this thought. Scipio is advised to turn away from "un cierto blando y pegadizo amor de la gloria" (1947, 1.664). He ought to turn his attention to the heavens: "Levanta tu ánimo y tu mente a esas celestiales realidades" (1947, 1.664). The Scipio of Cicero, Macrobius, and Vives drinks deeply from his grandfather's learning. The only one who teaches Cipión in *La Numancia* is the child Bariato, as he jumps from the tower:

Tú con esta caída levantaste
tu fama, y mis vitorias derribaste.
. . . .
Lleva, pues, niño, lleva la ganancia
y la gloria que el cielo te prepara,
por haber, derribándote, vencido
al que, subiendo, queda más caído.
          (vv. 2406–7, 2413–16)

Although there are traces of anagnorisis in Cipión's generous speech as he acknowledges the child's power over him, it is uncertain whether he will attain to the understanding of his contextual self.

There is no question that the play stresses earthly glory and fame. Following Cipión's concession that the child has acquired for Numantia fame and glory, the winged figure of Fame arrives to reassert the claim and end the action. We have seen how such a figure can be equated with vainglory. Even don Quijote, the knight who has often been accused of vainglory, contrasts fame with eternity: "Puesto que los cristianos, católicos y andantes caballeros más debemos de atender a la gloria de los siglos venideros, que es eterna en las regiones etéreas y celestes, que a la vanidad de la fama, que en este presente y acabable siglo se alcanza; la cual fama, por much que dure, en fin se ha de acabar con el mesmo mundo, que tiene su fin señalado" (1978, 2.8.96). And yet, *La Numancia* emphasizes precisely this perishable notion rather than the Platonic or Christian eternity. The Spanish text thus battles with contexts that assert that there is a higher virtue than political prudence or courage and that Fame pales in the light of eternity. Why is *La Numancia* so anxious to defeat its ideological models and proclaim the triumph of Fame, a figure tainted with vainglory in other texts by Cervantes? Why is this figure straining for closure in a text that delights in Socratic questionings and oppositions?

In *La verdad embadurnada*, Juan Luis Vives portrays public Fame as a mendacious monster: "La fama pública, que es un monstruo de muchas cabezas, libre, licensiosa, desbocada, sin freno, descomedida, gran maestra de errores, inventará, fingirá, compondrá, arreglará, retocará la *Verdad* todo cuanto se le antojare" (1947, 1.891). If Fame can alter truth, then the figure in Cervantes's play could, like Proteus, partake of mendacity. But why is she allowed to have the last word? Vives adds: "Los . . . poetas, si lo pusieren por escrito, no quedarán incursos en responsabilidad ni fraude" (1947, 1.891). Poets, then, often borrow from the false words of Fame to fashion their works. Indeed, the poets are figures akin to Fame since they often refashion "truth" with clever inventions and thus scatter their fancies throughout the world. Their works often grant glory to forgotten figures or illusive events. The poet can be a maker of history. Who would remember the fictions and truths of Troy if Homer had not sung the death of the city? Who would remember Numantia if Cervantes had not dramatized its fall? The similitude between Fame and Poetry in *La Numancia* is based on their elemental origin. Fame's words, her wings, and her trumpet denote her relationship to air. Calling up the image of Poetry from the Stanza della Segnatura (Fig. 4), we recall that she is also a winged figure. She carries a sign: *Numine afflatur*, "to be moved by air." Thus, both poetry and fame partake of this element.

Both Cervantes, the rebuilder of Numantia's ruins, and Scipio, the destroyer of the Celtiberian city, were poets. In his *Republic* Cicero records the formation of Scipio's Circle. Acknowledging that recent critics have concluded that it was not a school per se,[23] Carlos Fuentes describes the Circle's main adherents and its major contribution: "No había, propiamente, una literatura romana hasta que tú te rodeaste de gente como Terencio y Polibio, el satírico Lucilio y el estoico griego

Panecio. La literatura, hasta entonces, era asunto menor, obra de esclavos y libertos. Contigo y tu círculo, se convirtió en preocupación de estadistas, guerreros aristócratas" (1993, 139). Scipio, then, transformed literature into a worthy pursuit, gathering around him artists such as Polybius, who sought the causes of Roman greatness; Lucilius, whose satires would inspire Juvenal; and Terence, whose plays caused commotion through their *contaminatio*. Cervantes makes Scipio's Circle one of his models, searching for the causes of Spanish greatness, satirizing people and events that do not rise up to the challenge, and constructing through *contaminatio* a play that attempts to surpass the ancients. When Cipión confesses at the end of Cervantes's play that he has been defeated by a child, he is confessing that his literary circle has been surpassed by a young poet, by a modern offspring of the Romans who seeks to make literature as worthy in Spain as it was in ancient times. Bariato's death announces the demise of Cervantes the soldier and the rise of the poet. From the ashes of Numantia, from the misfortunes of his early career, Cervantes forges a new art that will transform his leaden failures into golden verses.[24] *La Numancia*, then, is creating not only a myth of empire but also a legend of a soldier turned poet, one that will last at least as long as the memory of Scipio's deeds. Both Scipio and Cervantes seek fame through war and poetry. Scipio acquires it through Cicero, Macrobius, and the Roman historians. Cervantes forges his own fame in the play. By having the figure of Fame end his work, he is surrendering to this winged figure not only the deeds of the past but also his own poetic endeavor. Even though Fame rests in his retelling of history, her contexts battle the author, whispering of vainglory and oblivion while speaking of glory and eternal memory. The battle within the text thus continues to the very end and beyond.

The epic battle that rages within *La Numancia* points to a constellation of cultural, ideological, and ethical conflicts that permeate the text and spill upon its contexts. Greek culture competes with Roman ideals; the ancients battle with the moderns, while Christianity fights paganism. Philip II is engaged in a contest of power with the Vatican; Raphael's frescoes and their political agenda are subverted by irreverent graffiti. Imperialism seeks to supplant republicanism; liberty is proclaimed in the same breath as vengeance. The ashes of Numantia sparkle with the cinders of Troy and the ruins of Rome. Does empire fall within the cycles of time, or can a particular political entity become eternal through *renovatio*? Who is the greatest of ancient epic poets: Homer or Virgil? Virgil or Lucan?

What is the greatest quality of the epic hero: wisdom or courage? Cunning or fortitude? What is more virtuous, suicide or surrender? And who represents the future Spanish Empire: the Numantians or Cipión? Is Fame a boon to be desired or does she hide the perils of mendacity and vainglory? Does poetry give meaning to history? Or are they both mendacious arts? Is drama a Socratic dialogue that seeks out hidden truths? Or is it a play of power, a vehicle for imperial propaganda? Will the poet attain to glory finding similitudes in random events? Or is his creative quest a demonic and vainglorious one?

Whatever the answers to these questions may be, and whoever may win the battles that rage textually and contextually, the besieged city triumphs through an archeology that endows it with the glories of Troy and Rome. The ancient enemy becomes a fellow architect. Scipio's Circle aids the poet in the construction of his text and in the attainment of fame.[25] The ghost of Homer once told Ennius in a dream that he now inhabited Ennius's body and would make him a new Homer. Cervantes's dream does not allow for this type of contamination. He sings of Spain in his own voice, but modulated to the magic of a lost civilization. He calls upon the specter of Homer to dance in the fires of destruction. Having washed in the Virgilian waters of imperial prophecy, he summons the dead bodies of liberty through a foul feat of necromancy. He conjoins apocalyptic frenzies with the fires of *ekpyrosis* to warn once again of the consequences of imperial expansion. Winged Fame praises the ancient deeds and his own poem, while her Ciceronian contexts warn of their futility. Yet the play rejoices in the theater of the mind, in the joy of artfully placing the images in an Empedoclean elemental universe, in the bliss of meandering meanings. Recalling the colors and images of the Vatican, the play succeeds in creating one more theater for memory: "pues de esto se encarga la memoria" (v. 2447). Memory is thus given a vehicle for "eternity."

Notes

1: The politics of imitation

1. In the prologue to the *Novelas ejemplares* Cervantes calls *Persiles y Sigismunda* "libro que se atreue a competir con Heliodoro" (1982b, 1.65). In the prologue to *Don Quijote*, Part 2 (1615), he announces that he is finishing *Persiles y Sigismunda* and the second part of *La Galatea* (1978, 2.37).
2. Spenser's career pattern is, of course, much more complicated. For Spenser's career and his continuing epic impulses see Cheney 1994.
3. The description of Mercury, for example, is far from burlesque:

   En el gallardo talle y compostura,
   en los alados pies, y el caduceo,
   símbolo de prudencia y de cordura,
   digo que al mismo paraninfo veo.
   (Cervantes 1984b, 60).

   Indeed, this god has come to praise Cervantes's poetry, calling him twice a "raro inventor" (1984b, 61). But, being a satirical poem, the *Viaje del Parnaso* does poke fun at the antique pantheon. The Muses, for example, "andan las cinco en pie, las cuatro a gatas" (1984b, 96). The humanization and anachronisms of which Gaos speaks surface in the descriptions of Apollo "en calzas y en jubón vistoso" (1984b, 96) and Venus "vestida de pardilla raja / una gran saya entera" (1984b, 126). Elias Rivers sees Apollo as "a ridiculous figure belonging to a debunked Parnassian mythology that no one can really take seriously" (1991, 211). At the same time, this critic has to admit: "The final part of this dialogue with Apollo obviously represents an inner dialogue of Cervantes with himself and is an eloquent defense of his own career and a rationalization for his lack of public recognition" (1991, 213). Apollo thus assumes a most serious role in certain portions of the poem. As for Venus, although she is depicted in modern dress, she does arrive in her chariot pulled by doves. Neptune's conveyance is drawn by dolphins. Thus, throughout the poem, there is a constant exhibition of classical learning. And the deities are not without power. It is "el ingenio del divino Apolo" (1984b, 65) who creates a ship made out of poetry. Indeed, the very description of Poetry leading a troop of nymphs is totally devoid of burlesque elements (1984b, 106).
4. For verbal reminiscences of Horace, see Cervantes 1984b, 94; of Virgil, see 1984b, 79.

5. *Viaje del Parnaso* refers to authors such as Homer (1984b, 77), Lucan (69), Ovid (159), Tacitus (71), Virgil (59, 135), and Zoilus (72).

6. As Cervantes scholars know quite well, the avowed purpose of the work is far from controlling the action. Some would even argue that *Don Quijote* is the best of the romances of chivalry. For Bataillon, Cervantes's critique of chivalry is Erasmian in nature, partaking of "l'esprit dont s'inspirent les érasmistes dans leur critique du roman de chevalrie" (1937, 821).

7. When in the *Viaje del Parnaso* Cervantes depicts Lope de Vega as descending from a cloud, rather than ascending through his own efforts the mountain of learning and poetry, he is illustrating once again Lope's lack of intellectual credentials (Lokos 1989, 66).

8. Riley clearly shows in his *Don Quixote* (1986) how Cervantes's prologue is an attack on Lope's pretentiousness.

9. Studying Cervantes's *Retablo de las maravillas* and Carpentier's *El arpa y la sombra*, González concludes that "la necesidad de pasar juicios éticos es una característica de toda ficción, a la vez que afirma la imposibilidad de llegar a un juicio ético concluyente. Para que haya ficción, tiene que haber ética: la contemplación y adjudicación de valores en pugna" (1994, 502).

10. The Platonic question of writing as *pharmakon* comes into play here. On Cervantes and the *pharmakon*, see González 1994 and Parr 1991.

11. As Avalle-Arce states: "El tema más apasionante para Cervantes a lo largo de su vida fue el de la verdad. Pero entendamos bien, no la verdad absoluta, revelada y encarnada en los dogmas . . . sino la verdad relativa" (1979, 1.22).

12. Castro underlines the differences, rather than the similarities, between Lope and Cervantes: "Pero Lope no era solamente un rival dichoso, cuya gloria estorbase, sino un modelo del cual había de huir" (1960, 236).

13. "Encierro los preceptos con[n] seis llaues; / Saco a Tere[n]cio y Plauto de mi estudio" (Lope de Vega 1971, 284).

14. Jameson (1937) shows that among the sources of Lope's "classical" erudition are Renaissance writers such as Ravisius Textor, Rodiginio, and El Volaterrano (Raffaello Maffei).

15. A detailed discussion of this topic would lead us far astray. I have treated Lope de Vega's and Claramonte's use of mythology in a series of essays (e.g., de Armas 1989, 1992a).

16. For arguments for and against the "uniqueness" of the *comedia*, see Reichenberger 1959, 1970; Bentley 1970.

17. In spite of extensive work by Gómez Santacruz, (1914), Schevill and Bonilla (1920–2), Shivers (1970), and others, much remains to be done on the relationship between ancient history and Cervantes's play.

18. In "Las dos Numancias," a novella included in the collection *El naranjo*, (1993) Fuentes tells of the relationship between Polybius and Scipio. The Greek historian, captured by the Romans, became Scipio's tutor. Although he wrote of the Punic Wars, "me abstuve de narrar lo que vi en Numancia acompañando a mi discípulo y amigo el joven Escipión" (1993, 150). The

reason was that he did not want to make his pupil suffer ("por respeto al sufrimiento" [1993, 150]).

19. According to Appian, Scipio takes a number of Numantians to Rome for his triumphal parade: "Having chosen fifty of them for his Triumph, Scipio sold the rest and razed the city to the ground" (1962, 1.293).

20. Ambrosio de Morales repeats this anecdote, citing Valerius Maximus: "Como celebra Valerio Maximo, Teogenes, un principal Numantino, puso fuego a todo su barrio . . . convidando a sus vecinos que se matasen con El, y que el que venciese, echase al vencido muerto en el fuego" (1791, 4.45).

21. "Appiano Alexandrino cuenta algo diferente la matanza y destruicion que los Numantinos hicieron de sí mismos, diciendo que quedaron algunos vivos, y los tomó Scipion. Mas yo sigo a Tito Livio, Orosio, Floro y Valerio Maximo, que concuerdan, y son de mucha autoridad" (Morales 1791, 4.46).

22. "Raphael's reputation in poetry was important to Vasari; the association of poetry and painting is an important component of this *Life*. Vasari quotes an epitaph by Castiglioni at its conclusion, in addition to the tomb inscription by Pietro Bembo" (Rubin 1995, 364–5)

23. For Raphael as "an image of the artist that best fit the didactic aims of *The Lives*" (Rubin 1995, 359), see Rubin 1995, 357–401. Philip Sohm, on the other hand, explains how Vasari placed Raphael second to Michelangelo since the latter was "the most masculine of all artists" (1995, 774). Raphael, "whose *grazia* and *leggiadria* most perfectly embodied the feminine qualities of beauty, was cast by Vasari as a follower of Michelangelo (a contention that has been actively disputed into this century)" (1995, 774).

24. Homer rules the third and the first half of the fourth act, while Cicero/Macrobius is limited to the end of Act 4. The first and second acts can be viewed as a contest between Virgil and Lucan.

2: Raphael: A Vatican of the mind

1. For a brief summary of antiquarianism in the Renaissance (and the destruction of many Roman ruins) see Stiebing 1993, 143–5.

2. On imitation as necromancy see Greene 1982, 37–8.

3. Whereas Villamediana and other exponents of the poetry of ruins mournfully stress the *ubi sunt* motif – "¿no adviertes . . . / tantas en polvo hoy fábricas divinas?" (1990, 424, no. 338), Cervantes's text foregrounds another aspect of the tradition, the life of fame that allows the memory of such cities and glorious events to survive. Cervantes's inclusion of the figure of Fama at the end of his play will be echoed in a line by Villamediana: "con aliento vivaz Fama conserva" (1990, 314, no. 234).

4. Even though Foucault argues that *Don Quijote* can be seen as the end of this type of knowledge, *La Numancia* was conceived long before the knight became "the man who is *alienated* in *analogy*" (Foucault 1973, 49).

5. "Así pues, el 22 de diciembre de 1569, Rodrigo de Cervantes certifica ante el teniente de corregidor de Madrid, Duarte de Acuña, que Miguel no es

bastardo y que entre sus ascendientes no cuenta ni moros, ni judíos, ni conversos ni reconciliados por el Santo Oficio. Esta es la fórmula clásica que encontramos en todos esos certificados de limpieza de sangre" (Canavaggio 1987, 49).

6. I would like to thank Edward Dudley for having provided me with a typescript of his essay "Goddess on the Edge: The Galatea Agenda in Raphael, Garcilaso, and Cervantes," which has now been published in the first issue of *Caliope* (1995).

7. Citing the reference to Raphael and Michelangelo, Canavaggio wonders if Cervantes "se limitó a acumular de esa forma las lecturas, las imágenes, los recuerdos, o si aprovechó sus ocios para ponerse a escribir" (1987, 67–8).

8. Ortel Baledre's tale contains an example of Cervantes's archeological interests. It takes place near the town of Talavera, which was preparing to celebrate the feast of Monda. The story connects this Christian feast with a pagan festival for Venus: "La gran fiesta de la Monda, que trae su origen de muchos años antes que Cristo naciese, reducida por los cristianos a tan buen punto y término, que si entonces se celebraba en honra de la diosa Venus por la gentilidad, ahora se celebra en alabanza de la Vírgen de las vírgenes" (Cerrantes 1969, 312). See de Armas 1993, 407.

9. As Pérez Sánchez has noted, most sixteenth- and seventeenth-century Spanish references to Raphael pair him with Michelangelo: "Se le halla siempre – al menos en el siglo XVI y hasta mediados del XVII – estrechamente asociado a Miguel Angel, pero ocupando el segundo lugar, aunque con extrema ponderación" (1985, 34). He cites, among others, Francisco de Quevedo's *Silva al pincel*, Fray Hortensio Félix Pallavicino's *Oraciones evangélicas*, and Vicente Carducho's *Diálogos de la pintura*. Francisco Pacheco's *Arte de la pintura* and Jusepe Martínez's *Discursos practicables del nobilísimo arte de la pintura*, on the other hand, praise Raphael's art above Michelangelo's (1985, 37).

10. Referring to how Rodaja leaves Rome for Naples in *El licenciado vidriera*, Canavaggio asks: "¿Es el discípulo de Erasmo, hostil a las prácticas de una devoción supersticiosa, el que lanza esta pulla por boca de Tomás? Tal vez sea, más simplemente, el ex-camarero de Acquaviva, que aún conserva en la memoria el recuerdo de las intrigas del Vaticano" (1987, 64).

11. "Que faltando la sobredicha (Sixtina) fueran estas las primeras" (Pérez Sánchez 1985, 31).

12. For a description of the mechanics of executing a fresco during the Renaissance, see Beck 1993, 7–8.

13. For the theory of ekphrasis, see Krieger 1992. On the importance of ekphrasis in Spanish poetry, see Bergmann 1979. Although Cervantes's utilization of Raphael's frescoes is seldom ekphrastic, he must have been well aware that ekphrasis was a common element in epic poetry, since its locus classicus was the shield of Achilles in Homer's *Iliad* (Book 18). Perhaps the brief description of Attila's threat to Rome in *La Numancia* can be seen as a distant echo of epic ekphrasis.

14. For a detailed outline of the relationship between art and theater during the Spanish Golden Age, see Damiani 1989.

15. It is said that Simonides "called painting mute poetry and poetry painting that speaks." Yates cites from Plutarch's *Glory of Athens* (1966, 28).

16. Lodovico Dolce also recommends such images, giving as an example Titian's painting on the rape of Europa (Yates 1966, 164).

17. Ricci was at Saint Andrew's Quirinale in Rome as a novice in 1571. He went on to study in Florence in 1572–3 and was at the Jesuit College in Rome from 1573 to 1577 (Spence 1984, xi).

18. García de la Concha (1983) has studied the fifteenth-century work *Arte memorativa*, and Muñoz Delgado (1975) has examined Juan de Aguilera's *Ars memorativa* from the following century. Indeed, both Egido (1983, 1994) and Gerli (1984) have written on Santa Teresa and the art of memory.

19. "Vasari's report that Raphael saved . . . Sodoma's framework in the Stanza della Segnatura, invites the speculation that Raphael was trying to avoid making himself totally unpopular with his colleagues" (Nesselrath 1992, 37).

20. Rosselius was a Florentine Dominican who wrote a small book on memory. He utilizes Hell for one of his loci, dividing it into eleven places. He also describes "the making of 'real' places in abbeys, churches and the like" (Yates 1966, 122).

21. Kempers reminds us that Vasari's interpretation of *The School of Athens* has been disregarded by modern critics: "how astronomy, geometry, philosophy and poetry can be reconciled with each other by theology" (1987, 253). Indeed, Kempers claims that this Christian interpretation should be reevaluated. But Rubin has shown that Vasari's interpretation was based on a print by Agostino Veneziano that foregrounds the Pythagoras group: "Instead of the pagan philosopher the print shows the Evangelist Luke, a transformation probably intended to facilitate the sale of the print as a sacred subject" (1995, 365). Thus, although Vasari was attempting accuracy by consulting a print of the painting, this very print misled him into elaborating an erroneous interpretation of the fresco.

22. The name *segnatura* reflects the ecclesiastical court held here in the years following Julius II's pontificate.

23. Redig de Campos understands Plato's gesture as pointing to the realm of Ideas: "Platone . . . indica con la diestra l'empireo delle Idee, ultima realtà" (1965, 15).

24. Pope-Hennessy (1970) follows H. B. Gutmann in asserting that the program of the wall frescoes is based on Saint Bonaventure. *The School of Athens*, as well as the *Disputa*, reflects "Bonaventure's distinction between the natural and rational sciences" (1970, 139). However, Pope-Hennessy also points to failures in this theory and refers to Raphael's archeological impulses (1970, 139–41). This chapter will view the frescoes in an entirely different light.

25. Hersey concludes that the larger scenes on the vault are "all by Raphael" but that the "rest of the vault is decorated with imprese and emblems of Julius II, and is the work of the earlier artists whom Raphael supplanted" (1993, 142).

26. Beck claims that the number 8 is the key structuring principle: "The central

octagon seems to have given rise to the scheme of the entire ceiling. The eight main scenes are each related to one of the sides. . . . Furthermore, there are tiny depictions, four in imitation of Antique marble reliefs (perhaps executed by Sodoma) and four related to mosaic, again reinforcing the number eight" (1993, 19). Considering the importance of the tetractys in *The School of Athens* and following Wind's (1938) interpretation of the eight scenes as representing the four elements, I would argue for the four elementals as key. The ceiling has four sets of pictures with four paintings each. We thus have a quaternity of a quaternity, further emphasizing the elemental 4.

27. This was the Camera di Torre Borgia, which Vasari calls "camera del fuoco" (Rubin 1995, 368).

28. The middle halls are the more difficult to interpret in terms of elements. The Stanza della Segnatura, as will be seen, also contains numerous references to air. The ceiling of this hall and that of the Stanza d'Eliodoro depict all four elements.

29. Fludd came to Spain around 1600 (Yates 1966, 63) but would have been too late to influence Cervantes's conception of *La Numancia* since the play was written in the 1580s.

30. Studying the relationship between Fludd's memory system, his use of a theater to illustrate it, and the curiously similar shape of Spanish public theaters, Varey concludes: "There is no evidence, therefore, to support the view that the design of any sixteenth-century public theater in Spain reflected the memory theaters of Camillo, Fludd, and the like" (1991, 47). Varey does concede, however, that the plays themselves may reflect this type of Renaissance thinking. Beyond using the art of memory to remember and replicate images from Italian art, Cervantes could well have conceived of the staging of *La Numancia* as an art of memory.

31. As Pedro de Medina states: "Destos quatro elementos, los dos son leves y ligeros y los dos graves y pesados. Los dos leves son fuego y aire, estos siempre apetecen subir hasta ser en su sphera. Los dos graves son agua y tierra, estos sienpre apetecen decender hasta su centro" (Lamb 1972, 108).

32. Beck is here following Redig de Campos's statement on the figure of Philosophy: "La tunica mostra i colori dei quattro elementi" (1946, 24). It is tempting to relate the different colored waters used by Marquino in his necromancy to the colors of Philosophy. However, the disinterment scene seems to emphasize the number 3 instead of 4. The three colors may relate instead to three basic steps in alchemy: *nigredo* (black), *albedo* (clear waters), and *rubedo* (yellow/reddish). They are imparted backward in the play to imply that necromancy is the opposite of the alchemical process.

33. It is curious to note that although fire relates to theology in the Stanza della Segnatura, it is linked to the suicide of the inhabitants of the city in *La Numancia*, an act that goes against Christian precepts. In this context, one of the figures of *The School of Athens* may carry additional significance in terms of Cervantes's play. The legend that Empedocles committed suicide by plunging himself into the fires of Mount Etna could also have a bearing on

La Numancia since the suicide of the inhabitants of the city is associated with the fires of destruction.

34. "Cuando Mucio en las llamas abrasaba / el atrevido fuei te brazo y fiero, / esta el incendio horrible resfriaba" (1984b, 142).

35. Hall has compared Castiglioni's *Superbi colli* to a letter by Raphael to Pope Leo X and has concluded that they share a similar humanist historical perspective of the city of Rome: "The present, whatever its potential, hardly measures up to the glorious past to which the ruins bear witness – an imperial past valued for its art, its achievement, its stability, and *not* deplored for its corruption and cruelty or its enslavement of other peoples" (1974, 162). By metamorphosing the ruins of Rome into the ruins of Numantia, Cervantes rejects Raphael's unquestioning admiration of the past. *La Numancia* contains a praise of classical art and a critique of Roman politics.

36. While Hoogewerff asserts that the three represent the tragic poets (1947–9, 326), Jones and Penny reject this attribution (1983, 72).

37. In Thomson's translation of the *Ethics*, he gives "sagacity" and "prudence" as alternate translations for "practical wisdom" (1953, 319).

38. I am citing from a different translation than the one used by Parr in his review.

39. I would like to thank Kenneth Chandler for allowing me to read the section on Plato from his manuscript "The Awakened Mind: The Higher Stages of Development of Human Consciousness," vol. 2. I have followed his choice of translations.

40. This principle is more ancient than Greek philosophy and is found in ancient Vedic literature. Maharishi's Vedic Science explains that when people reach the deepest level of the self, Being, a state of restful alertness, they have "come into contact with the unlimited creative intelligence of the cosmic life" (1986, 465).

41. Although I generally cite Plato from the Hamilton and Cairns edition, at times I refer to the Jowett translation (indeed, Hamilton and Cairns include several dialogues translated by Jowett). I always note the shift in translation to Jowett.

42. Parr (1994) makes this statement in connection with Aristotle's *Ethics*.

43. This new future, however, is far from perfect. Although in the *Fourth Eclogue* Virgil shows universal peace through empire, Cervantes's text also reflects the problems of an imperial agenda that revels in revenge and expansionism.

44. This anecdote is found in Pliny, *Natural History*, 7.29. Pliny declares that Alexander uses Darius's case of gold, pearls, and precious stones in order to preserve the works of Homer. Pliny's praise of Homer parallels Alexander's: "Unless perhaps it is agreed that no genius has ever existed who was more successful than Homer the bard of Greece, whether he be judged by the form or by the matter of his work" (7.577).

45. According to Marasso, Cervantes borrowed this story from a translation of Claudius Donatus's *Vida de Virgilio* included in Hernández Velasco's Spanish version of the *Aeneid* (1954, 83).

46. According to Hersey (1993, 135), these scenes in the Dado were painted by Raphael's disciple Perino del Vaga (1501–47).

47. For a discussion of how Dante fashioned a new type of limbo separate from the *limbus patrum* and the *limbus puerorum* in order to save the virtuous pagans from Hell, see Iannuci 1993. He carefully discusses the significance of the classical poets in relation to Dante's own poetic ambitions. In *Don Quijote*, Cervantes wavers between an orthodox condemnation of the ancients (as in Part 2, Chapter 8, where the knight claims that all classical heroes are in Hell) and an almost Erasmian appreciation of virtuous pagans (as in Part 2, Chapter 53). On the condemnation, Bataillon asks: "Cervantes a-t-il souri en précipitant tous des dentils en enfer?" (1937, 828). On Cervantes's appreciation of the ancients, he states: "l'humanisme de Cervantes n'est plus assez fervent pour qu'il songe à incorporer les sages antiques à la cohorte des saints. Il n'ingnore pourtant pas qu'ils ont pu, par les seules lumières de la raison, attaindre des vérités assez hautes, comme l'immortalité de l'ame" (1937, 828).

48. As they proceed further, Dante and Virgil encounter the "filosofica famiglia" ("philosophic family" [1982, Canto 4.133–44]). There are clear parallels between these figures and the ones depicted by Raphael in *The School of Athens*. Both artists include, for example, Socrates, Plato, Empedocles, Euclid, Ptolemy, and Averroes.

49. Ambrosio de Morales, however, favors the distinction in his *Corónica*: "Queda aun otro Séneca, que es el que escribió las tragedias que tenemos . . . que el uno era Filósofo, y ayo de Neron, y el otro imitando a Esquilo y a Eurípides, compuso las tragedias" (1791, 4.436).

50. Sancho laughs and stops four times after the adventure of the fulling mills: "Cuatro veces sosegó, y otras tantas volvió a su risa con el mismo ímpetu que primero" (Cervantes 1978, 1.20.248). This passage transforms a Virgilian triad into a quaternity (Virgil, 1991, 3.567–70, 4.690, 6.32). See Marasso 1954, 66.

51. "[H]echo enemigo de la tierra que me sustentaba, negándome el aire aliento para mis suspiros y el agua humor para mis ojos; sólo el fuego se acrecentó" (Cervantes 1978, 1.27.339).

52. "Todos los elementos vi turbarse: / la tierra, el auga, el aire, y aun el fuego / vi entre rompidas nubes azorarse" (Cervantes 1984b, 79).

53. While Cicero praises Scipio's role in the siege of the city, Cervantes claims that Roman hopes for victory have become nothing but smoke and wind (vv. 2261–62). Cervantes's play thus rivals Cicero's own representation of Scipio, as the fires of destruction turn a Roman victory into defeat.

54. I am using the term "moral" since Seneca and Cicero were thus referred to in Dante's *Commedia*.

3: Raphael: The archeology of power

1. The division is as follows: fire (Abraham's altar), earth (Promised Land), air (angels in Jacob's dream), and water (the Flood, recalled by God's appear-

ance to Noah). According to Nesselrath: "Raphael changed the vault after he had finished all frescoes on the walls following Leo X's elevation to the papacy" (1992, 31). The four scenes on the ceiling have been attributed to Raphael's assistant, Guillaume de Marcillat (Hersey 1993, 150).

2. According to Kempers, the fresco's thrust is even more specific, dealing with the pope's fiscal power, "the papal right to collect taxes" (1987, 262).

3. "El fresco es una alegoría sobre la victoria del Papa sobre los cardenales franceses, que por razones políticas habían intentado causar un cisma en la Iglesia" (Antal 1988, 90). It refers to the Council of Pisa called by Louis XII in 1511.

4. Elliott explains that "during the pontificate of the fanatically anti-Spanish Paul IV (1555–59) Spain and the Papacy actually went to war" (1970, 228).

5. An early drawing for the fresco shows Pope Julius II carried on a chair. But since this pope died early in 1513, he is replaced in the final fresco by Leo X on horseback (Dussler 1971, 81–2; Pope-Hennessy 1970, 115). In fact, Kempers notes that Raphael made several designs for this painting, and that the earliest represented neither of the popes in the fresco: "the expulsion was entirely the work of Peter (without a sword) and Paul" (1987, 263).

6. This quote from Arnold Nesselrath is found in an article in the *New York Times* (1996): "Vatican Museum Shows a Spruced-Up Raphael."

7. Sebastiano del Piombo was the first restorer in the 1530s. He had to deal with the many holes and scratches put there by the invading soldiers.

8. Chastel's information is derived from D. Redig de Campos, who explains, for example: "Un altro curioso ricordo del Sacco si e scoperto nel corso dell'ultimo restauro della *Disputa*: un graffito inciso in basso, poco a diestra del centro con una invocazione a Carlo V . . . e il nome fatale *Martinus Lutherus*" (1965, 19–20).

9. For Derrida, inscription and textuality can be found in all forms of knowing. Charles Oriel has applied Derrida's notion of inscription to Golden Age theater: "Drama as a literary genre literalizes Derrida's notion that there is a form of inscription behind even the most seemingly spontaneous activities and that speaking is, in fact, 'a type of writing'" (1992, 15).

10. "In the Marandro–Lira episode, there is a quasi-Christian counterpart of the earlier sacrifice" (Whitby 1962, 209).

11. The motto *maiora tibi* prophesies greater triumphs for Philip's son, Fernando, born December 1571. However, the child died in 1578. Wethey believes that the "dull character of the allegorical machine" of this painting was provided by Alonso Sánchez Coello. The *Allegory* was shipped from Venice in 1575 and was displayed in the Alcazar of Madrid (Wethey 1969, 3.132).

12. Numerous verbal similitudes such as "Eucharistia = Hic Austria" (Tanner 1993, 221) existed in the period.

13. Bergmann's quote has the word "they" instead of "he" at this point, since she includes Fernando as a deified figure. Could he represent the child who is to bring about a new Golden Age as described in Virgil's *Fourth Eclogue*?

14. Rather than sacrificing Fernando/Isaac, the king is raising him up in triumph, helping him receive the palm of victory from the "angel."

15. Panofsky warns us to ignore most of the elements that appear on the edges of the painting (including the "vanquished Turk and the trophies" [1969, 72]) because these are the work of Vicente Carducho, who was paid on 24 December 1625 for enlarging the painting.

16. The apocalyptic imagery in the third act of the play may arise from the belief that Philip, fulfilling history, "yields the terrestrial rule back to Christ" at the end of time (Tanner 1993, 145).

17. Raphael started painting in the Stanze dell'Incendio "around 1 July 1514, but this was certainly preceded by a period in which the fresco was designed and the cartoon produced" (Nesselrath 1992, 44). Although Nesselrath points to Julius II as the first to order the redecoration of this hall (Nesselrath 1992, 36), it must be remembered that this pope died in 1513, so his direction could have lasted only a few months. Certainly, the frescoes in the hall have nothing to do with Julius but praise his successor, Leo X.

18. Nesselrath argues that the vault frescoes should "probably be attributed" to Perugino's workshop, and in particular to Giovanni Battista Caporali. Perugino "had demonstrated technical mastery of the fresco technique," but the vault shows inexperience with fresco (Nesselrath, 1992, 41). While *The Temptation of Christ* and *God the Father* are attributed to Perugino's workshop, *Christ between Justitia and Misericordia* shows Perugino's "higher quality of painting and technique" (Nesselrath 1992, 44). This is the fresco that stands above *The Fire in the Borgo*. The opposition between justice and mercy could well have entered into the characterization of Scipio in Cervantes's play since Scipio asserts that he would have shown mercy for the besieged city if it had surrendered.

19. Kempers claims that Charlemagne's features "are those of Francis I" (1987, 267).

20. He received the Frankish crown at Aachen on 23 October 1520 and the iron crown of Lombardy on 22 February 1530 at Bologna.

21. There are, as with many of these frescoes, contradictory opinions on the authorship and worth of *The Victory of Leo IV at Ostia*. Jones and Penny claim that "*The Battle of Ostia* does not look as if it was executed by Raphael, and the composition is too clumsy to be entirely his, but it incorporates some figures Raphael had invented" (1983, 153). Burckhardt, on the other hand, praised it as worthy of Raphael: "The fight, the conquest, and the taking of prisoners are here in a masterly manner united in a most energetic, simple and beautiful picture" (1879, 155).

22. "Pero el cielo lo ordenó de otra manera, no por culpa ni descuido del general que a los nuestros regía, sino por los pecados de la cristiandad, y porque quiere y permite Dios que tengamos siempre verdugos que nos castiguen" (Cervantes 1978, 1.39.478).

23. Although acknowledging the *Liber Pontificalis* as the ultimate source, Jones and Penny propose "the popular and official lives of the Popes written by Sixtus IV's librarian Platina" as the more immediate model (1983, 150).

24. These statements by Ettore Camesasca and Hermann Dollmayr are cited by Badt (1959, 36, 38).

25. Morgan's translation of Vitruvius does not seem as accurate: "Tragic scenes are delineated with columns, pediments, statues and other objects suited to kings" (1960, 150).

26. Nesselrath argues that the building to the right of Saint Peter's in the background of the fresco is a palace and not "the tower built by Leo III and restored by Leo IV" (1992, 48).

27. According to Jones and Penny, Raphael consulted ancient literature to design a number of his late works, including *Galatea* and *The Nuptials of Alexander and Roxane*, for which "Raphael follows Lucian's description [in *Herodotus* 5–7] of a famous painting" (1983, 179).

28. The page number is from West's (1991) edition. The book and line numbers are from Fairclough's (1978) Latin edition and English translation.

29. Aeneas and Anchises also appear in *El condenado por desconfiado*, attributed to Tirso, and in *Alejandro el segundo*, attributed to Lope. The authorship of both of these plays has been questioned.

30. The phrasing of Fairclough's (1978) translation is well known: "For these I set neither bounds nor periods of empire; dominion without end have I bestowed" (1.261).

31. E. Camesasca, *Tutta li pittura di Rafaello* (as cited in Badt 1959, 43), discusses the relationship between the temples of Mars and Saturn and Raphael's fresco. For a description of Saturn's temple, see Richardson 1992, 343–4.

4: Giulio Romano: Remembering Rome

1. Hersey's illustration of *The Donation of Constantine* attributes it to Gian Francesco Penni (1993, 175).

2. Some believe that *The Apparition of the Cross to Constantine* was actually executed by Raffaellino, one of Giulio Romano's assistants: "The *Vision of Constantine*, while it must certainly follow fairly exactly a cartoon by Giulio, and while the color scheme is precisely that of the *Battle*, is in general much coarser in detail, at times very crudely handled. In spite of such excellent preparatory studies by Giulio . . . , the assistant produces uniformly faulty and weak forms" (Hartt 1958, 49).

3. For a discussion of the classical *allocutio* in Renaissance paintings, see Panofsky 1969, 74–7.

4. The pyramid that was thought to be Romulus's tomb was "demolished during Alexander VI's pontificate" (Stinger 1985, 249).

5. In locating Numantia, Cervantes follows not only Ambrosio de Morales but also Antonio de Guevara's *Epístolas familiares*.

6. Early Christian images of Jesus owe much to Apollo, as Thomas F. Mathews has suggested. As "god of light and health" and as "perpetually adolescent," with abundant hair, Apollo was an often imitated model for mosaics and sarcophagi depicting Christ (1993, 126–7). Indeed, the feminine aspects of Dionysus and Apollo were also translated into "Christ's feminine bodily traits" (1993, 135).

7. Another standard, the one closest to Constantine, shows the eagle of

empire. This emblem did not have to be "corrected" by the cross of Christian victory, because it became the emblem of the Christian Habsburg empire. Indeed, the bird appears in *La Numancia* when a priest sees the "águilas imperiales vencedoras" as an omen for the triumph of Cipión. The irony, of course, is that the eagle will eventually pass to the new empire, and other peoples and nations will live in fear of the Christian empire's expansionist aims.

8. The earthly Venus stands above the bestial Venus, the goddess who induces wantonness and luxury. The highest, or celestial, Venus inspires a love of the spirit. For Marsilio Ficino there are twin Venuses, one of divine beauty and another of procreation (1985, 118). To the divine and active loves he adds a third, or bestial, category (1985, 120).

9. The opposition between the two Venuses was a common notion in Renaissance Platonism and is reflected in two paintings by Botticelli: *The Birth of Venus*, presenting the celestial figure, and *Primavera*, depicting the vulgar one (Wind 1968, 138).

10. In his chapter "What things are under the power of Mars and are called Martial," Agrippa finds that "all such Animals as are warlike, ravenous, bold, and of clear fancy, as the Horse, Mule, Goat, Kid, Wolf, Libard, the wild Ass," are dedicated to the god of war (1987, 58).

11. Chastel identifies the dwarf as Ippolito de' Medici's jester (1983, 58). Pagden identifies him as Gradasso Berattai da Norcia (1989, 86).

12. Although this Venus is "higher" than that of the Romans, she still does not attain to the lofty Ficinian heights of divine beauty untainted by physical contact.

13. Taken from Jesus' words in Matthew 11:30.

14. Hersey provides a different interpretation: "Eternity clad in white and gold. In her right hand she holds a quill and in her left an inkpot and book. Eternity, then, is achieved through history, through fame. A phoenix, symbol of rebirth – the "eternity" of rebirth – is by her side" (1993, 164). If he is correct in identifying the bird with the phoenix rather than the rooster, this would also be of significance for *La Numancia* since the destruction of the city and the rebirth of the empire correspond to the renewal of the mythical bird. The figure of Fame appears at the end of the play. Like Giulio Romano's Eternity, she can represent the eternalizing power of the poet. Cervantes, through his "historical" tragedy, gives Numantia new life through fame.

15. The rooster is a most appropriate bird to place as a frame for Saint Peter. Covarrubias says of the apostle: "toda su vida, a la ora que cantava el gallo, llorava amargamente el pecado de la negación, y la Yglesia Santa lo celebra en el himno de las laudes del Domingo, que empieáa, *Aeterne rerum conditor*" (1987, 623). Thus, Peter is related both to the rooster and to the eternal.

16. This tale is found in Livy's *Histories*, 26.50, 1–12; Polybius's *History*, 10.2.19; and Valerius Maximus's *Memorabilia*, 4.3.1 (Salet, Jestaz, and Bacou 1978, 46).

17. This tapestry is not included in the set owned by Philip II.

18. The result of Cervantes's imitation is far from simple. Many questions arise,

for example: Why is the *discordia concors* exemplified by Marandro included, since it is so at odds with the excessive martial spirit of Numantia, a spirit that demands total destruction, a blood sacrifice? What is the relation of Spain as the new Roman Empire to Rome itself, now the seat of the "new" religion? Has Giulio Romano's defense of the papacy been transformed into a defense of the Christian empire in order to "paganize" the new Spain?

5: Aeschylus: Praising the enemy

1. This citation from Albertino Mussato's *Vita Senecae* is taken from Braden 1985, 102.
2. Even though it has been customary to reject the Senecan influence, recent studies are showing its great impact in the Renaissance. See Braden 1985.
3. On Bertaut and Calderón, see Thomas 1929.
4. On *La vida es sueño* as a wild text that must be tamed by its French and English adaptors, see de Armas 1983 and 1987. On Spain's marginality, see Smith: "que la cultura española ha estado marginada, desterrada a las fronteras de una tradición europea consagrada" (1995, 197).
5. See, e.g., Watson 1963.
6. Braden utilizes certain lines from *El médico de su honra* to show "the normality of this kind of outburst in Seneca and on the Renaissance stage." For him, this rhetoric has "a corporate coherence as instruments of a particular style of selfhood" (1985, 65–6).
7. Toro's article (1985) shows Aristotelian anagnorisis to be found in the protagonist. In this, he differs from Ruano de la Haza (1983), who finds tragedy in Calderón but sees the anagnorisis as part of the audience. Through tragic irony, the protagonist is never conscious of his error, although the audience sees it clearly.
8. See, for example, the tragic elements of Calderón's *La dama duende*, as outlined by Mujica (1969).
9. For a comparison between these plays and *La Numancia*, see Friedman 1977.
10. See de Armas 1974. This chapter is based on this essay but reformulates some of the concepts. Willard King argues that since Scipio "is capable of perceiving the meaning of the catastrophe" this "confers on him something of the dignity of the classical tragic hero" (1979, 200).
11. "Cervantes presentó en su obra el cuadro de la destrucción de todo un pueblo, y por más que se diga que un desastre tan general no produce tanta impresión en el ánimo de los espectadores como los infortunios de una o pocas personas, es indudable que un argumento de esta clase, sobre todo si es nacional, puede excitar el terror y la compasión que recomienda Aristóteles en la tragedia" (Menéndez Pelayo 1941, 1.260).
12. For Whitby (1962), the "caída–levantamiento" is subsidiary to the theme of sacrifice.
13. Sólo se ha de mirar que el enemigo
    no alcance de nosotros triunfo o gloria;

antes ha de servir él de testigo
que apruebe y eternice nuestra historia.
(vv. 1418–21)

14. "[M]erece ser eterna en la memoria" (v. 2266).

15. Lewis-Smith (1987) links this to the tragedy of "double issue" as defined by Aristotle. I will discuss this subject in Chapter 6.

16. It was part of a tetralogy which included three tragedies (*Phineus*, *The Persians*, and *Glaukus*) and a satyr play (*Prometheus*).

17. All references to *The Persians* are from Lembke and Herington's edition (1981). I have also consulted Potter's translation in *The Complete Greek Drama* (1938). Broadhead's edition (1960) has also been taken into account.

18. *Prometheus Bound* was also imitated by Jacques-Auguste de Thou in his tragedy *Parabata vinctus* (1595) (Mund-Dopchie 1984, 330). In the nineteenth century Shelley wrote *Prometheus Unbound* as a sequel to Aeschylus's *Prometheus Bound*. Highet explains that "Shelley's own *Hellas* was 'a sort of imitation' of *The Persians* of Aeschylus" (1949, 419).

19. According to Highet, Greek drama was seldom translated into the vernacular during the Renaissance due to "the existence of handy Latin translations, such as those by Erasmus and Buchanan" (1949, 120). As we will see later, Cervantes could have read a Latin translation of Aeschylus.

20. There is a lengthy tradition of fictional manuscripts that are "discovered." See, for example, Montalvo's claim in the prologue to *Amadís de Gaula* that *Sergas de Esplandián* was found near Constantinople by a Hungarian merchant. Note the use of Constantinople as the source for manuscript traditions.

21. Marasso has argued that the second of these plays could have been used by Cervantes: "Pero también Cervantes escribió la *Numancia*, la ciudad sitiada, y si se acordó de Troya, pensó más en los *Siete contra Tebas* de Esquilo" (1954, 62).

22. *Ajax* was also available in published Latin translations. Henri Estienne's *Tragediae selectae* includes Sophocles' play using a translation by Joachim Camerarius (Mund-Dopchie 1984, 182).

23. Tar claims that "in Aristotelian terms, *hamartia* does not indicate an error of judgment hinging upon morality or an innate wickedness of character; rather, its cause lies in a misunderstanding of circumstance or facts surrounding the circumstance (*Poetics* 1453a)" (1990, 26). Although this is correct, Greek tragedies such as *The Persians* depict a tragic hero whose flaw is hubris. Furthermore, sixteenth-century theory emphasized the moral purpose of literature and thus transformed Aristotelian hamartia into a moral flaw (as in Robortello, Maggi, and Varchi). However, many of these texts preserved a sense of paradox (nobility vs. error) and a sense of fate that are the marks of canonical tragedies.

24. As Martín has shown, the Numantians are also said to be proud, but theirs is a positive quality, which saves them from oblivion (1996, 20).

25. On "soy quien soy," see Spitzer 1947.

26. It should be remembered that Spain, as part of the Habsburg Empire in the sixteenth century, used the eagle as a device. Thus, Spain inherits the bird of empire from the Romans.

6: Homer: An epic contest

1. Agustín García Arrieta (1805), Francisco María Turbino (1862), Ramón León Maínez (1876), and many others rejected such parallels, giving as reasons the tone of Cervantes's work and its originality (for a summary of their views see Drake 1974). They did not seem to have read Vicente de los Ríos very carefully since this critic emphasizes the differences in tone between the Homeric epics and *Don Quijote*. He states that whereas Homer narrates a heroic action, Cervantes composes a ridiculous one (1819, 24–5). Whereas the epic poet "presentó a los hombres toda la magestad de sus dioses, toda la grandeza de sus héroes," the Spanish writer, "menos atrevido," decided to only represent everyday human beings and "retratarles al natural sus defectos" (1819, 15). Although contemporary criticism rejects the view of Cervantes as "menos atrevido," it should take into account other insights by Vicente de los Ríos.

2. Other interesting parallels include (1) Camacho's wedding compared to the funeral games for Patroclus in the *Iliad* and the games celebrated by Aeneas on Anchises' anniversary (Ríos 1819, 37–9); (2) the Cave of Montesinos, as many critics have noted since, resembles both Odysseus's and Aeneas's journey to the underworld (1819, 45); and (3) Sancho's soliloquy about the search for Dulcinea recalls Juno's monologues in Homer (1819, 47).

3. López Férez asserts that there were fifteen editions between 1490 and 1597 (1993, 365).

4. For an excellent outline of the impact of Greek epics on Spanish medieval and Golden Age literature, see López Férez 1993. On Trojan subjects in Spanish art and literature of the Golden Age see López Torrijos 1985, 187–230.

5. We have seen in Chapter 2 how Raphael's *Parnassus* served as a model for *La Numancia* and could have inspired the *Viaje del Parnaso*.

6. The son's critical attitude toward Homer recalls that of Zoilus, the grammarian, who was always finding fault with the epic poet. Cervantes refers to him in the *Viaje del Parnaso* (1984b, 72).

7. For this and other reminiscences of Homer in *Don Quijote*, see Marasso 1954, 70, 109, etc. On the *aliquando* mistake, see Marasso 1954, 190–1.

8. See MacCurdy 1960, 100; and 1958, 12.

9. Rey Hazas also speaks of the "espíritu épico" of the work (1992, 72).

10. Lodovico Castelvetro, for example, in his *Poetica d'Aristotele vulgarizzata et sposta*, compares at length epic and tragedy. See Gilbert 1962, 354–5.

11. For a careful analysis of the *Poetics* and its relation to the neo-Aristotelian treatises of the sixteenth century, see Rabell 1992, 5–33. She also provides a chart of the similarities and differences between epic and tragedy (1992, 24).

12. This painting, now at the National Gallery in London, was originally located

at the Palazzo Borghese in Rome (Dussler 1971, 6). Cervantes could have seen it during his Italian sojourn.

13. It is believed that this painting illustrates an episode from the *Punica* by Selius Italicus.

14. Hercules had to choose between Virtue and Pleasure.

15. A possible model for Raphael's painting was thought to be Macrobius's commentary on Cicero's *Dream of Scipio.* Chapter 10 will show that Cervantes also utilized this commentary as a model for *La Numancia.* It is possible that Raphael's painting led the Spanish writer to think of Macrobius as one of the classical models for his play.

16. Gaos asserts that "el sentido último de la obra . . . es, como en el Quijote, el enfrentamiento entre locura y cordura, y sus misteriosas interrelaciones" (1976, 147).

17. In his *Peregrinación sabia,* for example, a wise canine asks of his valiant friend: "Si hubieras querido juntar tu valor con mi consejo ¿quién tuviera fuerzas bastantes contra Aquiles y Ulises?" (cited and discussed by Navarro 1964, 297).

18. Feijóo (1993) cites Florus rather than Cervantes, thus emphasizing the "historical" nature of his account.

19. Casalduero notes the use of *antanaclasis* in order to foreground the difficulty of Cipíon's endeavor (1966, 259–60).

20. Lewis-Smith argues that "Scipio's *hamartia* is his unshakable assumption that the Numantians will surrender if imprisoned in their city and starved to the point of death" (1987, 17). But he later rejects Scipio as tragic hero since the fall which he suffers is "thoroughly just" (1987, 16, 18). Tar accepts Scipio's hamartia as an "inadequate reading of the other" but rejects Lewis-Smith's assertion that Scipio is not a tragic hero (1990, 26). I would argue that it is Scipio's hubris which does not allow him to read the other correctly. Although Aristotle does not describe hamartia in moral terms, Renaissance commentaries on the *Poetics* interpret the flaw as moral. Cervantes, I believe, is following such interpretations. As Rabell notes: "La crítica española . . . interpretó este fin de la tragedia como un fin didáctico moral" (1992, 25).

21. Homer speaks of "resourceful Odysseus" (1919, 303/8.412).

22. Although I am citing from West's (1991) translation, I have also consulted the Latin edition and English translation of H. R. Fairclough (1978). Although the page number (the first number given) refers to West's translation, the book and verse numbers are from the latter edition.

23. For a discussion of Cervantes's ambiguity when dealing with the question of empire, see Johnson 1980 and King 1979.

24. Gaos asserts that "Cervantes comprende por igual a numantinos y a romanos . . . funde lo irracional y lo racional en fórmula única" (1976, 147).

25. For the historicity of the foray, see Shivers 1970, 9–10.

26. Appian had also spoken of a secret foray "on a cloudy night" (1962, 1.287).

27. In Florus's *Epitome of Roman History* the women go even further: "Finally they made up their minds to flee, but this was prevented by their wives, who cut

the girth of their horses – a grievous wrong, but due to their affection" (1929, 155).

28. Güntert explains this frenzy, or *furor*, in terms of poetic furor. While the Numantians represent poetic inspiration, the Romans stand for the rules of art (1986, 671ff.).

29. In calling the Numantians "bestias" the Spanish text is echoing Appian's history where the city's inhabitants are called "wild beasts" (1962, 1.293).

30. Zabaleta uses the term *maña* in a somewhat positive sense in his *Errores celebrados*. Hano, a Carthaginian, is able to tame lions. But his amazing ability only earns him exile: "no era seguro en la República hombre de danta osadía y tanta maña" (1972, 49).

7: Virgil: Prophesying empire

1. On the question of authority see Greene 1982, 12.

2. The impetus to include Neptune comes not only from Virgil and Raphael but also from Aeschylus's *The Persians*, in which Xerxes incurs the wrath of the sea god when he "yokes" the Hellespont.

3. Even though many classical deities and heroes are at play in the play, only some have significant roles. The text often reveals these beings through foregrounding, a term defined by Bohuslav Havránek (1964) and Keir Elam (1980), but which I will apply only to the classical gods and heroes within theater. I have also expanded the definition to include not only an unusual utterance but also a narrative or situation that not only is unusual but also calls attention to itself. Havránek defines "foregrounding" as "the use of the devices of the language in such a way that this use itself attracts attention and is perceived as uncommon, as deprived of automatization" (1964, 10). Automatization, on the other hand, is the use of unusual devices of language where "the expression itself does not attract any attention" (1964, 9). He gives as an example the French expression "s'il vous plait," a formula with an automatized meaning that, when translated literally into Czech, would then become foregrounded.

4. I would like to thank William R. Blue for allowing me to cite this passage from his manuscript *Spanish Comedy in the 1620's*. The book has now been published by Pennsylvania State University Press (1996).

5. Fernando Cantalapiedra associates the image of Spain with that of Italy as it appears in an emblem by Cesare Ripa (1994, 387).

6. His book was published in Brussels in 1636.

7. Benito de Peñadosa, *Libro de las cinco excelencias del Español* (Pamplona, 1629).

8. This denouement is prefigured by Spain when she invokes the image of the phoenix: "do acabará su vida, y no su fama, / cual fénix renovándose en la llama" (vv. 389–90).

9. According to Marasso, Cervantes probably read in his youth a translation of the *Aeneid* by Hernández de Velasco. He could have also known the critical

edition of the works of Virgil published in Valladolid in 1601 by Diego López. But Marasso believes that although Cervantes might have used Velasco's translation and López's "versión inelegante," he also turned to the original. When he chooses to renew the art of Virgil in *Don Quijote*, "el ingenioso autor del *Quijote* preferirá . . . el texto latino" (1954, 52–3). It is not my purpose to decide whether Cervantes utilized a Latin version or a Spanish translation (or both). I am more interested in showing how Cervantes dealt with the authorities he proposed. I will also deal with the politics of imitation.

10. But for Johnson, there is a structure of ambiguity in the play, one based on historical contexts: "The Romans in the play also grew up to be the Spaniards: cruel, imperialistic, in no sense the bearers of a superior civilization. The Romans in the play are like the Spaniards in Flanders and like the Romans at Masada as reported by Josephus" (1980, 89).

11. Juan de Horozco y Covarrubias shows it to be a commonplace: "La figura de los ríos se ponía con una urna debajo del brazo que vertía agua" (cited in Fernández Arenas 1982, 82).

12. For the development of the river god in Renaissance Italian literature and in the Spanish Golden Age, see de Armas 1985. The river god is particularly prominent in Jacopo Sannazaro's *Arcadia* and in Gil Polo's *Diana enamorada*.

13. As noted in the previous chapter, I am citing from the West translation of the *Aeneid*, to which the first number given (the page number) refers. I have also consulted the Latin text and English translation by H. R. Fairclough (1978). The book and verse numbers are from this edition. Here, Aeneas is "tristi turbatus pectora bello."

14. Hamilton points to Johannes Sturm's *Nobilitas liberata* (published in Germany in 1549 and translated into English in 1570) as a very complete text on imitation. It teaches students how to write well, following as models the best authors, particularly Homer and Virgil. Sturm taught how to conceal imitations: "to shewe us how we may hide and cover lyke thinges by unlike using and handling" (Hamilton 1990, 15).

15. Juan de Caramuel y Lobkowitz, for example, attempts to locate the four rivers of Paradise in Spain: "De allí salen los cuatro ríos que pintó Moises, y explican con curiosidad muchos autores" (cited in Herrero García 1966, 23). The four rivers of Hell are Acheron, Pyriphlegeton, Cocytus, and Styx.

16. Although Cervantes is exhibiting a Virgilian model, it is difficult to determine whether he borrows directly from the Latin or whether he is approaching Virgil's *Fourth Georgic* through an intermediary. It is possible that Cervantes had in mind Boscán's *Historia de Leandro y Hero*, which was included in the third book of *Las obras de Boscán y algunas de Garcilaso de la Vega repartidas en quatro libros* (1543), a work that enjoyed some twenty editions before 1569. Although Boscán's poem is a translation/adaptation of Mussaeus's love epic, it also includes the tale of Aristaeus and Proteus. Juan Luis Calvo Martínez has recently argued that Boscán's passage borrows from Book 4 of the *Odyssey* (1993, 341). I view it, instead, as an adaptation of Virgil's *Fourth Georgic*, with an original section where Proteus criticizes Aristaeus in front of Neptune.

17. I am following here the Fairclough translation (1978).

18. On the notion of *catabasis*, see de Armas (1985).
19. "Proteus ('first man') is the grandson of Sky and Earth, and thus reminds us that our natures are a fusion of opposing characteristics such as spirit and matter, intellect and emotions, will and appetite. The parents of Proteus are Oceanus, god of the sea, and Tethys, a sea goddess" (McCune, Orbison, and Wilter 1980, 11). Proteus's appearance before the destruction of Numantia is most apt since Tethys is the mother of both Achilles and Proteus. If the city represents the valor of Achilles, then it can be said that Proteus understands the courage of his half-brother and offers him this prophecy of imperial *renovatio*.
20 Giamatti (1968) uses for this discussion Juan Luis Vives's *Fabula de homine*.
21. The wiles of imitation can be connected with the Homeric figure of Odysseus. Indeed, Cipíon's cunning is modeled after this classical hero. In the first part of *Don Quijote*, Ulysses (Odysseus) is seen as a worthy figure of imitation (1978, 1.25.303).
22. This episode is an imitation of Homer's *Odyssey* (1919, 145–61/4.360–570) where, once bound, Menelaus recounts his fate along with the destiny of Ajax, Agamemnon, and Odysseus.
23. Both the Latin and the Spanish versions of emblem number 182 contain both positive and negative characteristics of the god. Cervantes may have also chosen Proteus since he stands as a symbol for classical antiquity. In López's version, the god claims: "Muestro las señales de la antiguedad y del siglo primiero del qual cada uno sueña a su parecer, y como quiere, y inventa lo que le parece" (1670, 621). Like the dreamers, Cervantes invents his own "myth of origins" for the Spanish Empire.
24. "The Sophist himself is the being of the simulacrum, the satyr or centaur, the Proteus who meddles and insinuates himself everywhere. For this reason, it may be that the end of *The Sophist* contains the most extraordinary adventure of platonism; as a consequence of searching in the direction of the simulacrum and of leaning over its abyss, Plato discovers, in the flash of an instant, that the simulacrum is not simply a false copy, but that it places in question the very notions of copy and model" (Deleuze 1990, 256).
25. For examples from France, Alciati, Stephanus, and Thomas More, see Giamatti 1968, 453 n. 40. Rousset, in his study of the Baroque in France, links the enchantress Circe to Proteus (1953, 22).
26. Bataillon (1925) points to the criticism of vengeful wars as one of the Erasmian traits found in Cervantes.
27. Although viewing the prophecy as praise of Spanish imperialism, Avalle-Arce is aware that the failure to mention the Moors could be interpreted from the opposite perspective: "Se evita mencionar la conquista de España por los moros, omisión que si bien puede parecer obvia en la retórica patriótica de un *laus Hispaniae*, creo que no deja de tener su interés al enfilarla deste otra perspectiva" (1962, 58).
28. Cardinal Cisneros ordered the conversion of these Moors in 1499 "against the advice of the local authorities and in violation of the promise made by the Catholic Kings" (Braudel 1973, 2.783).

29. "En 1566, el rey publica, contra la opinión del duque de Alba, una serie de disposiciones que prohíben el uso de la lengua morisca en público y en privado . . . manda entregar todos los libros moriscos a las Chancillerías; ordena renunciar a ritos, costumbres y trajes moriscos (Hermenegildo 1976, 48).

30. Although this is said regarding the kings of Spain, it can encompass the whole population.

31. Events such as the comet of 1527 and the flood of 1530 received much attention as prodigies.

32. The first engraving portraying the sack of Rome as one of Charles V's triumphs did not appear until thirty years later.

33. Sebastiano del Piombo restored Raphael's *stanze* in the 1530s. Did traces remain of the graffiti?

34. "[P]arcere subiectis et debellare superbos": I am following here David West's translation rather than H. R. Fairclough's "to spare the humbled, and to tame in war the proud!" (1978, 566/6.853).

35. In a typical doubling of history, the fresco also alludes to the "rout of the French troops after the battle of Ravenna," in which Pope Leo X took part (Chastel 1983, 52).

36. The empire partakes of Scipio's tragic hubris, whereas papal behavior can be compared to the state of the Roman soldiers before the general's arrival in Spain. Their surrender to Venus and Bacchus recalls attacks on the papacy for its paganism, Bacchic feasts, and luxury.

37. Bataillon makes it clear that although Cervantes was a believer in Catholicism, he could also criticize and smile at certain aspects of its practice: "C'est un croyant éclairé pour qui tout dans la religion, n'est pas sur le meme plan, qui sourit de bien des choses" (1937, 827).

38. Zapata's imprisonment may have been the result of his criticisms of Philip II. According to Márquez Villanueva, Cervantes echoes these criticisms in *El celoso extremeño* (1973, 154–8).

39. Not all critics believe that Erasmus influenced Cervantes. For a rejection of this influence, see Ciriaco Morón Arroyo: "Los análisis practicados creo nos obligan a olvidar la leyenda del erasmismo del *Quijote*" (1994, 173ff.).

40. Vilanova notes how Cervantes includes in his texts both Erasmian and Counter-Reformation ideals: "este último representante del espíritu erasmista encaja sin dificultad alguna en el mundo de la Contrarreforma, aun cuando no puede ser considerado como su expresión más genuina" (1949, 15).

41. King wonders why "he does not seize the opportunity to appeal to the thrilling memories of the Navas de Tolosa, the conquest of Granada and the New World, San Quintín or even his beloved Lepanto. Both in its overt references and in its obvious reticences the speech is puzzling" (1979, 214). I would argue for more than puzzlement – subversion.

42. "Y aquel día, que fue para la cristiandad tan dichoso, porque en él se desengañó el mundo y todas las naciones del error en que estaban, creyendo que los turcos eran invencibles por el mar" (Cervantes 1978, 1.39.477).

43. Gaylord (in press) makes a very shrewd assertion concerning this claim: "For

Cervantes to assert that this sonnet has redounded to the great honor of his writings may sound like a straightforward expression of authorial pride. But invocation of a poet's honor, made in one satiric poem in reference to another satiric poem, surely warrants some suspicion, particularly when the brunt of satire falls heavily in both instances on the boastfulness and vainglory of the poet–speakers in question."

44. See also the sonnets "A la entrada del Duque de Medina en Cádiz" and "De otro valentón, sobre el túmulo de Felipe II."

45. "On 14 December 1587, eight months before the defeat of the Armada, Lucrecia witnesses a naval battle in which an English fleet routs a Spanish armada commanded by Santa Cruz" (Kagan 1990, 75).

46. Stressing the ending of this line, "y a su estado antiguo unirse" (v. 520), Peraita (in press) asserts: "El derecho a la anexión de Portugal está ratificado por una legitimidad providencial."

47. The preponderance of *divinatio* in the second act creates a countercurrent to Protean deceitfulness. In addition, Proteus's rhetoric serves to "veil" a hidden "truth" – a critique of empire. Furthermore, the epic nature of *La Numancia* conspires against the break with resemblance. According to Foucault, Don Quijote's task is "to recreate the epic, though by a reverse process: the epic recounted (or claimed to recount) real exploits, offering them to our memory; Don Quijote, on the other hand, must endow with reality the signs-without-content of the narrative" (1973, 47). Contrary to *Don Quijote*, *La Numancia* seems to inscribe a plenitude of marks filled with content that can be deciphered through *divinatio*. Consequently, the text foreshadows the future break but does not partake of it.

48. And yet, it can be argued that the Delphic Oracle was often "deceitful," that it often used rhetoric to conceal its ambiguity.

49. On *aemulatio*, see Foucault 1973, 19–21. This form of knowing is also related to the imitation of the ancients. It is akin to the "sacramental type of imitation" described by Greene (1982, 38).

50. "By insisting that aesthetic judgment should rest upon the intrinsic qualities of a work of art, Vasari and Cervantes separate the work's prestige from a historically prior origin. . . . The claim to historical priority is vitiated since no human work of art is absolutely prior, originating outside of history" (Quint 1983, 4).

51. Aristaeus's pursuit of Eurydice caused her death and Orpheus's lament. He must thus sacrifice to them.

8: Lucan: The necromancy of imitation

1. "[A]ny discourse ought to be constructed like a living creature, with its own body, as it were, it must not lack head or feet; it must have a middle and extremities so composed as to suit each other and the whole work" (Plato 1990, 264c).

2. The book was attributed to one of two kings of Portugal: Juan II or Juan III. Cervantes read a poor translation by Luis de Hurtado. In his edition of *Don*

Quijote, Murillo calls it a "versión bastante desaliñada" (1978, 2.15.115, n. 20).

3. The *Commentarii* adopts an unadorned style that bespeaks of historical objectivity. Caesar's work thus seems to contrast with Virgil's later laudatory epic. Modern criticism, however, has shown that Caesar's works include tendentious interpretations. Thus, both Caesar's commentaries and Virgil's epic seem to follow a political agenda.

4. Quint gives this definition of "epic continuity" (1993, 8) based on Greene 1963.

5. His assassination does not take place within the epic, although the witch Erichto envisions the death of the two rivals, Pompey and Caesar: "One passion only and one anxiety she feels – what part may she snatch from the exposed body of Magnus [Pompey], and on what limbs of Caesar may she pounce" (Lucan 1962, 6.586–7).

6. Of course, we have seen that even Proteus's imperial prophecy is in many ways problematic and even subversive.

7. We have seen in Chapters 3 and 7 how the Duero's prophecy seems to skip hundreds of years of history and focus on both important and less significant events. This apparent aimlessness, of course, has a definite function in Cervantes: to question the imperial construction of Spanish history.

8. All references to Lucan's *Pharsalia* are from Duff's translation (1962). At times I have chosen Graves's translation (1957) over Duff's. I have noted this fact every time. I have also consulted Haskins and Heitland's (1971) Latin edition. Cervantes could have used either the Latin text or a translation by Martín Lasso de Oropesa. The Spanish version was first published between 1530 and 1540. There were numerous editions: 1541, 1544, 1551, 1585, and 1588. See Beardsley 1970, 33. According to Marasso, Cervantes uses the *Pharsalia* as an integral element of Grisóstomo's "Canción desesperada" in *Don Quijote* (1954, 86–99).

9. Quint notes that "this image of imperial conquest would, in turn, be imitated by Milton to compare the causeway between Hell and Earth that Sin and Death build on the tracks of Satan in Book 10 of *Paradise Lost*" (1993, 7).

10. In Pérez de Villagrá's *Historia de la Nueva Mexico*, for example, the defeated Indians use an "if" clause in their curse: "Que si bolver podemos a vengarnos" (cited in Quint 1993, 100). And in Girolamo Fracastoro's *Syphilis* (1530) the curse is neutralized in the end and made positive: "we should note that it ends *not* simply with the disease . . . but rather with the prospect of its *cure*: by means of the guaiacum tree growing in the American forests" (Quint 1993, 127).

11. The witch envisions Pluto's punishment for the victors: "The lord of that stagnant realm throws wide his dim abode; he sharpens his steep rocks and the hard steel for fetters, preparing punishment for the victorious rival" (Lucan 1962, 6.799–802).

12. As a rival to Neptune who in the Titans' rebellion attempted to gain control over the waters, Adamastor shares an aquatic link with Cervantes's Proteus.

13. Quint sees Dido's curse as an imitation of Polyphemus's curse in the *Odyssey* (1993, 107–13).

14. "En algunos de sus pasajes dice San Agustín que no pudo cohibir sus lágrimas, como en el lugar donde Dido dice a Eneas: '¡Traidor! ¿Imaginaste que podrías encubrir tamaña maldad y salir de mi tierra clandestinamente?' (Vives 1947, 1.547).

15. Although not reflected in the West translation, Dido is called an "infelix animi Phoenissa" (1978, 97/4.529), a "soul-racked Phoenician queen," in the Fairclough edition and translation.

16. The phoenix becomes a commonplace in the literature of the Spanish Golden Age. Long narrative poems are dedicated to it and it adorns many of the pages of seventeenth-century *comedias*. In Lope de Vega's *El caballero de Olmedo*, as in *La Numancia*, it may represent a surmounting of tragic fate through the life of fame.

17. Fairclough translates it as "dust." Later, when West translates as "Arise from my dead bones" (1991, 101), Fairclough translates *ossibus* as "ashes" (1978, 4.625), which preserves the phoenix-like image.

18. On the complex relationship between Caesar, Scipio, and Hannibal, see Ahl 1976, 108–12. For the Anteus–Hercules myth, see Ahl 1976, 94–6.

19. Friedman, for example, asserts: "The sacrifice of the ram by the Numantian priests serves as a ritual reenactment of the death of the townspeople" (1977, 83).

20. "Prophetic frenzies" were a common way of foregrounding the presence of a classical subtext within the *comedia*. The term appears repeatedly in West's translation of Virgil's *Aeneid* (1991, 70/4.444). Cassandra's prophecies, for example, are described as "praecepta furentis" (1991, 40/2.345). Not only was prophecy central to many classical texts, but also, through Ficino's commentaries, Renaissance thinkers became fascinated by the four Platonic frenzies and their link to the gods (Ficino 1985, 170–1). Indeed, Plato can be seen as a model for the use of a mythological subtext within a theatrical dialogue, something quite common in Golden Age theater. See Mattéi 1988.

21. I owe a debt of gratitude to Nicolopulos, for, on reading his manuscript, I was alerted to the importance of Lucan's necromancy.

22. Canavaggio recognizes reminiscences from Seneca's *Oedipus* and Lucan's *Pharsalia*, along with Spanish imitations of these antique texts such as Juan de Mena's *Laberinto de la fortuna* and Ercilla's *Araucana* (1977, 43).

23. The weakness of the sacrificial flame in Cervantes's play and the different course taken by the flame and the smoke suggest to Canavaggio (1977, 79 n. 34) a *contaminatio* from Seneca's *Oedipus* (1979, vv. 304–15).

24. Book 5 contains a digression on the Delphic Oracle. For a discussion of these three seers, see Morford 1967, 62–6.

25. The youth in Cervantes had been buried for only three hours (v. 954), and in Lucan the soldier "but lately was alive" (1962, 6.716). Although in Cervantes the youth has died of famine, in Lucan he died of a wound. Although Duff translates "the flesh divided by mortal wound" (1962, 6.723), Graves's translation provides a closer link with *La Numancia*, since the soldier is "dead

of a deep belly-wound" (1957, 146). In a sense, they have both died of similar causes: since lack of food in the stomach can be imagined metaphorically as a wound in the belly.

26. Marquino has a clear, a black, and a saffron colored liquid for his necromancy (see stage directions following v. 938). The black liquid is said to come from the waters of the Styx (v. 1015), an element that appears at least twice in Erichto's invocation (1962, 6.698, 749; 1957, 147).

27. Morford contends that Ovid's *Metamorphoses*, Book 7, and Seneca's *Medea* are the most important influences for Lucan's magic (1967, 68). Canavaggio claims that the magic waters carried by Marquino recall the waters held by Fitón in Ercilla's *Araucana* (1977, 79 n. 47).

28. Graves's translation foregrounds voice, while Duff writes: "Then she went on to speak plainly in a Thessalian spell, with accents that went down to Tartarus" (1962, 6.693–4).

29. On Scipio's *cordura*, see Chapter 5.

30. Avalle-Arce (1962) and Johnson (1980) have discussed parallels between *La Numancia* and Virgil's epic. See Chapter 7.

31. Heitland states: "But I do think that bitter loathing of the Empire is one of the chief, if not the chief, influences that animate the poem." However, he disagrees with Graves in that he does not believe that Lucan wanted "the overthrow of the imperial monarchy and the reestablishment of an aristocratic Republic." See his introduction to Haskins and Heitland's edition of the *Pharsalia* (1971, xli).

32. For this series of oppositions, see Graves's introduction to the *Pharsalia* (1957, 11–14). Heitland explains that throughout Lucan's poem "the ruling divinity is the capricious abstraction *Fortuna*." He adds that Virgil's reverence is not found in Lucan: "In no respect do the two writers differ more than in their relations to the religions of their respective ages." See Heitland's introduction to the *Pharsalia* (1971, li). As for magic and divination, Heitland relates it to Lucan's Stoicism (1971, xlv).

33. On this topic see Avalle-Arce 1961.

34. Greene explains that a "sacred original . . . can never be adequately reproduced." Eclectic or exploitative imitation "treats all traditions as stockpiles to be drawn upon ostensibly at random" (1982, 38–9).

9: Contaminatio: *Epic flames/textual ashes*

1. Raphael's *Parnassus* was known in Spain through a print made by Marcantonio Raimondi (Avila 1985, 48).

2. As noted in Chapter 1, I am using *contaminatio*, in contradistinction to Greene, as the blending of a discrete number of ancient texts: either two key texts or one central text and a couple of subsidiary ones.

3. In order not to confuse the reader, I will continue to use the Roman names of the gods.

4. See Ovid's *Metamorphoses*, 4.169–89 and *The Art of Love*, 2.561–94.

5. See Plutarch's essay *Isis and Osiris*, included in his *Moralia* (6.193). Plutarch

compares the opposition between Venus and Mars with philosophic concepts found in Heraclitus, Empedocles, Pythagoras, and Plato.

6. On *El gallardo español*, see de Armas 1981. On *La casa de los celos*, see Correa: "La comedia fluctúa entre los hechizos peligrosos de la diosa Venus y los austeros dictados del dios Marte" (1959, 295).

7. Venus is mentioned at least seven times in the novel. At one point, Antonio, narrating his life, states: "No tuve amistad en mis verdes años ni con Ceres ni con Baco y así en mí estuvo Venus fría" (Cervantes 1969, 72). Avalle-Arce, in his edition of *Persiles y Sigismunda*, states that Antonio is repeating a phrase from Terence: "Sine Cerere et Baccho, friget Venus" (*Eunnuchus* 4.5). A reference to Mars follows immediately in Antonio's speech: "Fueme Marte favorable, alcancé nombre de buen soldado" (Cervantes 1969, 73). Thus, we see the opposition between Venus and Mars.

8. Gaos uses a similar argument to relate the representations of myth in the *Viaje del Parnaso* to Velázquez's paintings (Cervantes 1984b, 32–3).

9. Scipio returns to the subject later in his exhortation, alluding to Venus's "blandas camas" and to Bacchus's "juego y vino" (vv. 153–4).

10. "It is precisely this fusion of the qualities of Mars and Venus, which was admired and often considered the ideal of the Renaissance courtier. It is an ideal which the Romans could neither recognize nor were capable of" (Selig 1971, 685).

11. For a discussion of the Homeric elements in this episode, see Chapter 6.

12. As Helen Solterer has shown, the image of conquest which relates woman to city and vice versa was very common during the Middle Ages (1995, 107).

13. In the Fairclough translation Dido shouts: "False One!"

14. As mentioned in Chapter 5, Marasso (1954) believes that *La Numancia* evokes Aeschylus's *Seven against Thebes*.

15. T. S. Eliot's famous essay on Stoicism in Shakespeare (1964) notwithstanding, English critics have resisted the notion of a deep Senecan strain in the literature of the sixteenth and seventeenth centuries, in spite of Cunliffe's early and important book on the subject (1893). Gordon Braden explains: "And the case for Seneca's pertinence to the development of Renaissance drama, including English, has not been so much refuted as shown to have been badly conceived and developed. It has not, for one thing, been based on a firmly held sense of what is powerful and significant in Senecan tragedy on its own terms" (1985, 64). The critical history of Spanish Golden Age theater is very similar. In spite of repeated but cursory comparisons between the *comedia* and Senecan texts, and despite MacCurdy's important essay on the subject (1964), most critics either neglect or reject this link. Castro's well-known assessment of the situation is still quoted: "Sólo una laucinación, explicable por una especie de psicosis colective, pudo hacer de Séneca y de su filosofía un fenómeno español. Aun admitiendo que el pensar estoico hubiese tenido hondas y originales repercusiones en el pensamiento español (no las tuvo), de ahí no cabría deducir ningún españolismo en Séneca" (1962, 146–7). Castro goes on to state that "conviene subrayar que el pensamiento crítico de Séneca y su interés por la ciencia natural nunca

interesaron a la casta cristiana que, desde fines del siglo XVI, fue la que total-
mente representó la forma de vida española" (1962, 147). Bluher, although
attempting a balanced and cautious approach, claims that "el teatro español
se desarrolló en el siglo XVII en una dirección tal que casi no dejó sitio para
una imitación *directa* de las tragedias de Seneca" (1983, 329).

16. "From the left quarter of the sky rushes a star, dragging a murky trail. The
wine, poured upon the fire, changes from wine and flows as blood; from the
king's head falls the crown twice and again, and the ivory statues in the temples weep" (*Thyestes*, 1979, 2.700–2).

17. For Cantalapiedra, these figures recall similar ones in Cesare Ripa's
emblems (1994, 388).

18. We have seen how Jupiter and Mars pervade the play. Saturn is also present
through the evocation of a future golden age. Venus is not mentioned in the
dire predictions of the astrologers since it is the planet of harmony and good
fortune. Venus's presence in *La Numancia* reflects how Empedoclean harmony attempts to counter the principle of strife.

19. Campanella and Salazar add a fifth universal monarchy, the Medes (the
Chaldeans).

20. Hercules is said to have saved Spain from the tyranny of Gerion and is thus
the founder of Spanish monarchy. (On the legend of Hercules and its
impact on Spain, see Tate 1954.) It is not by chance that Charles V picked as
an emblem of his empire the columns of Hercules. By changing Hercules'
warning "Non plus ultra" to "Plus ultra," Charles is asserting that his dominion can go beyond the Straits of Gibraltar into a New World. Thus his universal empire is greater than the holdings of the ancient Romans (Yates
1975, 23).

21. For a discussion of *ekpyrosis* in Seneca, see de Armas 1986, 10–14.

22. For Belli, the Bariato episode derives from Euripides: "A tower resembling
the Trojan one exists in Numancia. And there is a boy resembling Astyanax"
(1979, 126).

10: Cicero/Macrobius: Intimations of immortality

1. The expression "from Batro to Tile" (Tule) represents the ends of the world,
from Asia to an archipelago in the North Atlantic. See Stagg 1954.

2. Schevill and Bonilla note this possibility in a footnote to their edition of the
Viaje del Parnaso (1920, 5.355). Listing the forces that will fight against Caesar at Pharsalia, the poem includes the "nomad peoples of Scythia, bounded
by the cold stream of Bactros and the endless forest of Hyrcania"
(3.169–70). The Asian land of Bactra, or Bactria, also plays a part in the
poem (8.299, 423).

3. In Vicente Gaos's edition the poem is simply entitled "Canción primera a la
Armada Invencible" (1981, 2.359); the Schevill–Bonilla edition labels it
"Cançion nacida de las varias nuevas que an venido de la catholica armada
que fue sobre Inglaterra."

4. See also Schevill and Bonilla 1922, 6.55.

5. Both of their stories are told by Titus Livius. Let us recall that Scaevola's heroic deed was depicted in the ceiling of the Stanza della Segnatura among the paintings dedicated to fire. Although the legend emphasizes Scaevola's love of Rome, Cervantes underlines his desire for glory both in *Viaje del Parnaso* and in *Don Quijote* (see Chapter 2 for a discussion of the painting). Juan de Zabaleta criticizes Scaevola's desire for fame: "Quiso sólo hacer fama" (1972, 110).

6. Of course, the *Viaje del Parnaso* does contrast fame and vainglory. The first belongs to those poets who have labored to enter the circle of the chosen, and the second, to those who have pretensions to greatness and "mere" popular fame. Ellen Lokos has shown how the figure of Vainglory in the *Viaje del Parnaso* is closely related to Lope de Vega. Lokos also points out the contrast between Cervantes's and Lope's fate in the poem: "El contraste marcado entre las fortunas de los dos ingenios, tanto en riqueza como en éxito popular, nos convence que el paralelo entre la apariencia de Lope y de la Vanagloria no es casual; la visión de ésta constituye un retrato vivo del Fénix" (1989, 68).

7. Macrobius discusses three types of prophetic dreams: the oracular, the prophetic vision, and the enigmatic dream (1952, 90).

8. All citations of Cicero's *Dream of Scipio* derive from Stahl's 1952 edition of Macrobius's commentary.

9. Vives does not tell the full story: "En el proemio de los *Annales* . . . confesaba Enio haber tendio un sueño, en el que se le aparecía un *simulacrum* de Homero, que entre otras cosas, le comunicaba que su alma había transmigrado a Enio, lo que le convertía en un *alter Homerus*, un *Homerus rediuiuus*" (Pociña 1993, 321). Ennius is also present in Macrobius's *Saturnalia*, which contains numerous fragments from his poems.

10. Stahl claims that these elements "do not necessarily indicate that he was not a Christian at the time he wrote. Paganism died very slowly throughout the empire. . . . The more Christianity succeeded in spreading, the stronger seemed to be the yearning for the preservation of the antiquities and thoughts of the pagan past" (Macrobius 1952, 7–8).

11. Although generally Greek cunning (as represented by Odysseus) is contrasted with Roman valor, in *La Numancia* Cervantes endows the Romans with cunning and the Numantians with valor, thus reinventing the previous struggle to fit the war between Rome and Spain. But Cervantes was not the first to see Roman warfare in terms of cunning. See below for a discussion of his models.

12. The relationship between history and poetry is constantly being questioned in Cervantes's texts. Américo Castro (1972) long ago demonstrated the opposition between "lo universal poético" and the specific events of history in Cervantes's thought.

13. Américo Castro demonstrates how in *Don Quijote* both elements are represented: "Don Quijote hablará en nombre de la verdad universal y verosímil; Sancho defenderá la verdad sensible y particular. La oposición, como es natural y cervantino, no se resuelve" (1972, 33). Nor is it resolved in *La*

Numancia, where Scipio could well represent Sancho's common sense and the city stand for Don Quijote's visionary poetics.

14. At the time this book was being sent to press, I came across a new article by Rachel Schmidt, who problematizes the portrayals of "good" and "bad" Poetry in the *Viaje del Parnaso,* showing how they are both connected to Vainglory (1996, 40).

15. Arturo Marasso asserts: "por esa ironía lucianesca y a veces socrática, el contenido del *Quijote* es inagotable" (1954, 15).

16. Macrobius is said to have interpreted the *Timaeus* through a lost commentary by Porphyry (1952, 196).

17. For an extended discussion of this concept as presented by Plato, Pythagoras, and Macrobius, see Heninger 1974, 160–70.

18. Raphael's *stanze* demonstrate harmony rather than conflict since the Stanza dell'Incendio (fire) and the Sala di Constantino (earth) stand at opposite ends, being mediated by the Stanza della Segnatura (water) and the Stanza d'Eliodoro (air).

19. Macrobius cites Plato, Porphyry, and Plotinus in this context.

20. Georges Güntert asserts: "La prudencia de Escipión, tan admirada por Cicerón y la cultura renacentista, aparece como *cordura*, por prometer una victoria sin pérdida de sangre." He cites in this context Cicero's *Tusculanae disputationes* 1.5, 81, 110, 2.62, 4.5, 50; and *De republica* (1986, 674).

21. Cicero asks: "Has your name or that of any Roman been able to pass beyond the Caucasus, which you see over here, or to cross the Ganges over yonder?" (1952, 75).

22. This fraction of the year is computed by Macrobius from a Great Year of 15,000 years (1952, 222). The fraction for Cervantes is based on the more common 36,000-year cycle, which is found both in Plato and in Hipparchus's precession of the equinoxes. For a more complete explanation of this topic, with bibliographical data, see de Armas 1986, 1–2 nn. 1–2.

23. "[Q]ue no será ninguna escuela, sino un círculo" (Fuentes 1993, 137). Scipio's Circle has recently been described as a "community of Hellenizing interests and tendencies among some eminent Roman aristocrats" (Conte 1994, 73).

24. There are a number of alchemical images in the play. The three colored waters used by Marquino (p. 73), for example, recall three of the major stages of the alchemical *opus*: "negra" (nigredo), "azafrán" (rubedo), and "clara" (albedo). While the nigredo represents the corruption of the dead body, the latter two point to the resuscitation of the dead. In a similar manner, Cervantes's tragedy brings back to life the actions of Numantia, which have long been corrupted by death and time.

25. Georges Güntert sees the battle between the Numantians and the Roman general as symbolic of opposing definitions of poetic creation: "una contienda – y al mismo tiempo una colaboración – entre el *arte*, con su disciplina y sus reglas, y la inspiración poética, a la que los platónicos llamaban *furor*" (1986, 676).

Works Cited

Aeschylus. 1981. *The Persians.* Trans. and ed. Janet Lembke and C. J. Herington. Oxford: Oxford University Press.

Agrippa of Nettesheim, Henry Cornelius. 1987. *Three Books of Occult Philosophy.* 2d ed. London: Chthonios Books.

Ahl, Frederick M. 1976. *Lucan: An Introduction.* Ithaca: Cornell University Press.

Alciati, Andrea. 1577. *Omnia emblemata.* Antwerp: Christophori Plantini.

Antal, Frederick. 1988. *Rafael entre el clacisismo y el manierismo.* Madrid: Visor.

Appianus. 1962. *Roman History.* Trans. Horace White. 4 vols. London: William Heinemann.

Aristotle. 1941. *The Basic Works of Aristotle.* Ed. Richard McKeon. New York: Random House.

　　1953. *Ethics.* Trans. J. A. K. Thomson. London: Penguin.

Arrowsmith, William. 1981. Editor's Foreword to *Persians*, by Aeschylus, trans. and ed. Janet Lembke and C. J. Herington. Oxford: Oxford University Press.

Avalle-Arce, Juan Bautista. 1961. "Grisóstomo y Marcela (la verdad problemática)." In *Deslindes Cervantinos*, pp. 97–119. Madrid: Historia, Geografía y Arte.

　　1962. "Poesía, historia, imperialismo: *La Numancia*." *Anuario de letras* 2: 55–75.

　　1979. "Estudio preliminar." in *Don Quijote de la Mancha*, by Miguel de Cervantes, 1.3–47. Madrid: Alhambra.

Avalle-Arce, Juan Bautista, and E. C. Riley. 1973. "*Don Quijote.*" In *Suma Cervantina*, ed. J. B. Avalle-Arce and E. C. Riley, pp. 47–80. London: Tamesis.

Avila, Ana. 1985. "Influencia de Rafael en la pintura española del siglo XVI a través de los grabados." In *Rafael en España: Museo del Prado, Mayo–Agosto 1985*, pp. 43–53. Madrid: Ministerio de Cultura.

Aylen, Leo. 1964. *Greek Tragedy and the Modern World.* London: Methuen.

Badt, Kurt. 1959. "Raphael's *Incendio del Borgo.*" *Journal of the Warburg and Courtauld Institutes* 22: 35–59.

Barkan, Leonard. 1986. *The Gods Made Flesh: Metamorphosis and the Pursuit of Paganism.* New Haven: Yale University Press.

　　1995. "Making Pictures Speak: Renaissance Art, Elizabethan Literature, Modern Scholarship." *Renaissance Quarterly* 48: 326–51.

Bataillon, Marcel. 1925. "Alfonso de Valdés, auteur du *Diálogo de Mercurio y Carón.*" In *Homenaje ofrecido a Menéndez Pidal*, vol. 1, pp. 403–15. Madrid: Hernando.

　　1937. *Erasme et l'Espagne.* Paris: Droz.

Beardsley, Theodore S. 1970. *Hispano-Classical Translations*. Pittsburgh: Duquesne University Press.

Becatti, Giovanni. 1969. "Raphael and Antiquity." In *The Complete Works of Raphael*, pp. 491–568. New York: Reynal.

Beck, James. 1993. *Raphael: The Stanza della Segnatura*. New York: George Braziller.

Belli, Angela. 1979. "Cervantes' *El cerco de Numancia* and Euripides' *The Trojan Women*." *Kentucky Romance Quarterly* 25: 121–8.

Bentley, Eric. 1970. "The Universality of the *Comedia*." *Hispanic Review* 38: 147–62.

Bergmann, Emilie. 1979. *Art Inscribed: Essays on Ekphrasis in Spanish Golden Age Poetry*. Cambridge: Harvard University Press.

——— 1984. "The Epic Vision of Cervantes' *La Numancia*." *Theatre Journal* 36: 85–96.

Bernardo, Aldo S. 1962. *Petrarch, Scipio, and the "Africa": The Birth of Humanism's Dream*. Baltimore: Johns Hopkins University Press.

Bloom, Harold. 1973. *The Anxiety of Influence*. Oxford: Oxford University Press.

Blue, William R. 1996. *Spanish Comedy in the 1620's*. University Park: Pennsylvania State University Press.

Bluher, Karl Alfred. 1983. *Seneca en España*. Trans. Juan Conde. Madrid: Gredos.

Braden, Gordon. 1985. *Renaissance Tragedy and the Senecan Tradition*. New Haven: Yale University Press.

Braudel, Fernand. 1973. *The Mediterranean and the Mediterranean World in the Age of Philip II*. Trans. Sian Reynolds. 2 vols. New York: Harper and Row.

Broadhead, H. D. 1960. *The "Persae" of Aeschylus*. Cambridge: Cambridge University Press.

Brown, Jonathan. 1991. *The Golden Age of Painting in Spain*. New Haven: Yale University Press.

Burckhardt, Jacob. 1879. *The Cicerone. An Art Guide to Painting in Italy*. Trans. A. H. Clough, ed. J. A. Crowe. London: John Murray.

Calvo Martínez, Juan Luis. 1993. "La figura de Ulises en la literatura española." In *La épica griega y su influencia en la literatura española*, ed. Juan Antonio López Férez, pp. 333–58. Madrid: Ediciones Clásicas.

Camamis, George. 1988. "Cervantes and Botticelli." *Cervantes* 8: 183–223.

Canavaggio, Jean. 1977. *Cervantés dramaturge: Un théatre à naitre*. Paris: Presses Universitaires de France.

——— 1987. *Cervantes*. Trans. Mauro Armiño. Madrid: Espasa-Calpe.

Cantalapiedra, Fernando. 1994. "Las figuras alegóricas en el teatro cervantino." In *Cervantes en la víspera de su centenario*, vol. 2, pp. 381–400. Kassel: Editio Reichenberger.

Carruthers, Mary J. 1990. *The Book of Memory: A Study of Memory in Medieval Culture*. Cambridge: Cambridge University Press.

Casalduero, Joaquín. 1966. *Sentido y forma del teatro de Cervantes*. Madrid: Gredos.

Castro, Américo. 1960. "Los prólogos al *Quijote*." In *Hacia Cervantes*, pp. 231–66. 2d ed. Madrid: Taurus.

——— 1962. *La realidad histórica de España*. 2d ed. Mexico City: Porrúa.

——— 1972. *El pensamiento de Cervantes*. Ed. Julio Rodríguez-Puértolas. Barcelona: Noguer.

——— 1974. *Cervantes y los casticismos españoles*. Madrid: Alianza.

Cervantes, Miguel de. 1920–22. *Obras completas de Miguel de Cervantes.* Vols. 5–6. Ed. Rodolfo Schevill and Adolfo Bonilla. Madrid: Gráficas Reunidas.

1968. *La Galatea.* Ed. Juan Bautista Avalle-Arce. Madrid: Espasa-Calpe.

1969. *Los trabajos de Persiles y Sigismunda.* Ed. Juan Bautista Avalle-Arce. Madrid: Castalia.

1978. *El ingenioso hidalgo don Quijote de la Mancha.* Ed. Luis Andrés Murillo. 5th ed. 2 vols. Madrid: Castalia.

1981. *Poesías completas II.* Ed. Vicente Gaos. Madrid: Castalia.

1982a. *Entremeses.* Ed. Nicholas Spadaccini. Madrid: Cátedra.

1982b. *Novelas ejemplares.* Ed. Juan Bautista Avalle-Arce. 3 vols. Madrid: Castalia.

1984a. *El cerco de Numancia.* Ed. Robert Marrast. 2nd ed. Madrid: Cátedra.

1984b. *Poesías completas I: "Viaje del Parnaso" y "Adjunta al Parnaso."* Ed. Vicente Gaos. Madrid: Castalia.

Chandler, Kenneth. Forthcoming. "The Awakened Mind: The Higher Stages of Development of Human Consciousness." Vol. 2. Typescript.

Chastel, André. 1983. *The Sack of Rome, 1527.* Trans. Beth Archer. Princeton: Princeton University Press.

Cheney, Patrick. 1994. *Spenser's Famous Flight: A Renaissance Idea of a Literary Career.* Toronto: Toronto University Press.

Cirlot, J. E. 1971. *A Dictionary of Symbols.* Trans. Jack Sage. 2nd ed. New York: Philosophical Library.

Clemencín, Diego, ed. 1933. *El ingenioso hidalgo Don Quijote de la Mancha,* vol. 1, by Miguel de Cervantes Saavedra. Madrid: D. E. Aguado.

Conte, Gian Biagio. 1994. *Latin Literature: A History.* Trans. Joseph B. Solodaw, rev. Don Fowler and Glenn W. Marst. Baltimore: Johns Hopkins University Press.

Conti, Natale. 1988. *Mitología.* Ed. and trans. Rosa María Iglesias Montiel and María Consuel Alvarez Morán. Murcia: Publicaciones de la Universidad de Murcia.

Correa, Gustavo. 1959. "El concepto de la fama en el teatro de Cervantes." *Hispanic Review* 27: 208–302.

Cotarelo y Valledor, A. 1915. *El teatro de Cervantes.* Madrid: Tipografía de la Revista de Archivos, Bibliotecas, y Museos.

Covarrubias, Sebastián de. 1978. *Emblemas morales.* Ed. Carmen Bravo Villasante. Madrid: Fundación Universitaria Española.

1987. *Tesoro de la lengua castellana o española.* Ed. Martín de Riquer. Barcelona: Editorial Alta Fulla.

Culler, Jonathan. 1982. *On Deconstruction; Theory and Criticism after Structuralism.* Ithaca: Cornell University Press.

Cunliffe, John William. 1893. *The Influence of Seneca on Elizabethan Tragedy.* London: Macmillan and Co.

Curtius, Ernst Robert. 1953. *European Literature and the Latin Middle Ages.* Trans. Willard R. Trask. New York: Harper and Row.

Damiani, Bruno M. 1989. "Los dramaturgos del Siglo de Oro frente a las artes visuales: prólogo para un estudio comparativo." In *El mundo del teatro español en su Siglo de Oro: Ensayos dedicados a John E. Varey,* ed. J. M. Ruano de la Haza. pp. 137–49. Ottawa: Dovehouse.

Dante Alighieri. 1982. *Inferno*. Trans. Allen Mandelbaum. New York: Bantam.

de Armas, Frederick A. 1974. "Classical Tragedy and Cervantes' *La Numancia*."
   Neophilologus 58:34–40.

——— 1981. "Los excesos de Venus y Marte en *El gallardo español*." In *Cervante: Su obra
   y su mundo*, ed. Manuel Criado de Val, pp. 249–59. Madrid: Edi-6.

——— 1982. "The Four Elements: Key to an Interpretation of Villamediana's
   Sonnets." *Hispanic Journal* 3: 61–79.

——— 1983. "The Dragon's Gold: Calderón and Boisrobert's *La vie n'est qu'un songe*."
   Kentucky Romance Quarterly 30: 335–48.

——— 1985. "Caves of Fame and Wisdom in the Spanish Pastoral Novel." *Studies in
   Philology* 82: 332–58.

——— 1986. *The Return of Astraea: An Astral–Imperial Myth in Calderón*. Lexington:
   University Press of Kentucky.

——— 1987. "Rosaura Subdued: Victorian Views of Calderón's *La vida es sueño*."
   South Central Review 4: 43–62.

——— 1989. "Diomedes' Horses: Mythical Foregrounding and Reversal in
   Claramonte's *Deste agua no beberé*." *Gestos* 4: 47–64.

——— 1992a. "La estructura mítica de *Los comendadores de Córdoba*." In *Actas del X
   Congreso de la Asociación Internacional de Hispanistas*. vol. 1, pp. 763–72.
   Barcelona: PPU.

——— 1992b. "Interpolation and Invisibility: From Herodotus to Cervantes' *Don
   Quixote*." *Journal of the Fantastic in the Arts* 4: 8–28.

——— 1993. "A Banquet of the Senses: The Mythological Structure of *Persiles y
   Sigismunda, III*." *Bulletin of Hispanic Studies* 70: 403–14.

——— 1996. "The Necromancy of Imitation: Lucan and Cervantes' *La Numancia*." In
   *El arte nuevo de estudiar comedias: Literary Theory and Spanish Golden Age
   Drama*, ed. Barbara Simerka, pp. 246–58. Lewisburg: Bucknell University
   Press.

de Armas Wilson, Diana. 1987. "Passing the Love of Women: The Intertextuality
   of *El curioso impertinente*." *Cervantes* 7: 9–28.

Deleuze, Gilles. 1990. *The Logic of Sense*. Trans. Mark Lester. New York: Columbia
   University Press.

Domínguez Ortiz, Antonio, Concha Herrero Carretero and José A. Godoy. 1991.
   *Resplendence of the Spanish Monarchy: Renaissance Tapestries and Armor from the
   Patrimonio Nacional*. New York: Harry N. Abrams.

Dorius, R. J. 1965. "Tragedy." In *Princeton Encyclopedia of Poetry and Poetics*, ed. Alex
   Preminger, pp. 860–4. Princeton: Princeton University Press.

Drake, Dana B. 1974. *"Don Quijote" (1894–1970): A Selective Annotated
   Bibliography*. Vol. 1. Chapel Hill: University of North Carolina Department
   of Romance Languages.

Dudley, Edward. 1995. "Goddess on the Edge: The Galatea Agenda in Raphael,
   Garcilaso, and Cervantes." *Caliope* 1: 27–45.

Dunn, Peter. 1973. "Las *Novelas ejemplares*." In *Suma Cervantina*, ed. J. B. Avalle-
   Arce and E. C. Riley, pp. 81–118. London: Tamesis.

Dussler, Luitpold. 1971. *Raphael: A Critical Catalogue of His Pictures, Wall-Paintings,
   and Tapestries*. London: Phaidon.

East, W. Gordon. 1967. *The Geography behind History*. New York: W. W. Norton.

Egido, Aurora. 1983. "La configuración alegórica de *El castillo interior.*" *Boletín del Museo e Instituto "Camón Aznar"* 10: 69–93.

——. 1994. "La memoria ejemplar y *El coloquio de los perros.*" In *Cervantes: Estudios en la víspera de su centenario,* vol. 2, pp. 465–81. Kassel: Edition Reichenberger.

Elam, Keir. 1980. *The Semiotics of Theatre and Drama.* London: Methuen.

Eliade, Mircea. 1954. *The Myth of the Eternal Return.* Princeton: Princeton University Press.

Eliot, T. S. 1964. "Shakespeare and the Stoicism of Seneca." In *Elizabethan Essays,* pp. 33–54. New York: Haskell House.

Elliott, J. H. 1970. *Imperial Spain, 1469–1716.* London: Penguin.

El Saffar, Ruth. 1975. *Distance and Control in "Don Quixote": A Study in Narrative Technique.* North Carolina Studies in the Romance Languages and Literatures, vol. 147. Chapel Hill: University of North Carolina Press.

Fajardo, Salvador J. 1994. "Instructions for Use: The Prologue to *Don Quixote I.*" *Journal of Interdisciplinary Literary Studies* 6: 1–17.

Feijóo, Benito Jerónimo. 1993. *Teatro crítico universal.* Ed. Angel Raimundo Fernández González. 5th ed. Madrid: Cátedra.

Fernández Arenas, José. 1982. *Renacimiento y barroco en España. Fuentes y documentos para la historia del arte.* Vol. 6. Barcelona: Gustavo Gili.

Ficino, Marsilio. 1985. *Commentary on Plato's "Symposium."* Ed. and trans. Sears Jayne. Dallas: Spring Publications.

Florus, Lucius Anneus. 1929. *Epitome of Roman History.* Trans. Edward Seymour Foster. London: William Heinemann.

Forcione, Alban K. 1970. *Cervantes, Aristotle, and the "Persiles."* Princeton: Princeton University Press.

Foucault, Michel. 1973. *The Order of Things. An Archeology of the Human Sciences.* New York: Random House.

Foulché-Delbosc, R. 1904. "Notes sur le sonnet *Superbi colli.*" *Revue hispanique* 11: 225–43.

Friedman, Edward H. 1977. "*La Numancia* within Structural Patterns of Sixteenth-Century Spanish Tragedy." *Neophilologus* 61: 74–89.

Fuentes, Carlos. 1993. *El naranjo.* Madrid: Alfaguara.

Gaos, Vicente. 1976. "Significado cervantino de *La Numancia.*" *Cervantes – Novelista, Dramaturgo, Poeta.* Barcelona: Planeta.

García Arrieta, Agustín. 1805. *Principios filosóficos de la literatura: Obra escrita en francés por M. Batteux, profesor real de la Academia francesa, y de las de inscripciones y bellas letras: traducida al castellano, ilustrada y completada con various suplementos, y los correspondientes apéndices sobre la literatura española.* Madrid: Sancha.

García de la Concha, Víctor. 1983. "Un *Arte memorativa* castellana." In *Serta philologica F. Lázaro Carreter,* vol. 2, pp. 187–97. Madrid: Cátedra.

Gaston Hall, H. 1974. "Castiglioni's *Superbi colli* in Relation to Raphael, Petrarch, Du Bellay, Spencer, Lope de Vega, and Scarron." *Kentucky Romance Quarterly* 21: 159–81.

Gaylord, Mary Malcom. In press. "*Yo el soneto*: Cervantes' Poetics of the Cenotaph." *Bucknell Review.*

Gerli, E. Michael. 1984. "*El castillo interior* y el *Arte de la memoria.*" *Bulletin hispanique* 86: 154–63.

——— 1989. "*El retablo de las maravillas*: Cervantes' *Arte nuevo de deshacer comedias.*" *Hispanic Review* 57: 477–92.

——— 1995. "Aristotle in Africa: History, Fiction, and Truth in *El gallardo español.*" *Cervantes* 15: 43–57.

Giamatti, A. Bartlett. 1968. "Proteus Unbound: Some Versions of the Sea God in the Renaissance." In *The Disciplines of Criticism. Essays in Literary Theory, Interpretation, and History,* ed. Peter Demetz, Thomas Greene, and Lowry Nelson Jr., pp. 437–76. New Haven: Yale University Press.

Gilbert, Allan H. 1962. *Literary Criticism. Plato to Dryden.* Detroit: Wayne State University Press.

Gómez Santacruz, Santiago. 1914. *El solar numantino.* Madrid: Imprenta de la Revista de Archivos, Bibliotecas, y Museos.

González, Aníbal. 1994. "Etica y teatralidad: *El retablo de las Maravillas* de Cervantes y *El arpa y la sombra* de Alejo Carpentier." *La torre* 7: 485–502.

Grant, Michael. 1993. *Constantine the Great.* New York: Charles Scribner's Sons.

Greene, Thomas M. 1963. *The Descent from Heaven: A Study in Epic Continuity.* New Haven: Yale University Press.

——— 1982. *The Light in Troy.* New Haven: Yale University Press.

Güntert, Georges. 1986. "Arte y furor en *La Numancia.*" In *Acta del VIII Congreso de la AIH,* ed. A. David Kossoff et al., pp. 671–83. Madrid: Istmo.

Gutiérrez Cortines Corral, Cristina. 1989. "La fortuna de Giulio Romano en la arquitectura española." In *Giulio Romano: Atti del Convegno Internazionale di Studi su Giulio Romano e l'Espansione Europea del Rinascimento.* Mantova: Gariplo.

Hamilton, Donna B. 1990. *Virgil and "The Tempest": The Politics of Imitation.* Columbus: Ohio State University Press.

Harsh, Philip Whaley. 1944. *A Handbook of Classical Drama.* Palo Alto: Stanford University Press.

Hartt, Frederick. 1944. "Raphael and Giulio Romano with Notes on the Raphael School." *Art Bulletin* 26 (1944): 67–94.

——— 1958. *Giulio Romano.* New Haven: Yale University Press.

Hatzfeld, Helmut. 1952. "Artistic Parallels in Cervantes and Velázquez." In *Estudios dedicados a Menéndez Pidal,* vol. 3, pp. 265–97. Madrid: Consejo Superior de Investigaciones Científicas.

Havránek, Bohuslav. 1964. "The Functional Differentiation of the Standard Language." In *A Prague School Reader on Esthetics, Literary Structure, and Style,* ed. and trans. Paul L. Garvin, pp. 3–16. Washington: Georgetown University Press.

Hegyi, Ottmar. 1992. *Cervantes and the Turks: Historical Reality versus Literary Fiction in "La Gran Sultana" and "El amante liberal."* Newark, Del.: Juan de la Cuesta.

Heiple, Daniel L. 1994. *Garcilaso de la Vega and the Italian Renaissance.* University Park: Pennsylvania State University Press.

Heninger, S. K. 1974. *Touches of Sweet Harmony: Pythagorean Cosmology and Renaissance Poetics.* San Marino: Huntington Library.

Herendeen, W. H. 1981. "The Rhetoric of Rivers: The River and the Pursuit of Knowledge." *Studies in Philology* 78: 107–27.

Hermenegildo, Alfredo. 1973. *La tragedia en el Renacimiento español.* Barcelona: Planeta.

———. 1976. *"La Numancia" de Cervantes.* Madrid: Sociedad General Española de Librería.

———. 1994. "La semiosis del poder y la tragedia del siglo XV: Cristóbal de Virués." In *Teatro y poder,* ed. Francisco Ruiz Ramón. *Crítica hispánica* 16: 11–30.

Herrero García, Miguel. 1966. *Idea de los españoles del siglo XVII.* Madrid: Gredos.

Hersey, George L. 1993. *High Renaissance Art in St. Peter's and the Vatican.* Chicago: University of Chicago Press.

Hibbert, Christopher. 1975. *The House of Medici, Its Rise and Fall.* New York: Morrow.

Highet, Gilbert. 1949. *The Classical Tradition: Greek and Roman Influences on Western Literature.* Oxford: Oxford University Press.

Homer. 1919. *The Odyssey.* Trans. A. T. Murray. 2 vols. Loeb Classical Library. Cambridge: Harvard University Press.

———. 1924. *The Iliad.* Trans. A. T. Murray. 2 vols. Loeb Classical Library. Cambridge: Harvard University Press.

Hoogewerff, G. 1947–9. "La stanza della segnatura." *Atti della pontificia academia romana di archeologia* 23:326.

Hutchinson, Steven. 1992. *Cervantine Journeys.* Madison: University of Wisconsin Press.

Iannuci, Amilcare A. 1993. *Dante e la "bella scola" della poesia.* Ravenna: Longo Editore.

Jameson, A. K. 1937. "The Sources of Lope de Vega's Erudition." *Hispanic Review* 5: 124–39.

Johnson, Carroll B. 1980. *"La Numancia* and the Structure of Cervantine Ambiguity." *Ideologies and Literature* 3: 74–94.

Johnson, W. R. 1987. *Momentary Monsters.* Ithaca: Cornell University Press.

Jones, Roger, and Nicholas Penny. 1983. *Raphael.* New Haven: Yale University Press.

Jover, José María. 1949. "Sobre la conciencia histórica del barroco español." *Arbor* 12: 355–74.

Kagan, Richard L. 1990. *Lucrecia's Dreams: Politics and Prophecy in Sixteenth-Century Spain.* Berkeley and Los Angeles: University of California Press.

Kempers, Bram. 1987. *Painting, Power, and Patronage: The Rise of the Professional Artist in Renaissance Italy.* Trans. Beverly Jackson. London: Penguin.

King, Willard F. 1979. "Cervantes' *Numancia* and Imperial Spain." *Modern Language Notes* 94: 200–21.

Kitto, H. D. F. 1968. *Greek Tragedy.* London: Methuen.

Krieger, Murray. 1992. *Ekphrasis.* Baltimore: Johns Hopkins University Press.

Lamb, Ursula. 1972. *A Navigator's Universe: The "Libro de cosmographía" of 1538 by Pedro de Medina.* Chicago: University of Chicago Press.

Lewis-Smith, Paul. 1987. "Cervantes' *Numancia* as Tragedy and as Tragicomedy." *Bulletin of Hispanic Studies* 64: 15–26.

Lida de Malkiel, María Rosa. 1950. *Juan de Mena: Poeta del prerenacimiento español*. Mexico City: Colegio de México.

Lokos, Ellen. 1989. "El lenguaje emblemático en el *Viaje del Parnaso*." *Cervantes* 9: 63–74.

Longhurst, John E., with the collaboration of Raymond R. MacCurdy. 1952. *Alfonso de Valdés and the Sack of Rome*. Albuquerque: University of New Mexico Press.

Lope de Vega. 1971. *El arte nuevo de hacer comedias en este tiempo*. Ed. Juana de José Prades. Madrid: CSIC.

Lopez, Diego. 1670. *Declaracion magistral sobre los emblemas de Andres Alciato*. Valencia: Geronimo Vilagrasa.

López Férez, Juan Antonio. 1993. "Datos sobre la influencide la épica griega en la literatura española." In *La épica griega y su influenciaen la literatura española*, ed. Juan Antonio López Férez, pp. 359–409. Madrid: Ediciones Clásicas.

López Torrijos, Rosa. 1985. *La mitología en la pintura española del Siglo de Oro*. Madrid: Cátedra.

Lucan. 1957. *Pharsalia*. Trans. Robert Graves. New York: Penguin.

——— 1962. *Pharsalia*. Trans. and ed. J. D. Duff. Cambridge: Harvard University Press.

Lucanus, M. Annaeus. 1971. *Pharsalia*. Ed. C. E. Haskins and W. E. Heitland. Hildesheim: Georg Olms.

Macrobius. 1952. *Commentary on the Dream of Scipio*. Trans. and ed. William Harris Stahl. New York: Columbia University Press.

MacCurdy, Raymond R. 1958. *Francisco de Rojas Zorrilla and the Tragedy*. Albuquerque: University of New Mexico Press.

——— 1960. "The Numantia Plays of Cervantes and Rojas Zorrilla: The Shift from Collective to Personal Tragedy," *Symposium* 14: 100–120.

——— 1964. "La tragédie néo-sénéquienne en Espagne au XVIIe siècle, et particuliärment le thäme du tyran." In *Les tragédies de Sénäque et le théatre de la Renaissance*, ed. Jean Jacquot, pp. 73–85. Paris: Centre National de la Recherche Scientifique.

——— 1978. *The Tragic Fall. Don Alvaro de Luna and Other Favorites in Spanish Golden Age Drama*. Chapel Hill: North Carolina Studies in the Romance Languages and Literatures, vol. 197. University of North Carolina Press.

Maharishi Mahesh Yogi. 1967. *On the Bhagavad-Gita: A New Translation and Commentary, Chapters 1–6*. London: Penguin.

——— 1986. *Thirty Years around the World: Dawn of the Age of Enlightenment*. Vol. l. The Netherlands: MVU Press.

Maínez, Ramón León. 1876. *Vida de Miguel de Cervantes Saavedra*. Cádiz: La Mercantil.

Marasso, Arturo. 1954. *Cervantes: La invención del "Quijote."* Buenos Aires: Hachette.

Marín, Flavia. 1994. "Seneca's *Troades* and Cervantes' *La Numancia*: Women and Lamentation." M.A. thesis, Pennsylvania State University.

Márquez Villanueva, Francisco. 1973. *Fuentes literarias cervantinas*. Madrid: Gredos.

Martín, Adrienne Laskier. 1991. *Cervantes and the Burlesque Sonnet*. Berkeley and Los Angeles: University of California Press.

Martín, Francisco J. 1993. "Los prólogos del *Quijote*: La consagración de un género." *Cervantes* 13: 77–88.

—— 1996. "El desdoblamiento de la hamartia en *La Numancia*." *Bulletin of the Comediantes* 48: 15–24.

Mathews, Thomas F. 1993. *The Clash of Gods: A Reinterpretation of Early Christian Art*. Princeton: Princeton University Press.

Mattéi, Jean-François. 1988. "The Theater of Myth in Plato." In *Platonic Writings/Platonic Readings*, ed. Charles L. Griswold, pp. 66–83. London: Routledge.

McCune, Marjorie W., Tucker Orbison, and Philip M. Wilter. 1980. *The Binding of Proteus. Perspectives on Myth and the Literary Process*. Lewisburg: Bucknell University Press.

McGaha, Michael. 1980. "Cervantes and Virgil." In *Cervantes and the Renaissance*, ed. Michael McGaha, pp. 34–52. Newark, Del.: Juan de la Cuesta.

—— 1991. "Intertextuality as a Guide to the Interpretation of the Battle of the Sheep (*Don Quixote* I, 18)." In *On Cervantes: Essays for L. A. Murillo*, ed. James A. Parr, pp. 149–62. Newark, Del.: Juan de la Cuesta.

McKendrick, Melveena. 1980. *Cervantes*. Boston: Little, Brown.

Menéndez Pelayo, Marcelino. 1941. *Estudios de crítica histórica y literaria*. 7 vols. Santander: Consejo Superior de Investigaciones Científicas.

Moir, Duncan. 1965. "The Classical Tradition in Spanish Theory and Practice." In *Classical Drama and Its Influence. Essays Presented to H. D. F. Kitto*, pp. 193–228. London: Methuen.

Morales, Ambrosio. 1791. *Corónica general de España que continuaba Ambrosio de Morales cronista del rey nuestro señor don Felipe II*. Vols. 3–4. Madrid: Benito Cano.

Morford, M. P. O. 1967. *The Poet Lucan. Studies in Rhetorical Epic*. New York: Barnes and Noble.

Morón Arroyo, Ciriaco. 1994. "Erasmo y el texto del *Quijote*." In *Cervantes: Estudios en la víspera de su centenario*, vol. 1, pp. 173–95. Kassel: Editio Reichenberger.

Mujica, Barbara K. 1969. "Tragic Elements in Calderón's *La dama duende*." *Kentucky Romance Quarterly* 16: 303–28.

Mund-Dopchie, Monique. 1984. *La survie d'Eschyle à la Renaissance*. Louvain: Aedibus Peeters.

Muñoz Delgado, V. 1975. "Juan de Aguilera y su *Ars memorativa* (1536)." *Cuadernos de historia de la medicina española* 14: 175–90.

Nadeau, Carolyn. 1994. "*Women of the Prologue: Writing the Female in "Don Quijote"* Ph.D. diss., Pennsylvania State University.

Navarro, Alberto. 1964. *El "Quijote" español del siglo XVII*. Madrid: Rialp.

Nesselrath, Arnold. 1992. "Art-historical Findings during the Restoration of the *Stanza dell'Incendio*." *Master Drawings* 30: 31–60.

Nicolopulos, James. Forthcoming. "Prophecy, Empire, and Imitation in the *Araucana* in the Light of the *Lusiadas*." Typescript.

Oates, Whitney J., and Eugene O'Neill Jr., eds. 1938. The *Complete Greek Drama*. Vol. 1. New York: Random House.

Oriel, Charles. 1992. *Writing and Inscription in Golden Age Drama*. West Lafayette: Purdue University Press.

Ovid. 1921. *Metamorphoses.* Trans. Frank Justus Miller. 2 vols. Cambridge: Harvard University Press.

1979. *The Art of Love and Other Poems.* Trans. J. H. Mozley. Cambridge: Harvard University Press.

Pagden, Sylvia Ferino. 1989. "Giulio Romano pittore e disegnatore a Roma." In *Giulio Romano,* ed. Ernst H. Gombrich et al., Electa. pp. 65–96. Milan.

Panofsky, Erwin. 1969. *Problems in Titian.* New York: New York University Press.

Parker, Alexander A. 1962. "Towards a Definition of Calderonian Tragedy." *Bulletin of Hispanic Studies* 39: 222–37.

Parr, James. 1984. "Extrafictional Point of View in *Don Quijote.*" In *Studies on "Don Quijote" and Other Cervantine Works,* ed. Donald W. Bleznick pp. 20–30. York, S.C.: Spanish Literature Publications.

1991. "Plato, Cervantes, Derrida: Framing Speaking and Writing in *Don Quixote.*" In *On Cervantes: Essays for L. A. Murillo,* ed. James A. Parr, pp. 163–88. Newark, Del.: Juan de la Cuesta.

1994. Review of Steven Hutchinson's *Cervantine Journeys. Comparative Literature Studies* 31: 427–30.

Peraita, Carmen. In press. "Idea de la historia y providencialismo en Cervantes: Las profecías numantinas." In *Actas del Segundo Congreso de la Asociación Internacional de Cervantistas.*

Percas de Ponseti, Helena. 1988. *Cervantes the Writer and the Painter of "Don Quijote."* Columbia: University of Missouri Press.

Pérez Sánchez, Alfonso E. 1985. "Rafael en los tratadistas españoles." In *Rafael en España. Museo del Prado. Mayo–Agosto 1985,* pp. 29–42. Madrid: Ministerio de Cultura.

Plato. 1892. *The Dialogues of Plato.* Ed. and trans. Benjamin Jowett. 2 vols. New York: Random House.

1963. *The Collected Dialogues of Plato.* Ed. and trans. Edith Hamilton and Huntington Cairns. Princeton: Princeton University Press.

1990. *Plato's "Phaedrus."* Trans. R. Hackforth. Cambridge: Cambridge University Press.

Pliny. 1969. *Natural History II (Books III–VII).* Vol. 2. Trans. H. Rackham. Cambridge: Harvard University Press.

Plutarch. 1902. *Plutarch's "Lives."* Trans. A. H. Clough. New York: Harper.

1993. *Moralia.* Trans. F. C. Babbitt. Cambridge: Harvard University Press.

Pociña, Andrés. 1993. "La épica griega y la latina. El caso de Lucrecio." In *La épica griega y su influencia en la literatura española,* ed. Juan Antonio López Férez, pp. 313–32. Madrid: Ediciones clásicas.

Pope-Hennessy, John. 1970. *Raphael.* New York: New York University Press.

Quint, David. 1983. *Origin and Originality in Renaissance Literature.* New Haven: Yale University Press.

1993. *Epic and Empire.* Princeton: Princeton University Press.

Rabell, Carmen R. 1992. *Lope de Vega: El arte nuevo de hacer "novellas."* London: Tamesis.

Redig de Campos, D. 1946. *Raffaello e Michelangelo: Studi di storia e d'arte.* Rome: G. Bardi.

1965. *Raffaello nelle stanze*. Milan: Aldo Martello.

Reichenberger, Arnold. 1959. "The Uniqueness of the *Comedia*." *Hispanic Review* 27: 303–16.

1970. "The Uniqueness of the *Comedia*." *Hispanic Review* 38: 163–73.

Rey Hazas, Antonio. 1992. "Cervantes y Lope ante el personaje colectivo: *La Numancia* frente a *Fuenteovejuna*," *Cuadernos de teatro clásico* 7: 69–91.

Richardson Jr., L. 1992. *A New Topographical Dictionary of Ancient Rome*. London and Baltimore: Johns Hopkins University Press.

Riffaterre, Michael. 1983. *Text Production*. Trans. Terese Lyons. New York: Columbia University Press.

Riley, E. C. 1986. *Don Quixote*. London: Allen and Unwin.

Ríos, Vicente de los. 1819. "Juicio crítico o análisis del *Quijote*." In *El ingenioso hidalgo Don Quijote de la Mancha*, by Miguel de Cervantes Saavedra, vol. 1, pp. 13–159. 4th ed. Madrid: Imprenta Real.

Rivers, Elias L. 1991. "Genres and Voices in the *Viaje del Parnaso*." In *On Cervantes: Essays for L. A. Murillo*, ed. James A. Parr, pp. 207–26. Newark, Del.: Juan de la Cuesta.

Rosenmeyer, Thomas G. 1982. *The Art of Aeschylus*. Berkeley and Los Angeles: University of California Press.

Ross, Sir David. 1964. *Aristotle*. New York: Barnes and Noble.

Rousset, Jean. 1953. *La littérature de l'age Baroque en France*. Paris: Corti.

Ruano de la Haza, José. 1983. "Hacia una nueva definición de la tragedia Calderoniana," *Bulletin of the Comediantes* 35: 165–80.

Rubin, Patricia Lee. 1995. *Giorgio Vasari: Art and History*. New Haven: Yale University Press.

Salet, Francis, Bertrand Jestaz, and Roseline Bacou. 1978. *Jules Romain: L'histoire de Scipion*. Paris: Editions de la Réunion des Musées Nationaux.

Sandys, John E. 1962. *A History of Classical Scholarship*. 2 vols. New York: Hafner.

Schevill, Rudolph. 1907–8. "Studies in Cervantes." *Transactions of the Connecticut Academy of Arts and Sciences* 13: 475–548.

1919. *Cervantes*. London: Murray.

Schmidt, Rachel. 1996. "Maps, Figures, and Canons in the *Viaje del Parnaso*." *Cervantes* 16: 29–46.

Selig, Karl Ludwig. 1967. "Nuevas consideraciones sobre la temática y estructura de las *Novelas ejemplares*." In *Das literarische Werk von Miguel de Cervantes*, Beitrage zur romanischen Philologie.

1971. "*La Numancia*: A Reconsideration of the Duero Speech." In *Homenaje a William L. Fichter*, ed. David A. Kossoff and José Amor y Vázquez, pp. 681–5. Madrid: Castalia.

1983. "Apuleius and Cervantes: *Don Quixote* (I, XVIII)." In *Aureum Saeculum Hispanum*, ed. Karl-Hermann Korner and Dietrich Briesemeister, pp. 285–7. Wiesbaden: Franz Steiner Verlag.

Seneca. 1979. *Tragedies*. Trans. Frank Justus Miller. 2 vols. Cambridge: Harvard University Press.

Shivers, George. 1970. "La historicidad de *El cerco de la Numancia* de Miguel de Cervantes." *Hispanófila* 39: 1–14.

Simonde de Sismondi, J. C. L. 1853. *The Literature of the South of Europe*. 2 vols. London: H. G. Bohn.

Smith, Paul Julian. 1995. *Escrito al margen. Literatura española del Siglo de Oro*. Madrid: Castalia.

Sohm, Philip. 1995. "Gendered Style in Italian Art Criticism from Michelangelo to Malvasia." *Renaissance Quarterly* 48: 759–808.

Solterer, Helen. 1995. *The Master and Minerva: Disputing Women in French Medieval Culture*. Berkeley and Los Angeles: University of California Press.

Spatz, Lois. 1982. *Aeschylus*. Boston: Twayne Publishers.

Spence, Jonathan D. 1984. *The Memory Place of Matteo Ricci*. New York: Viking.

Spitzer, Leo. 1947. "Soy quien soy." *Nueva revista de filología hispánica* 1: 113–27.

Stagg, Geoffrey. 1954. "Cervantes' 'De Batro a Tile.' " *Modern Language Notes* 49: 96–9.

Stiebing Jr., William H. 1993. *Uncovering the Past: A History of Archeology*. Buffalo: Prometheus Books.

Stiegler, Brian N. 1996. "The Coming of the New Jerusalem: Apocalyptic Imagery in *La Numancia*." *Neophilologus* 80: 569–81.

Stinger, Charles L. 1985. *The Renaissance in Rome*. Bloomington: Indiana University Press.

Tanner, Marie. 1993. *The Last Descendant of Aeneas. The Hapsburgs and the Mythic Image of the Emperor*. New Haven: Yale University Press.

Tar, Jane. 1990. "*Hamartia* in Cervantes' *La Numancia*." *Aleph* 5: 22–8.

Tate, Robert B. 1954. "Mythology in Spanish Historiography in the Middle Ages and the Renaissance." *Hispanic Review* 22: 1–18.

Thomas, L. P. 1929. "François Bertaut et les conceptions dramatiques de Calderón." *Revue de literature comparée* 4: 199–221.

Toro, Alfonso de. 1985. "Tipos de tragicomedia de honor en Lope de Vega." *Iberorromania* 22: 1–28.

Turbino, Francisco María. 1862. *El "Quijote" y "La estafeta de Urganda."* Sevilla: La Andalucía.

Turyn, Aleksander. 1967. *The Manuscript Tradition of the Tragedies of Aeschylus*. Hildesheim: Georg Olms.

Urbina, Eduardo. 1987. "Gigantes y enanos: De lo maravilloso a lo grotesco en el *Quijote*." *Romanistisches Jahrbuch* 38: 323–38.

Valbuena Prat, Angel. 1968. *Historia de la literatura española*. 4 vols. Barcelona: Gustavo Gili.

Valdés, Alfonso de. 1975. *Diálogo de las cosas ocurridas en Roma*. Ed. José Luis Abellán. Madrid: Editora Nacional.

———. 1992. *Diálogo de las cosas acaecidas en Roma*. Ed. Rosa Navarro Durán. Madrid: Cátedra.

Valerius Maximus. 1888. *Factorum et dictorum memorabilum, libri novem*. Ed. Carolus Kempf. Leipzig: Teubner.

Varey, John. 1991. "Memory Theaters, Playhouses, and *Corrales de Comedias*." In *Parallel Lives: Spanish and English National Drama, 1580–1680*, ed. Louise

Fothergill-Payne and Peter Fothergill-Payne, pp. 39–51. Lewisburg: Bucknell University Press.

Vasari, Giorgio. 1971. *Lives of the Artists*. Trans. George Bull. Rev. ed. London: Penguin.

Vega Carpio, Félix Lope de. 1971. *El arte nuevo de hacer comedias en este tiempo*. Ed. Juana de José Prades. Madrid: CSIC.

Vilanova, Antonio. 1949. *Erasmo y Cervantes*. Barcelona: Publicaciones del Instituto "Miguel de Cervantes."

Villamediana, Conde de. 1990. *Poesía impresa completa*. Ed. José Francisco Ruiz Casanova. Madrid: Cátedra.

Virgil. 1978. *Virgil*. Trans. H. R. Fairclough. Cambridge: Harvard University Press. 1991. *The Aeneid*. Trans. David West. London: Penguin.

Vitruvius. 1960. *The Ten Books on Architecture*. Trans. Morris Hicky Morgan. Cambridge: Harvard University Press, 1914. Reprint, New York: Dover.

Vives, Juan Luis. 1947. *Obras completas*. Ed. and trans. Lorenzo Riber. 2 vols. Madrid: Aguilar.

Voegelin, Ermine W. 1972. "Dwarves." In *Standard Dictionary of Folklore, Mythology, and Legend*, ed. Maria Leach and Jerome Fried. New York: Funk and Wagnalls.

Watson, Irving. 1963. "*El pintor de su deshonra* and the Neo-Aristotelian Theory of Tragedy." *Bulletin of Hispanic Studies* 40: 17–34.

Wethey, Harold E. 1969. *The Paintings of Titian*. 3 vols. London: Phaidon.

Whitbread, Leslie George. 1971. *Fulgentius the Mythographer*. Columbus: Ohio State University Press.

Whitby, William. 1962. "The Sacrifice Theme in Cervantes' *Numancia*." *Hispania* 45: 205–10.

Wind, Edgar. 1938. "The Four Elements in Raphael's Stanza della Segnatura." *Journal of the Warburg Institute* 2: 75–9. 1968. *Pagan Mysteries in the Renaissance*. 2d ed. New York: Norton.

Winnington-Ingram, R. P. 1983. "Zeus in the *Persae*." In *Studies in Aeschylus*, pp. 1–15. Cambridge: Cambridge University Press.

Wittkower, R. 1977. "Interpretation of Visual Symbol." In *Allegory and the Migration of Symbols*, pp. 173–87. London: Thames and Hudson.

Wofford, Susanne Lindgren. 1992. *The Choice of Achilles: The Ideology of Figure in the Epic*. Stanford: Stanford University Press.

Wolford, Chester L. 1986. "Don Quixote and the Epic of Subversion." In *Cervantes and the Pastoral*, ed. José J. Labrador Herraiz and Juan Fernández Jiménez, pp. 197–212. Cleveland: Cleveland State University Press.

Yates, Frances A. 1966. *The Art of Memory*. Chicago: University of Chicago Press. 1969. *Theatre of the World*. London: Routledge and Kegan Paul. 1975. *Astraea: The Imperial Myth in the Sixteenth Century*. London: Routledge and Kegan Paul.

Zabaleta, Juan de. 1972. *Errores celebrados*. Ed. David Hershberg. Madrid: Espasa-Calpe.

Zimic, Stanislav. 1992. *El teatro de Cervantes*. Madrid: Castalia.

Index